Table of Con

MW00928685

Preface

Scala: A programming language that uniquely supports object-oriented Programming merges with the functional [1] that is preparing to move Java from To throne and to program with that is really fun.

In the summer semester of 2010, in addition to Haskell, I also taught Scala for the reading "Advanced Functional Programming" and many I have had good experiences. I saw how my students medium functional concepts with Scala could be transferred very well to the JVM. ten. From the 2010/11 winter semester, I started using Scala instead of Java for the

Use programming training of the freshman students. In Scala there arele things have been implemented in a simpler and cleaner way. For example, the Printout println ("Hello World") all by itself in a file as a script

or type directly into the interactive Scala interpreter. In Scala you can Let's stay so close to Java at first that a later switch is hardly possible Likely to cause problems [2] . That I also distributed Scala for programming Discussing systems goes without saying thanks to the actors and akka. With this book I would like to bring you closer to everything Scala has to offer, in which, in addition to the programming language itself, I also give you the essentials I will introduce tools and frameworks. My warmest thanks go to everyone who made this book possible and to me in this one Supported the project: Above all my family. Important discussions and Patrick Baumgartner, Jürgen Dubau,

Christoph Schmidt, Heiko Seeberger and Bernd Weber contributed. Thanks a lot for this. For the good I thank Margarete on behalf of the cooperation with the Hanser Verlag Metzger and Irene Weilhart.

Chapter 1

introduction

Another new programming language, although: Scala is no longer like that New. The development began in 2001 at the École polytechnique fédérale de La- sanne (EPFL) in Switzerland by a team led by Professor Martin Odersky. The first release was published in 2003. Version 2.0 followed in 2006 In 2010, while this book is being written, version 2.8 will be released. which, according to Odersky, should actually be 3.0 [1] . Professor Odersky is no stranger to the Java world. 1995 he started with Phi- lip Wadler [2] with the development of the functional programming language Pizza [3] , which can be translated into bytecode for the Java Virtual Machine (JVM). These Work led to GJ [4] and finally to the new javac compiler and the one with Java 5 introduced Java Generics [5] . When Odersky came to EPFL in 1999, he shifted his focus a little. He had still the goal of object-oriented and functional programming tooconnect, but no longer wanted to be burdened with the restrictions of Java. After developing the programming language Funnel [6] , he took on additional goals the practicality and interoperability with standard platforms and designed Scala [7] .

Scala is a hybrid language that uniquely combines features of objective connects entertaining and functional programming languages. Scala design goal is a concise, elegant and type-safe programming. Scala isn't just inBytecode compiled for the JVM, any Java code can also be extracted directly Use the Scala and vice versa.

Scala is a purely object-oriented programming language. That means, in Scala everythe value of an object. Scala uses a concept of classes and traits. With traits Rich interfaces can be implemented, because traits can already be implemented mentions included. Classes are extended through inheritance, traits are mixed into a class or an object. So as not to get into typical problems running with multiple inheritance, traits are linearized.

Whether Scala may call itself a functional programming language has been shortened on the web. lich first discussed in detail. Odersky finally refers to Scala in [Ode10a]as post-functional language. What is certain is that Scala has a number has features that are either attributable to functional programming or come from their environment.

In Scala, each function is a value of [8] and can be equated with other values. th are treated. This means, for example, that a function can ment or result of another function [9] , functions can be in lists and functions can be nested within one another.

In addition, Scala also supports features such as Pattern Matching [10] and Cur- rysing [11] .

In contrast to many modern and trendy programming languages, Sca- la statically typed. That is, the type of all expressions becomes compile-time checked and not at runtime, as is the case with dynamically typed languages the case is. After a large number of programming errors type errors, we believe that static typing is generally preferable.

to draw. The main disadvantage, namely the need to have types everywheremust be specified is countered in Scala with a type inference mechanism.net. This means that it is not necessary to specify types in most places. At the When translating, the type is then inferred and it is checked whether everything fits together. Scala has a very sophisticated type system that, in addition to generic classes and polymorphic methods also include variance annotations, upper and lower bounds and much more.

Another feature of Scala, which by the way stands for Scalable Language, is the easy expandability. Scala is therefore predestined for the creation of do- main Specific

Languages (DSLs). Last but not least, Scala can also work with support for the .NET platform. But that's still the case not a stand that can be described as "production ready". Scala on the JVM has long since grown up and can in all situations, can also be used in a business-critical manner. The further development of Scala is very active, from bug fix releases to new features will be announced in the next
Expect some more time. For the coming years, the focus of the Scala- Teams on the even better support of multicore architectures.

1.1 What managers should know about Scala

Scala is a mature, very well thought-out programming language. With Scala you can You can do everything that can be done with Java without restriction.
After Scala is compiled in bytecode for the JVM, i.e. in Java bytecode, you can of course also use the Scala code created once from Java. Zen. In summary, this means: Scala can be tried out safely. Even if you should switch back to Java, working in Scala is otherwise. And the entire range of tools used for Java development
such as Eclipse, NetBeans or Maven, is used to develop Scala- Code just continued to use.
But why should you switch to Scala at all? Scala increases productivity vity! Scala offers a variety of features that allow you to use shorter and elegant write other code. Certainly the sheer number of lines of code is not very meaningful, but with less code there is at least statistical also seen fewer errors. Scala is typed more strictly than Java. Also because of that
fewer errors slip through. And a major advantage when starting with Sca- la is that it feels almost like java and added features gradually can be braided.
Why then Scala and not one of the countless other languages? I would like to Let us give only a few quotations:
"If I were to pick a language to use today other than Java, it would be Scala."
James Gosling, creator of Java *"Scala, it must be stated, is the current heir apparent to the Java throne. No other*
language on the JVM seems as capable of being a "replacement for Java" as Sca- la, and the momentum behind Scala is now unquestionable. While Scala is not a dynamic language, it has many of the characteristics of popular dynamic language-

ges, through its rich and flexible type system, its sparse and clean syntax, and its marriage of functional and object paradigms. "
Charles Nutter, creator of JRuby
"Though my tip though for the long term replacement of javac is Scala. I'm very impressed with it! I can honestly say if someone had shown me the programming in Scala book by Martin Odersky, Lex Spoon & Bill Venners back in 2003 I'd probably have never created Groovy. "
James Strachan, creator of Groovy
Who still uses Scala? Scala is now in a number of companies such as Sony, Siemens and Xerox arrived. Let us consider two examples of success layers:

1. Électricité de France Trading (EDFT) is a subsidiary of France largest energy company EDF, which deals with the energy market. In the last n years ago, EDFT held a substantial portion of the 300,000 lines of Java code for "Trading and Pricing" successfully replaced by Scala. EDFT speaks of a A significant increase in productivity and much improved Interfaces for your dealers. Team leader Alex McGuire has meanwhile le EDFT and founded his own company, Scala-Consulting for Financial service providers and trading companies offers.
2. Twitter 12 offers a very popular real-time messaging service, the world- well over 70 million users use it. The Twitter infrastructure processes ture, which now largely consists of Scala code in the backend, over 50 Millions of short messages, so-called tweets. And what about commercial support? There is already a wide variety of them Shape. There is a very active Scala community and first, also German, companies, who provide Scala Consulting. An essential step was the establishment of the companyma ScalaSolutions by Martin Odersky himself. The company offers Scala support,
-Consulting and training. And last but not least, interested and good Java programmers turned into good Scala developers within a very short time be trained.

1.2 Java Scala integration

Even if you have not yet got to know Scala, we want to take it here for further motivation, already read something about the seamless integration with Java gen. From Scala you can use Java classes and libraries in the same way how you would do that directly in Java 13 .
The reverse is almost as easy. Only in a few small places sen to know a bit more about the internals. Scala is what language features as far as more powerful than Java. However, all features are represented by Java bytecode.
sent. So we can get anywhere from Java, the only question is how.
In Scala, in contrast to Java, everything is an object. For better performance the objects that are represented in Java as primitive types, if possible Lich converted into a primitive value, e.g. the Scala Int into the Java int.
If this is not possible, e.g. because primitive data types are not used as type parameters in Java
meter are allowed for generic classes, the value is in the appropriate Wrapper instance converted. For example, the Scala Int is in a list translated into an instance of the java.lang.Integer class
Scala's pure object orientation does not allow static class members. Instead of- Scala has singleton objects. From a singleton object named MyObject a class with the name MyObject $ is created that contains the object can be used via the static field MODULE $.

If there is no associated class for the singleton object, it is is a so-called standalone object, there is also a class se named MyObject creates the static members for all members of the Scala object. This then points to member x of the Scala object MyObject is accessed in Scala as well as in Java with MyObject.x. It's a bit more complicated with Scalas Traits as Java doesn't have one Knows construct. A trait always becomes a Java interface and thus a
Type generated. All methods of the Scala objects be used. However, implementing a trait in Java is not practical. tikabel, unless the trait contains only abstract members. Java's annotations and exceptions are supported by Scala. Special Scala
Annotations such as @volatile, @transient and @serializable are transformed into the corresponding Java constructs. Scala does not know ne Checked Exceptions, but offers an @throws annotation for the Java
Interoperability.

1.3 About this book

With this book we want to introduce you to the fascinating world of Sca- la kidnap. To make your entry as pleasant as possible and so that you can try out what we have described in practice right away, begin-
in Chapter 2 with information about the Scala tools and the tools to support the development process.
Then we deal with the programming language Sca in three chapters. la. In chapter 3 we feel our way to the syntax and discuss the imperative ven programming concepts. We'll also show you how executable in Scala
Scripts are developed and create a first compilable program. Even if the features of Scala are not strictly object-oriented
and functional programming languages, we have one Division into two chapters 4 and 5. There is everything
which is more to be assigned to the area of object orientation, in Chapter 4, and the Features that originally come from functional programming or are more closely related to it, in Chapter 5.
The popularity and usability of a programming language is of course not alive only from the language core. In two chapters we turn our attention to the libraries brought by the Scala distribution. In Chapter 6 we give first
a rough overview before we look at some areas such as the collection framework and take a closer look at Scala's excellent XML support.
ten. Due to its increasing importance, the actor library is of secondary importance A separate chapter is dedicated to current and multicore programming, namely Chapter 7. Good quality software should be well documented and tested. In the
We present the usual approaches to Scala development in Chapter 8. The last three chapters give you an introduction to three Scala frameworks. In In each of the three chapters, we develop a small sample application. The
Talk Allocator created in Chapter 9 is a web application that runs on Lift [14] , a a very extensive web framework. The final grade calculator from Chapter 10 uses the very lightweight web framework Scalatra [15] . And Finally, with the MovieStore in Chapter 11, we dive into the fascinating World of Actors and Software Transactional Memory with Akka [16] . About the previous In addition to the frameworks provided, there are a lot of other very interesting questions
meworks such as ScalaModules, already described in [WBB10] has been. On the website for the book http://scala.obraun.net/ you will find links to Source code for some chapters. You can find more information about Scala on the Scala website http://www.scala-lang.org/, on many mailing lists in blogs etc. A number of English-language Scala books are also available, [OSV08] should be mentioned here as an example.

1.4 Typographical and other conventions

The shell commands are preceded by a $ sign, which when typing may not be entered. Lines without the dollar sign are outputs for example:

```
$ scala -version
```

Scala code runner version 2.8.0.final - Copyright 2002-2010, LAMP / EPFL

Commands in the interactive Scala environment is as prompt scala > pre-employed. If the entry extends over several lines, the following the lines with five spaces followed by a | symbol. Other lines are Output from the Scala interpreter, for example:

```
scale> for (i <- 1 to 3)
|
println (i)
1
2
3
```

For the sake of better readability, this book does not include any indicate the feminine and masculine form of the position, such as "the reader the reader "or" the reader ". With the usual form then used, e.g. Of course, we would like readers to be "the reader" alike speak to.

And now we hope you enjoy reading and trying it out.

Chapter 2

Setting up the working environment

If you want to learn a foreign language, most of them will Other people recommend that you speak as much as possible in it. It is analogous with learning a new programming language. The most important thing is a lot in it to program. So that you can do it well and not get through it too much Selection and setup of the working environment from a quick start in the Scala
World, we would like to introduce you to the Scala tools and in this chapter present the support for the common development environments. In from- Section 2.1 we briefly explain the various command line programs of the
Scala distribution. We show the usual Scala build tools Maven and Sbt To you in section 2.2. Finally we take a look at the available bare IDE support in section 2.3.

2.1 The Scala shell and the command line

For the first steps in Scala, it is sufficient to install or unpack the Scala-Distribution. You can find this either at http://www.scala-lang.org/ or, if you work under Linux / * BSD / MacOS X / ..., with a high probability
included in your package management system. In addition to the standard library, the following are essentially installed
Shell scripts or batch files (with the extension .bat): scala - The Scala "interpreter". With the scala command, Scala applications, analogous to Java Applications or Scala scripts started in the Java runtime environment will. If no argument is passed when calling, the so-called *Scala shell* , an interactive command line interpreter, so a so-called *REPL* 1 , which is discussed in more detail below. scalac - The Scala compiler. The Scala compiler can be used to generate JVM 1.5 compatible. Class files or, if -target: msil is specified, MSIL assembly code
for the .NET platform 2 . fsc - The "Fast Offline" Compiler. In order not to initialize the JVM with every compilation process and having to load agile classes, fsc starts a *Compilation daemon* that can be reused for further translations can. This makes compiling the same classes particularly extreme accelerated. In order to change the content of the class path used in the To take into account compilation, the daemon must explicitly use fsc -shutdown to be terminated. The fsc is also used when a Scala- Script is to be executed with the scala command 3 .
scalap - The class file decoder. Analogous to javap, the Java class file disassembler, scalap the class files generated with the Scala compiler. When using javap provides you with the disassembled Java code, with scalap the
Scala code. scaladoc - the documentation generator. The Scala distribution contains its own tool to extract from the source code files generate the API as HTML files. Although the tags to use for the documentation essentially the same as those of Javadoc. men, your own tool is required, as a Scala API also includes objects and traits may contain. In addition, scaladoc has been revised with Scala 2.8 and better adapted to Scala. sbaz - The Scala Bazar System (SBaz)
The Scala Bazar system is intended as a package management system for a Maintain Scala installation. sbaz offers commands to install packages- ren, remove and upgrade to a newer version. Furthermore self-developed packages can be packed and distributed with the help of sbaz the. With the sbaz-setup, which is also included in the Scala distribution, a new directory can easily be initialized with Sbaz. The commands that access the JDK or JRE, scala, scalac and
fsc, consider the environment variables, if they are set: JAVACMD, the Java command to execute the Scala code, JAVA_HOME, the directory where the JDK / JRE programs

are installed, And JAVA_OPTS, options that are passed to the JAVACMD. In the following we will describe the various command line programs look a little closer. It is not necessary that you use the listed Source code, in particular the source code generated by tools such as scalap understand this point exactly. Rather, the goal is to gain insight what is possible with the commands.

2.1.1 The Scala interpreter

Although Scala source code is generally in bytecode for the JVM or for the .NET platform is translated, the distribution also brings an interactive ven interpreter with. This is started with the command scala without any more arguments.

Listing 2.1: Starting the interactive Scala interpreter

```
$ scala
```

Welcome to Scala version 2.8.0.final (Java HotSpot (TM) 64-bit server VM, Java 1.6.0_20).
Type in expressions to have them evaluated.
Type: help for more information.
scala>
After starting, expressions can be entered in the Scala shell. These are evaluated immediately after pressing the return key and the The result is output.

Listing 2.2: Simple calculations in the Scala shell

```
scale> 1 + 2
res0: Int = 3
scala> println ("Hello World!")
Hello World!
scala> println ("The result is" + (1 + 2))
The result is 3
scala> println ("The result is" + res0)
```

The result is 3

Listing 2.2 shows a few simple examples that you can calculate in the Scala shell can leave. First the integers 1 and 2 are added and the sum issued. The result is automatically assigned to the variable res0 and can thus be referenced again later. In addition, the inferior te type issued. The next result of a calculation is then the riables res1 assigned etc. The following three inputs do not calculate result but only have one side effect, which is something on the command line issues.
You can of course introduce your own variables, and it is possible to enter Scala code over several lines (see Listing 2.3). Additional 5 spaces, followed by a | symbol, automatic table preceded by the Scala shell. To allow an additional line, the shell must recognize that the entry is not yet a correct one Expression acts.

Listing 2.3: Own Variables and Multi-Line Code

```
scala> val sum = 1 until 100 reduceLeft {(x, y) => x + y}
sum: Int = 4950
```

```
scale> for (i <- 1 to 5)
|
if (i% 2 == 0)
|
println (i + "is even and between 1 and 5")
```

2 is even and between 1 and 5
4 is even and between 1 and 5

We will see later that the Scala shell is not quite equivalent to the Compile and run is [4]. With scala -i < filename > a Scala file can be placed in the Scala- Shell to be loaded. In the shell session itself, you can use the comm command: load < filename > a file can be loaded and interpreted with
: jar < filename > a JAR is added to the classpath. Since Scala 2.8.0 the shell masters autocomplete using the tab key. Thieves- The interpretation of some other commands can be queried with: help. Interesting to see the power of Scala directly on the command line is the -e flag, which can be used to specify a scala expression, the is evaluated immediately, as shown in Listing 2.4, for example.

Listing 2.4: Output of the absolute path on the command line using Scala

```
$ scala -e 'val file = new java.io.File (".")
println (file.getAbsolutePath ()) '
/ home / obraun / projects / scalabuch /.
```

If the scala interpreter receives a Scala script, i.e. a source code file with Scala Code, passed as an argument, this is compiled with the fsc and so- continued running. If the command line switch -nocompdaemon is used, then is compiled with scalac. To avoid repeated execution of an unchangeable To speed up scripts, -savecompiled can be specified. Anything entered in the interactive shell can be in a Scala script may be, i.e. variables, functions, classes and objects can be defined be ned. The script is processed line by line and when it is reached the end of the file. A Scala script can also be made executable yourself will. Under Unix this works with the shebang, as shown in Listing 2.5.
represents. However, in contrast to other shell scripts, the header must be used for the Scala script must be completed with! #.

Listing 2.5: Scala script executable under Unix

```
#! / bin / sh
exec scala "$ 0" "$ @"
! #
println ("Hello reader!")
```

On Windows, the executable script looks like the one shown in Listing 2.6.

Listing 2.6: Scala script executable under Windows

```
:: #!
@echo off
call scale% 0% *
goto. eof
::! #
```

```
println ("Hello reader!")
```

Last but not least, the command scala < objectname > *is used* analogously to java < classname > *is* used to create an object previously translated with the Scala compiler. project to execute. To do this, the object must contain a main method.

2.1.2 **The Scala (de) compilers**

The Scala compiler converts Scala source code files into class files for the JVM translated or with -target: msil MSIL assembler code for .NET generated. For normal use it is enough to know that the call is made

```
$ scalac <filename>
or.
$ fsc <filename>
```

translates the objects and classes contained in < filename > . Hereinafter let's go a little deeper for those interested in it.
The compiler goes through different phases such as parse, analyze and uncurry. With the command line flag -Xprint: < phases > it is possible to to output the file after the specified phase and thus to add something to see the scenery. For example, the object defined in Listing 2.7 after parsing as shown in Listing 2.8.

Listing 2.7: Hallo.scala

```
object Hello extends Application {
println ("Hello reader!")
}
```

Listing 2.8: Hallo.scala after parsing

```
[[syntax trees at end of parser]] // Scala source : Hello.
scale
package <empty> {
object Hello extends Application with scala.ScalaObject
{
def <init> () = {
super. <init> ();
()
};
println ("Hello reader!")
}
}
```

With the -print flag, the program can run without any Scala-specific features can be output (see Listing 2.9).

Listing 2.9: scalac -print Hallo.scala

```
[[syntax trees at end of cleanup]] // Scala source : Hello.
scale
package <empty> {
final class Hello extends java.lang.Object with
```

```
Application with ScalaObject {
<stable> <accessor> def executionStart (): Long =
Hello.this.executionStart;
private [this] val executionStart: Long = _;
<accessor> def scala $ Application $ _setter_
$ executionStart _ = (x $ 1: Long): Unit = Hello.this.
executionStart = x $ 1;
def main (args: Array [java.lang.String]): Unit = scala
.Application $ class.main (Hello.this, args);
def this (): object Hello = {
Hello.super.this ();
scala.Application $ class. / * Application $ class * / $ init $
(Hello.this);
scala.this.Predef.println ("Hello readers!");
()
}
}
}
```

Of course, the necessary paths such as class-path or sourcepath can be specified. Flags like -verbose, -optimise and
-explaintypes and a variety of *advanced options* offer further possibilities- to adapt the translation process to your own needs. The the respective meaning can be found in the document supplied in the Scala distribution
can be removed. The Fast Offline Compiler fsc starts a compilation daemon that works on a Socket accepts further translations. With the flag -verbose leaves watch yourself what happens the first time you call it up.
-Reset can be used to empty the caches used by the *compile server* . The daemon can be shut down with -shutdown. The translated class files can be processed with the command contained in the JDK. do javap be disassembled. For example, from the Scala file Hallo.scala (see Listing 2.7) the two JVM classes Hello and Hello $ testifies (see Listing 2.10)

Listing 2.10: javap hello and javap hello $

```
// This is Java
public final class Hello extends java.lang.Object {
public static final void main (java.lang.String []);
public static final void scala $ Application $ _setter_
$ executionStart_ $ eq (long);
public static final long executionStart ();
}
public final class Hello $ extends java.lang.Object
implements scala.Application, scala.ScalaObject {
public static final Hello $ MODULE $;
public static {};
public void main (java.lang.String []);
public void scala $ Application $ _setter_ $ executionStart
_ $ eq (long);
public long executionStart ();
}
```

If development is carried out in Scala, it naturally makes more sense to use the information as Scala-To be able to output code and not just as Java code. The Scala-Distribution the command scalap, the *scala class file decoder* , with. Since the If the current directory is not automatically in the classpath, it must be entered with -cp . to be added. Listing 2.11 shows the decoded Scala code of the two Files hello.class and hello $ .class.

Listing 2.11: scalap -cp. Hello and scalap -cp. Hello $

```
object Hello extends java.lang.Object with scala.
Application with scala.ScalaObject {
def this () = { / * compiled code * / }
}
package hello $;
final class Hello $ extends scala.AnyRef with scala.
ScalaObject with scala.Application {
final val executionStart: scala.Long;
def executionStart (): scala.Long;
def scala $ Application $ _setter_ $ executionStart _ = (scala.
Long): scala.Unit;
def main (scala.Array [java.lang.String]): scala.Unit;
def this (): scala.Unit;
}
object Hello $ {
final val MODULE $: Hello $;
}
```

2.1.3 The documentation generator

There is also a separate scaladoc for generating the API documentation.a tool. Did you see the documentation of the Java
The API documentation is still very similar, but the current Scala version now contains 2.8 a new documentation tool. The necessary documentation of the source codes still looks almost exactly like the one for Java and uses
The same tags are used to mark the information. Additionally can Macros are defined and a Wiki syntax can be used. From the source code With scaladoc, Listing 2.12 becomes the HTML page shown in Figure 2.1
generated. The documentation with scaladoc is described in more detail in Chapter 8 discussed.

Listing 2.12: Hallo.scala with source code documentation for scaladoc

```
/ **
* Hello reader application
* @ author Oliver Braun
* @ version 1.0.0
* /
object Hello extends Application {
println ("Hello reader!")
}
```

2.2 Build tools

There are many options for creating Scala applications. Hereinafter
let us introduce two ways. Especially those switching from Java, who are already familiar with

ven have worked, you will be able to start immediately with the Maven Scala plug-in. nen. Anyone who has no experience with Maven will find an introduction to it Section 2.2.1. In the following section 2.2.2 we present the simple build Tool (Sbt) before. Sbt is a tool written in Scala for Scala, which is used by Scala-Code can be configured and expanded. Within the Scala community Sbt is becoming more and more important.

2.2.1 The Maven Scala plugin

Apache Maven is a build and configuration management tool for the Software development that is widely used in the Java environment. With the help of With the so-called *Project Object Model* (POM), Maven can create the software re including dependencies, documentation, tests, etc. For more information For information on Maven, please visit http://maven.apache. org / or pick up one of the books about Maven, such as [Son08]. With plugins it is possible to adapt Maven to new fields of activity. The Maven Scala Plugin 5 is used to compile Scala source code with Maven
test and run as well as the generation of documentation. In order to work with Maven, it is sufficient first of all to have Maven in a len version to install 6 . Maven itself uses an existing Java
Installation ahead. A Scala distribution must be used with Maven. which will be present on the system yet to be installed. Was Maven successful A Maven project can be installed on the command line with $ mvn archetype: generate be created. The mvn command starts Maven. The argument arche- type: generate is a so-called *target* (Engl. *Goal*). Strictly speaking it stands the prefix archetype for the plugin which contains the target generate. If The first time you start Maven, a lot of data is in the local Maven repository downloaded. For example, it can be found on Unix under ~ / .m2 / repository /. Maven offers a number of archetypes, the numbering of which is always different can then change as new archetypes are added. For the Scala There is a scala-archetype-simple development under the current num- mer 272. With version 1.2 of the Scala plug-in, the GroupID, the ArtifactID and The version can then, for example, include the artifact my-app in the group org.obraun under version 1.0. The directory created by Maven nis structure looks like this in the concrete example:

```
my-app
| - pom.xml
+ - src
| - main
|
+ - scale
|
+ - org
|
+ - dark brown
|
+ - App.scala
+ - test
+ - scale
+ - org
+ - dark brown
| - AppTest.scala
|   MySpec.scala
```

The HelloWorld application generated in the App.scala file can then be selected from the directory my-app with
$ mvn compile
to be translated. The files stored in the AppTest.scala and MySpec.scala nerated tests can be used with
$ mvn test
are executed. With
$ mvn package
a Java archive (.jar file) is created that is saved with
$ scala -cp target / my-app-1.0-SNAPSHOT.jar \
org.obraun.scala.App
Hello World writes on the console.
The stated goals, compile, test and package, are standard Maven Targets that use the Scala plug-in and are based on the Maven specification build differently.
The Scala plug-in has a few special goals. To only use the appli- mvn scala: compile can be used to translate cation sources. The The mvn scala: testCompile command only compiles the test sources.
The target scala: cc is very interesting, with which all sources are immediately automatically translated. If the target is started with mvn scala: cc, it runs until it is explicitly canceled.
The goals site and scala: doc are used to generate the Scala documentation.
An application can be started via scala: run, via scala: console starts the interactive Scala shell.
Maven is configured in the pom.xml file. There, for example The Scala version to be used must be specified as a property. Becomes a version other than the predefined 2.7.0 is specified, e.g. 2.8.0, the Scala distribution cannot be installed, but is produced by Maven itself. downloaded, installed in the local repository and started.
A large number of other configurations can be stored in the file or in several ren hierarchically building *POMs can be* made. In order to for example the HelloWorld application with mvn scala: run without specifying To execute further arguments, a launcher can be specified, for example- wise:

```
<launcher>
<id> helloWorld </id>
<mainClass> org.obraun.scala.App </mainClass>
</launcher>
```

If multiple launchers are defined, the first one is selected unless the ID is used as an argument, e.g. mvn scala: run helloWorld.
Because a thorough introduction to Maven is beyond the scope of this book Let's end this overview. Further information
For information on the Maven Scala plugin, go to http://scala-tools.org/ mvnsites / maven-scala-plugin /.

2.2.2 Simple Build Tool

The Simple Build Tool *Sbt* is a build tool especially for Scala. It is as a jar File sbt-launch.jar available on the project homepage 7 . In the online Documentation, it is recommended to design the Jar with a heapsize of 512 MB. and best to build a script to start. Under Unix see that recommended single line script as follows from 8 : java -Xmx512M -jar /path/to/sbt-launch.jar "$ @"
It is recommended to use the following batch file under Windows 9 :

set SCRIPT_DIR =% ~ dp0
java -Xmx512M -jar "% SCRIPT_DIR% sbt-launch.jar"% *
A proxy server that may be present must be able to use the standard Java perties are set 10 . In order to then be able to easily use SBT in your projects nen, the directory in which it is located should be in the path or by a
Alias to be found 11 .
Like Maven, Sbt only requires an existing Java installation. The necessary The Scala distribution is installed by SBT itself. Should a project with Sbt are managed, a project directory must first be created and then sbt can be started.

Listing 2.13: Creating an Sbt Project

```
$ mkdir my-app
$ cd my-app
$ sbt
Project does not exist, create new project? (y / N / s) y
Name: my-app
Organization: org.obraun
Version [1.0]:
Scala version [2.7.7]: 2.8.0
sbt version [0.7.4]:
```

In Listing 2.13, a directory my-app is first created and inserted there changed. The call of sbt finds no existing directory in the current directory of the Sbt project and therefore asks whether a new one should be created. Will 's' for
scratch entered, no complete project is created, but an existing one Code can then be translated and executed immediately by typing run. If 'y' is entered as in Listing 2.13, Sbt asks for name, organization and version of the project as well as the Scala and Sbt version to be used. The The directory structure created by Sbt looks like this immediately afterwards
out:

```
my-app
| - lib
| - project
|
| - boat
|
+ - build.properties
| - src
|
| - main
|
|
| - resources
|
|
+ - scale
|
+ - test
|
| - resources
|
+ - scale
```

```
+ - target
```

In the directories src / main / scala and src / test / scala the Scala source code files for the application or for the tests are created and processed. If Java sources are also to be used, the Create subdirectories src / main / java or src / test / java and to use. So Sbt has the same structure for the sources as Maven. Files that are to be integrated into the main jar or the test jar, they must in the subdirectory resources. In order to integrate dependencies, the corresponding jars must be in the lib- Directory or a subdirectory of lib can be copied. But sbt can can also be configured to automatically download dependencies and copied into an additional directory lib_managed. The project directory contains the information for Sbt. The property file build.properties can be edited directly and accepts changes, which were carried out interactively. In a build directory, the project can be configured. Plugins are drawing project / plugins configured. Since Sbt is written in Scala, it takes place the configuration also directly in Scala. The boot directory contains the Sbt and Scala versions required for the project. If a project is translated, all generated files such as class files and documentation end up in the target Directory.

If sbt is entered in the shell without arguments, sbt starts in the interactive Mode. If actions and commands are used on the command line as arguments are transferred in batch mode.

Sbt knows a variety of *build actions* , e.g. clean, compile and run, and *Build commands* , e.g. exit and help. Of particular interest are the mandos of the form ~ < command > for the automatic execution of the command dos < command > as soon as a source file has changed, and ++ < version > < command > for changing to another Scala version. That means for example wisely, with ~ compile every changed source code file is compiled immediately, and with ++ 2.8.0.RC2 console a Scala shell in version 2.8.0.RC2 be started.

The possibilities of Sbt are very extensive and it can be perfect in Scala can be adapted to your own needs. In addition, there is already one Numerous extensions in the form of plugins such as *SbtEclipsify* to To equip the project with a .classpath and a .project file so that it can be edited smoothly in Eclipse. A detailed presentation from Sbt can be found at http://code.google.com/p/simple-build-tool/.

2.3 IDE support

There is a scale for common development environments in the Java environment Support in the form of plugins. With Scala version 2.8 is a lot of the code necessary for IDE support into the Scala distribution itself hiked. Based on this, there is the Scala IDE for Eclipse (see section 2.3.1), a plug-in for NetBeans (see section 2.3.2) and one for IntelliJ IDEA (see section 2.3.3). Of course there is also support for text Editors like VIM, Emacs or TextMate. As there are those who have a text editor will not be difficult to activate Scala support and the introductory tion become too extensive for everyone who does not know or use the editors we would simply skip a review in the context of this book all.

2.3.1 Eclipse

The Scala IDE for Eclipse [12] can be found at http://www.scala-ide.org/ . Eclipse and the JDK version are required to install the plug-in 1.6. The Scala IDE offers Scala support for editing and debugging and navigation in Scala projects. In addition, mixed Scala / Java Projects are processed. A Scala refactoring framework [13] , a source code Formatter

[14] and many other useful and important things like XML syntax Highlighting, code templates and quick fix imports are now also in- been integrated. To install the Scala IDE for Eclipse, open Eclipse and select the In the Help menu, select Install New Software. Enter the site as the desired URL, which you can download from http://download.scala-ide.org/
can choose [15] . Then choose both JDT Weaving for Scala and Scala IDE for Eclipse and install it. After a new
At the start of Eclipse, a Scala perspective and the Scala wizards are available Available. Figure 2.2 shows a screenshot of the Scala IDE for Eclipse.

2.3.2 NetBeans

The NetBeans [16] support is provided by the ErlyBird Project [17] and is located is currently still in beta. To install the Scala plugins, download download the zip file from the ErlyBird site [18] and unzip it at any Job. Then open NetBeans and select the "Tools" menu item wear "plugins". In the window that opens, you can click the "Download- ded "press the button" Add Plugins ". In the file dialog you navigate to where you unzipped the plugins and select all .nbm files. The names of the plugins then displayed indicate the scope of the scale Supports include: Scala Core, Scala Debugger, Scala Refactoring, to name a few to call. Then click "Install" and follow the instructions to install the plugins. In order to then actually develop Scala under NetBeans you just have to set the $ SCALA_HOME variable so that the Scala compiler etc. can be found under $ SCALA_HOME / bin. A single pressure from working with NetBeans should be conveyed in Figure 2.3.

2.3.3 IntelliJ IDEA

The third Java IDE that can offer Scala support is the IntelliJ IDEA [19] . The Community Edition is free and can be downloaded for free. After starting, the Scala plug-in can be selected via the plug-in manager and installed. The Scala plug-in includes support for editing data and formatting, compiling, testing and debugging, refactoring, navigation gation and search as well as various intention actions. After a restart you can start Scala development [20] . A new
Create the project as a Java project and select "Desired Technologies"Scala off. A look at the IntelliJ IDEA with the Scala plug-in installed shows

Chapter 3

Basics

After getting to know the tools, we finally want to start using the the first steps in Scala. We will do this first in Section 3.1
consider the syntax of Scala. Section 3.2 shows how imperative in Scala, ie is programmed with simple control structures.
To get to know Scala as quickly as possible and without major hurdles, recommend we will let you try out the examples while reading. The in section 3.1The code snippets given can be entered directly into the Scala shell. In
Section 3.2 shows you pieces of code that you can save to a file and can be executed as a script with scala < filename > .
Then in Section 3.3 we will show you how to write a program that does is translated into bytecode with the Scala compiler and then executed can be. The chapter closes with a brief look at annotations in cut 3.4.

3.1 A little bit of syntax

The Scala syntax is largely based on the Java syntax. In some areas but it differs significantly. A key goal of Scala in terms of the syntax is to be able to program as briefly and concisely as possible. That's why
are some things like the semicolon at the end of each line in Scala largely optional. Scala is statically typed. In contrast to Java, however, they are not necessarySpecify types everywhere in the code. Scala can use a type inference mechanism
must [1] determine the type yourself in most places [2] . Due to the fact, that the type can be omitted when defining a variable, for example it is not possible to use the Java and other C-like languages
keep the same syntax < type > < varname > . Instead, in Scala the identifier specified, followed by a colon and the type, e.g.
val age: Int If the type can be inferred and therefore omitted, the colon must also be used can be omitted, e.g.

```
var sum = 0
```

However, a variable definition in Scala must always start with var or val and contain an initialization of the variable, except as a member of a Class or a trait (see Chapter 4), ie the age variable specified above
must be declared in the context of a class or a trait. One with vargenerated variable can be changed. The variable defined with val (for *value*) is unchangeable and thus corresponds to a final variable in Java. Basically
the unchangeable variant should be preferred over what a functional Programming style.
That's how we make our lives as programmers often easier. For example, it only needs to be checked once whether the assigned
The indicated value is correct and we can, for example, also be sure that it is not from any other thread can be changed.
For parameterized types, the type parameter is in square brackets, e.g. Are defined

```
var list: List [Int] = List ()
```

a (changeable) variable list of the type "list of integers" 3 . Due to the Type inference can write the right side of the definition without the type parameter. be practiced. Of course, it is also possible to specify it:

```
val list: List [Int] = List [Int] ()
```

If no empty list is generated, but the list with elements 1, 2 and 3, the type of the variable can also be inferred and does not have to be specified will:

```
val list = List (1,2,3)
```

In the code snippets above, it is noticeable that list objects are generated, but not gends a new can be seen, although objects are also created in Scala with new the. The abbreviated notation is not a special feature of the lists, but can can basically be used anywhere if the apply method is defined is 4 . Namely, List () automatically expands to List.apply () becomes. The apply method then creates a new empty list object and returns this back. Similarly, List (1,2,3) becomes List.apply (1,2,3) and is created a list object that contains the numbers 1, 2, and 3. By the way, at this point new List () cannot be written, since the List class, as in Java, is is strakt. The use of the *factory method* apply also saves us the choice of a specific implementation. However, if we want a special implementation, e.g. a Java-ArrayList, this can of course also be made:

```
val list = new java.util.ArrayList [Int] ()
```

The above line of code shows how smoothly Java code integrates with Scala leaves. There a Java list is taken that contains Scala integers, the again by using the Java data type java.lang.Integer implement are animalized. Is even previously used with java.util.ArrayList import java.util.ArrayList

imported, enough to write:

```
val list = new ArrayList [Int] ()
```

In the case of the Java-ArrayList, the variable list can no longer use the Type List [Int] because it is not an implementation of the Scala class List. A sensible typing would be java.util.List [Int], the type inference mechanism calculates the type java.util.ArrayList [Int] without specifying the type. Arrays do not receive any special treatment in Scala. With

```
val array = array (1,2,3)
```

an immutable variable array is defined, which is an array of length 3 with the values 1, 2 and 3, which was generated using Array.apply (1,2,3),referenced. If an array is created with new, the parameter corresponds to the length of the array, e.g. an array of length 5 with

```
val array = new Array [Int] (5)
```

generated. With this definition, the parameter type Int must be specified, because otherwise no information is available from which the type can be derived that could. Defining it as val is like a final variable in Java only the reference to the array is immutable. The array itself can be for example wise with

```
array (1) = 6
```

can be changed so that it is then at the second position (the index starts at 0) contains the value 6. The index is in scala in round brackets written. This easy way to change the value at the point can be transferred to other classes. The code fragment array (1) = 6 is expanded to a normal method call, namely to
array.update (1.6)
This works for all classes that implement the update method. With
However, this does not work with the previously presented Scala list. It lies because the list generated by list () itself unchangeable (*immutable*)
is. For example, if a value is added to the beginning of the list with the *Cons operator* :: "Added", a new list, consisting of the value and the old list
te, generated. The old list remains unchanged. [5] The basic use from *immutable data* comes from functional programming and also represents in Scala is the preferred solution. In contrast to many functional ones Programming languages in Scala, however, remain the *imperative* way of changing tion of data is still possible, for example because in some cases is more efficient.
For example, if a list of many elements is gradually put together a ListBuffer can be used instead, which is then converted into a List is converted. [6] Listing 3.1 shows an example.

Listing 3.1: Using a ListBuffer

```
import scala.collection.mutable.ListBuffer
val listbuffer = ListBuffer [Int] ()
listbuffer + = 1
listbuffer ++ = List (2,3,4)
val list = listbuffer.toList
```

First the ListBuffer is imported in the first line, and in the second Line abbreviated ListBuffer. [7] In the second line,
an empty ListBuffer is generated via the apply method. On the third line the number 1 is appended, in the fourth line the numbers 2, 3 and 4.
Lich becomes the List (1,2,3,4) list from the ListBuffer in the last line generated.
Lines 3 and 4 are of particular interest with regard to the syntax. knows other C-like languages, would assume that listbuffer + = 1 is the Abbreviated notation for listbuffer = listbuffer + 1. In Scala this is not always the case. The character string + = is a valid identifier for a method that is defined in the ListBuffer class. Only if no such method de is present, the operator is interpreted as in C-like languages. This applies to any operator that ends with an =. Exceptions are the equals operators <=,> =,! = as well as all operators that are additionally preceded by an = begin. By the way, there is a special syntax like i ++ for the abbreviation of i = i
+1 not allowed in Scala.
In Scala, listbuffer + = 1 stands for listbuffer. + = (1), ie a method with the name + = and the argument 1. That this is possible is due to two Things: First, almost any name can be used in Scala methods (see further below), and secondly, in Scala, method calls with an argument ment without a dot or brackets, ie in *infix operator notation* written, will. This also makes it clear what the initially somewhat unusual ++ = in line

4 means: listbuffer. ++ = (List (2,3,4)).
If you look closely, even line 5 still seems a bit strange. We are
but from other languages used to having method names from argument lists
should be followed, i.e. we would rather have listbuffer.toList () with a
expected with the empty pair of brackets. Why this is possible or why the use
The use of brackets is not allowed here at all, is discussed in more detail in Chapter 4.
Now that you know that operators are actually just normal methods
let's look at the code fragment:
1 :: List (2,3,4)
that creates the list List (1,2,3,4). According to the previous rules
we now assume that we can explicitly write (1) .: :(List (2,3,4)) [8] . This
but would mean that the class Int (and all other classes whose ob-
objects we can store in lists) would have to implement the :: method.
After this is not only inexpedient, but also not manageable and
contradicts the idea of object orientation, according to which a list class for the
Generation of a list is responsible, of course it is not so. The method
de :: is implemented in the List class, which means the line above is actually called
List (2,3,4) .: :(1).
The code in Listing 3.2 is still correct. The rule is simple: Every-
the operator that ends with a colon is called the method of the right
Operands interpreted. The left operand is the argument. For all others
Operators (i.e. those that do not end with:) apply the other way round: The method
becomes
searched for the left operand, and the right operand is the argument. There
So it only depends on the colon at the end, you also have to do it yourself
remember the defined methods.
Any number of identifiers are not allowed in Scala. For education
There are three possibilities of valid identifiers:

1. The first character is a letter. Then any letters can be used on it
and numbers follow. After an underscore _, either book-
letters followed by numbers or operator signs. Examples: sum, unary_-
2. The first character is an operator character. Then any sequence of
Operator characters follow. Examples: ::, ++ =
3. Any string between *backquotes* . Examples: 'def', 'class'

Unicode is permitted for the entire source code (including the identifier).
Permissible operator characters are (in order of ascending ASCII value):
! #% & * + - /: <=>? @ \ ^ | ~
Since Scala Infix operators themselves can be defined, it is also defined
which operator binds stronger, i.e. whether an expression of the form:
expr1 <op1> expr2 <op2> expr3
with three expressions linked by two operators as:
(expr1 <op1> expr2) <op2> expr3
or:
expr1 <op1> (expr2 <op2> expr3)
is to be interpreted. To put it another way : Whether < op1 > binds more strongly than < op2 > or
vice versa.
Scala follows a simple rule: the further down the character with which the operator
rator begins, in Table 3.1, the stronger it binds. Characters in the same
Row have the same bond strength. So Scala follows what is also in Java
is common.

Table 3.1: Operator binding
(all letters)
|

^
&
<>
=!
:
+ -
* /%
(all other special characters)
Are < op1 > and < op2 > *the* same operator or have
they have the same strength of bond, associativity decides what to-
is calculated first. The following applies: The operators that end with: are right associative, all others are left-associative. That means for example 1 :: 2 ::

List () means 1 :: (2 :: List ()), and 1 + 2 + 3 means (1 + 2) + 3.
The following keywords are used in Scala, not or only under
Using backquotes as identifiers can be used:
abstract case
catch
class
def
do
else
extends false
final
finally
for
forSome if
implicit
import
lazy
match
new
zero
object
override package private protected
requires return
sealed
Super
this
throw
trait
try
true
type
val
var
while
with
yield
_
:
=
=>

<-
<:
<%
>:
#
@
In addition, the Unicode characters ⇒ (\ u21D2) and ← (\ u2190) are reserved.
In addition to the literals for numbers, characters, Boolean and
Strings, Scala also offers the option of adding multi-line strings.
ben, e.g.
"""This is
a multiline
String "" "
However, this string contains the spaces in front of a and character
Chain. In order to remove these automatically, the method stripMargin
be used, e.g.
"""This is
| a multiline
| String "" ". StripMargin
Comments in Scala either start with // and end with the
lenende or with / * and end with * /. In contrast to Java, multi-line
Comments are nested. However, this leads to a coming
tar of the form
*/ * This is one that begins with two "/ *", but not*
*correctly ended comment * /*
is not allowed.
Scala has a special syntax for tuples. Tuples look like parameter lists.
They start and end with an opening or closing parenthesis
and can have multiple components separated by commas, e.g.
val myTuple = ("Hello", 1, true, 5.7)
The components can be of different types. The type then becomes analog
written to the tuple, i.e. the tuple myTuple has the type (String, Int,
Boolean, Double). We can access the individual components with the
methods _ <position number>, where the position number is 1
begins. So it results in the interactive Scala-Shell for myTuple:
scala> val first = myTuple._1
first: java.lang.String = Hello
scala> val second = myTuple._2
second: Int = 1
scala> val third = myTuple._3
third: Boolean = true
scala> val fourth = myTuple._4
fourth: Double = 5.7
Tuples can also be used on the left side of an assignment to
assign the different components of a tuple to different identifiers
organize. For example, instead of the four individual assignments, we can only have one
use individual assignment, which all components at once to the corresponding
assigns the following identifiers:
scale> val (first, second, third, fourth) = myTuple
first: java.lang.String = Hello
second: Int = 1
third: Boolean = true
fourth: Double = 5.7
Scala has another possibility to have several identifiers at the same time

Assign value. It is possible to add several identifiers to the left of the assignment rator separated by commas and an expression on the right side specify, e.g.

```
scale> val i, j = 12
i: Int = 12
j: Int = 12
```

If we use a value of a variable data type on the right side, we each variable comes with its own value. In the following session we will assign initially m and n are a variable, empty set. Then we add a ne 12 in the set m and output both sets. As in the issue too can be seen, the set n remains unchanged:

```
scala> val m, n = scala.collection.mutable.Set [Int] ()
m: scala.collection.mutable.Set [Int] = Set ()
n: scala.collection.mutable.Set [Int] = Set ()
scale> m + = 12
res0: m.type = Set (12)
scala> println ("m =" + m + "\ nn =" + n)
m = set (12)
n = set ()
```

In this case, by the way, m + = 12 cannot abbreviate m = m + 12 be, because m is a val. The attempt to use the supposedly extensive spelling Using se leads to an error message:

```
scale> m = m + 12
<console>: 6: error: reassignment to val
m = m + 12
^
```

That is, in this case m + = 12 corresponds to the method call m. + = (12), which changes the set referenced by m.

Analogous to the variable definition with var or val, a function definition begins on always with the keyword def. It is followed by the function name and the pa- parameter list 9 . The return type, if it should or must be specified, given with a colon separated after the arguments, e.g.

```
def hello (name: String) {
println ("Hello" + name)
}
```

The local type inference mechanism implemented in Scala can change the parameter do not calculate types. Therefore, these must always be specified in the parameter list. be practiced. As expected, the function call consists of the function names and the argument list:

```
hello ("Oliver")
```

If, as in the hello function, no value is returned, the function has the result type Unit 10 . Should the return type in the function definition must be specified explicitly before the opening, curly bracket There is always an equal sign, ie the function hello can also be defined are made by:

```
def hello (name: String): Unit = {
println ("Hello" + name)
}
```

A function with the result type Unit is called a *procedure* in Scala . Usual The unit type and the equal sign are then usually omitted.

If a function is to calculate a result, an equal sign must always be used can be used, e.g. for:

```
def sum (x: Int, y: Int): Int = {
return x + y
```

}
If the last calculated expression is returned as the result, the key is
Keyword return optional, i.e. sum can also be defined by:
def sum (x: Int, y: Int): Int = {
x + y
}
If the function body consists of a single expression, the curly braces are omitted:
def sum (x: Int, y: Int): Int = x + y
Finally, in most cases, the result type of a function must be cannot be specified. That is, the shortest version of sum is:
def sum (x: Int, y: Int) = x + y
The result type can **not** be determined automatically in the following cases the:

1. The function contains an explicit return.
2. The function is recursive.
3. The function is overloaded and one of the functions is calling one of the others. Then the result type must be specified for the calling function.
4. The type should be explicitly restricted compared to the inferred one.

From version 2.8.0 there are *named arguments* and *default arguments* . It is with the former
possible to name the arguments explicitly when calling a function and to put them in in a different order. With the latter, the arguments for which a default value has been defined can be omitted. The following radio tion calls are all equivalent:
sum (1,2)
sum (x = 1.2)
sum (1, y = 2)
sum (x = 1, y = 2)
sum (y = 2, x = 1)
The last line, in which the two arguments were exchanged. If the function sum is defined with default arguments by:
def sum (x: Int = 1, y: Int = 0) = x + y
can therefore also be written:
sum (x = 1)
sum (y = 2)
The above expression sum (x = 1,2) is somewhat misleading as it is only used in the al case is allowed, in which the sequence is adhered to. Although he leads to the correct result, you should consider mixing named arguments and positional arguments adhere to the rule that all unnamed arguments must come before all named arguments, because the parameter list is first filled from the front in sequence, starting with the unnamed Arguments. The following two expressions are therefore not allowed:
sum (2, x = 1) // not allowed
sum (y = 2,1) // not allowed
It is also possible to allow a variable number of parameters. Displayed this is indicated with the * after specifying the common name for all parameters ter and the type of a single parameter. For example, the following Function can be called with any number of Int arguments. Every argument ment is then output on a separate line.
def printInts (ints: Int *) {
for (int <- ints) println (int)
}
The for loop used here is explained in section 3.2. As can be seen,

All arguments are hidden behind the name ints, in the form of a
Arrays. However, an array cannot be passed directly because the
the arguments expected individually. But it can simply be specified by specifying the type _ * in
individual values are converted, e.g. the following call of
printInts with the numbers array:

```
val numbers = array (1,2,3,4)
printInts (numbers: _ *)
```

The same procedure also works for other collections, for example:

```
printInts (List (100,200,300): _ *)
```

The function can also be called without any arguments. Fixed
given parameters and variable parameters can also be mixed. All-
however, the variable parameters must always be at the end of the parameter list, e.g.

```
def printStringAndInts (string: String, ints: Int *) {
//...
```

Scala can basically [11] all be nested, that is functioning
nes can contain other functions. This makes it possible, for example,
an auxiliary function, which is only necessary for one function, directly into it integrate.

[11] Not quite everything. For example, packages can only contain objects and classes.

Listing 3.3. A function that contains a function

```
def haveSameElements (xs: List [Any], ys: List [Any]) = {
def isSubsetOf (xs: List [Any], ys: List [Any]): Boolean = {
for (x <- xs)
if (! (ys contains x)) return false
true
}
isSubsetOf (xs, ys) && isSubsetOf (ys, xs)
}
```

Listing 3.3 shows an example. The haveSameElements function checks whether
two lists contain the same elements, i.e. whether the representation as a set
equals [12] . For this purpose it is checked whether one list is a subset of the other and
vice versa. To avoid redundant code for subset checking,
a function isSubsetOf is defined within haveSameElements.
This checks by means of a for loop [13] for each element x of the first list
xs whether it is also included in the second. Once an item is found
that is not in the second list, returns false. Can the Schlei-
fe are run through completely, all elements are included and the result
is therefore true.
After isSubsetOf contains an explicit return, the result type
Boolean must be specified. The type Any is the super type of all Scala types, ie
the most general type for any Scala object is Any. This enables the function
haveSameElements can be applied to lists with any elements.
Explain how the type can be restricted using a type parameter
we in section 5.7.
Scala has a so-called *semicolon inference mechanism* , ie on most
No semicolons need to be written in places. As a rule, the
lenende interpreted as a semicolon. If an expression is spread over several lines
it must be recognizable that the printout has not yet been completed.
For example, in the first line of the following function call, it is clear that
the expression cannot end with the +:

```
hello ("Oliver" +
"Brown")
```

Becomes the math function $f(x, y, z) = x * y + z$ in the following way defined, the result of f (1,2,3) is the number 3, not about 5:

```
def f (x: Int, y: Int, z: Int) = {
x * y
+ z
}
```

The inference mechanism puts a semicolon after the y so that the function + z returns as the result. For example, the deficiency is correctly calculated nition:

```
def f (x: Int, y: Int, z: Int) = {
x * y +
z
}
```

Scala allows the definition of type synonyms with the keyword type. At- for example, according to the definition you can:

```
type IntList = List [Int]
```

Use the IntList type in your programs. Are particularly useful Type synonyms to make programs more readable. For example, do we want to manage a price list in a program that includes the Saves price in cents, we can use a map [String, Int] 14 use. We can also use the following type syn- use onyme:

```
type ProductName = String
type Cent = Int
type PriceList = Map [ProductName, Cent]
```

The previous overview included the essential, but not all Aspects of Scala Syntax. Other specifics are related with the respective concepts explained in the following chapters. It now follows an introduction to the essential, built-in control structures.

3.2 Imperative programming

Although object orientation has been consistently implemented in Scala, it is not always necessary to define classes and objects. In Scala you can also Even for small tasks, simple scripts can be created and executed. Based In the following, we would like to give you the imperative programming of these scripts present in Scala.

Listing 3.4 is a complete Scala script and can be saved as a file with a any name, e.g. Hallo.scala, saved and then on the command do line with scala Hallo.scala and an optional argument will.

Listing 3.4: Hallo.scala

```
if (args isEmpty)
println ("Hello stranger")
else
if (args (0) == "Oliver")
println ("Hi")
else
println ("Hello" + args (0))
```

Command line arguments are used in Scala as in many other programming also talked about passing the args array. If no argument is passed

ben, ie if the args array is empty, the output reads hello stranger.
Analogous to the infix operator notation, we have the *postfix* for args *isEmpty Operator notation* selected. We have both the point and the empty argumentlist omitted. In detail we could write args.isEmpty (), where there is a Scala convention which states that the empty brackets should be left if the method has no side effects. So that would be according to the convention, verbose notation args.isEmpty.
If arguments are passed to the script, the first element with the String Oliver compared and then Hi or Hello < name > excluded where < name > *is* the first command line argument. In Scala compared the objects with ==. If you still prefer to use equals, can do this - preferably in the usual Scala operator notation name equals "Oliver". The comparison operator == is a synonym for equals. Should the ob-eq must be used.
The control structure if is in Scala an expression that the value of the executed Branch returns as a result and thus corresponds to the ternary?: Operator from C speaks. The hello script can therefore also be written as in Listing 3.5.

Listing 3.5: Hallo2.scala

```
println (if (args isEmpty)
"Hello Stranger"
else
if (args (0) == "Oliver")
"Hi"
else
"Hello" + args (0))
```

Scala also contains while and do-while loops as additional control structures fen. Listing 3.6 shows a script that uses a while loop to input the User until quit is entered.

Listing 3.6: Echo.scala

```
var input = ""
while (input! = "quit") {
input = readLine ()
println ("Echo:" + input)
}
```

You will be slowly wondering where the println and readLine are coming. They look like built-in functions, but they are normal methods. The trick is the Predef object. This object contains these and many other useful methods and is automatically included in every scale Program imported. In addition, the methods, as in the previous Some listings can be seen without specifying the Predef object.
The Predef object is discussed in Section 6.1.
Scala also has a for loop, which is more of a foreach loop corresponds. Listing 3.7 shows a complete Scala script that includes all command lines Outputs lenarguments on a separate line.

Listing 3.7: Args.scala

```
for (arg <- args) println (arg)
```

The expression arg < - args is called a *generator* and generates args for everyone Loop through a new element assigned to the variable arg until eventually the array is completely traversed. The introduced loop variable arg behaves like a val, ie arg can be inside the loop body cannot be changed.
The classic for loop with a loop variable such as for (int i =

0; i < 10; i ++) does not exist in Scala. If you still need a counter variable, can do this, for example, as in Listing 3.8.

Listing 3.8: Args2.scala

```
for (i <- 0 to args.length-1) println (args (i))
```

In Listing 3.8, the expression 0 to args.length-1 corresponds to the method invocation (0) .to (args.length-1), i.e. to is a method of class Int [15] and returns a Range object. Scalas for expression is a very powerful one Tool that will be considered in more detail in Section 5.6.

In Scala, as in many other programs, curly brackets define a so-called *scope* , a range of validity. Will be within of such a scope defines something, e.g. a variable or a function it only valid therein. The identifier simply does not exist outside the scope more. Since curly braces can be nested inside each other, there are Scopes that contain scopes. If an identifier is used in an inner scope det, which was already used in the outer scope, overshadows the inner one Definition the outer.

Listing 3.9: A function with a shaded variable

```
def fun (x: Int) = {
if (x == 3) {
val x = 7
println (x)
}
println (x)
}
```

As an example, consider the function in Listing 3.9. Although in function only println (x) occurs, when fun (3) is called first a 7, then a 3 is output. The identifier x is valid in the entire function Call fun (3) has the value 3. In the first branch of the if statement, the curly brackets create a new scope. A new x Are defined. This overshadows the outer x with the value 3. Therefore there is a 7 issued. After the closing curly bracket, the inner loses x its validity. Therefore a 3 is output for the second println (x).

3.3 An executable program

So far we have written Scala scripts dealing with scala < filename > have it carried out. With the Scala compilers scalac and fsc you can also executable programs are generated. Depending on how it was compiled, for the execution of a Java Virtual Machine or a .NET environment agile.

A Scala script cannot be translated directly into an executable program the. An object that implements the main method can be executed in Scala. Objects and methods are introduced in Chapter 4. At this point you want we only briefly introduce the necessary syntax.

The easiest way to make a script translatable is the so-called Extending the application trait [16] . Listing 3.10 shows the implementation of the Echo scripts from Listing 3.6 on page 41 as an application.

Listing 3.10. An Executable Echo Program

```
object Echo extends Application {
var input = ""
while (input! = "quit") {
input = readLine ()
println ("Echo:" + input)
}
```

}
In contrast to the echo script, two lines have been added: the first and the last. This defines an object with the name Echo (object Echo), that extends the application trait (extends application). All that belongs to the object, must then be enclosed within a pair of curly braces be written.
The source code file is then translated with
$ scalac Echo.scala
or.
$ fsc Echo.scala
To execute it, the object name is used as an argument to the scala command to hand over:
$ scala echo
Hello World
Echo: Hello world
Hello readers
Echo: Hello readers
quit
Echo: quit
The presented extension of the application trait, however, has some restrictions. It is essential at this point that the array args with the com-command line arguments so is not available. That is, the attempt to ting 3.7 on page 41 an executable by expanding the application trait Making program fails with the following error message when compiling fail:
$ fsc Args.scala
Args.scala: 2: error: not found: value args
for (arg <- args)
^
one error found
Programs that consist of several threads can use the application trait do not use, as this leads to so-called deadlocks 17 . And too good Lastly, some JVM implementations are unable to code optimize that is carried out by the application trait. Therefore, the application of the application trait only for very simple, from a single Thread existing programs recommended.
Without application trait, there must be a main method in the object that is should be implemented. The body of this method then becomes run at startup. The main method has an array as its only parameter from strings via which the command line arguments can be passed, and no result, i.e. the result type Unit. Listing 3.11 shows the implementation the code from Listing 3.7 as an executable program.

Listing 3.11. An executable program with an explicit main method

```
object Args {
def main (args: Array [String]) {
for (arg <- args)
println (arg)
}
}
```

The translated object can then be executed with the scala command:
$ scala Args "Hello World" and "Hello Reader"
Hello World
and

3.4 Annotations

Scala supports *annotations* to add metadata to a declaration.
Annotations are used in both Java and .NET, and in particular
In the field of enterprise applications, it is hard to imagine life without them. Java- and .NET annotations can be used directly in the Scala code.
Annotations begin with an @ sign followed by the name of the annotation.
The name can be followed by a list of arguments in round brackets. With Scala 2.8
Annotations can also be nested within each other. Typical annotations
ons are in Scala

```
@serializable class C {...}
@transient @volatile var m: Int
@deprecated ("Use g instead") def f = ...
(e: @unchecked) match {...}
```

Annotations can therefore precede classes or variable or function definitions. or after an expression and a colon. Furthermore
there is also the possibility to write an annotation after a type, e.g.
String @local. Some annotations, e.g. @throws, @unchecked, @tailrec and @specialized, we will introduce you to them later in the book.
In contrast to Java, however, the above examples show that Scala uses annotations in some places, for which there is a keyword in Java: transient or volatile. 18th
Annotations can also be easily defined yourself without special syntax the. All you have to do is write a class that is separated from annotation. is 19 . The use of the annotation with @ <annotationname> corresponds to then the constructor call of this class. There are already two specialized ones Versions you can infer from: scala.ClassfileAnnotation and scala.StaticAnnotation. A class file annotation is only used in the generated class file. Static annotation wherever there is an noted identifier is used.

Chapter 4

Pure object orientation

Scala is a purely object-oriented programming language 1 with a uniform Object model. That is, every value is an object and every operation is one Message to an object. In this chapter, the Basic building blocks, classes and objects presented. Then we go into 4.2 briefly discussed the organization of the code. Scala has no interfaces, but so-called traits (see Section 4.3). In addition to method signatures already contain implementations and also fields. The end Section 4.4 of the chapter on implicit conversions and pa-parameters and the so-called rich wrappers, with the help of which existing classes can be expanded.

4.1 Classes and Objects

The core of object orientation are objects and classes as blueprints for ob-jects. In contrast to many other object-oriented programming languages In Scala, not only classes with the keyword class, but also so-called *singleton objects,* i.e. independent objects without an associated class programmed with the keyword object.

4.1.1 Fields and Methods

Objects and classes can contain fields and methods, grouped together under the Names of *members* , included. Fields are defined like variables with var or val depending on whether they should be changeable. Methods are to the object resp. functions belonging to the class and are therefore introduced with def. All Members of a class or an object are at the top level. This means, Members cannot be other members, but of course functions and Contain variables.

Listing 4.1: The Hello object

```
object Hello {
var greeting = "Hello"
def hello () {
println (greeting)
}
}
```

Listing 4.1 defines an object (keyword object) with the name Hello which has a field 2 and a method. The field greeting is assigned the string Hello assigned. Due to the type inference, the type String does not have to be must be specified explicitly. The hello method has no arguments and returns the value of the greeting field with the Predef method println on the sole off. For example, if the object is defined in the interactive Scala shell 3 , so you can work with it afterwards, as the following session shows:

```
scala> Hello.hello ()
Hello
scala> Hello.greeting = "Hi"
scala> Hello.hello ()
Hi
```

In the above session, the message hello was first sent to the object Hello which then responds by executing its method hello. At-

Finally, the string Hi was assigned to the greeting field. The new one Executing hello then writes hi to the console as expected.

The definition of a class initially differs from that of an object once only by using the keyword class instead of object. In listing 4.2 the Hello class is defined, which is identical except for the class keyword to the object Hello from Listing 4.1.

Listing 4.2: The Hello class

```
class Hello {
var greeting = "Hello"
def hello () {
println (greeting)
}
}
```

Two things happen to the implementation of the class. On the one hand, with the keyword new any number of objects with the defined in the class th fields and methods can be generated. Second is through the class a *type* defined. Variables can now be of the Hello type, for example. Functional nen can accept values of the type Hello as an argument or as a result return.

In order to use the Hello class, objects with the key keyword new can be generated. Each of these objects then has its own field greeting and reacts to the message hello by executing the method hello. Variables to which the objects are assigned have the type Hello. The following session shows how to create and use two Hello objects:

```
scala> val say = new Hello
say: Hello = Hello @ 473eae6e
scala> say.hello ()
Hello
scala> val sayAgain = new Hello
sayAgain: Hello = Hello @ 569764bd
scala> say.greeting = "Hi"
scala> say.hello ()
Hi
scala> sayAgain.hello ()
Hello
```

First an immutable variable say is defined, a new hello Object created and assigned to the variable say. This means that for the riable say the Hello type is inferred. The message hello is then sent to sent the object with the name say, which is used to output the character chain Hello responds. With the third input a second object and a ne second variable generated. As is to be expected, the welcoming text of the sayAgain object Hello, although that of the say object with the following the input was changed to Hi, since each object has its own fields, so-called *Instance variables* , has.

At this point it becomes clear once again that an unchangeable variable ble can definitely reference a changeable object. The greeting say can be changed. say cannot reference any other object ren. The attempt say = sayAgain is returned with error: reassignment to val acknowledged.

If an object is created with new in the Scala shell, it is created using the to-

String method returned. Since the Hello class does not have its own to- String method, the standard implementation is used. Since we ourselves are on the Java platform, it is about the implementation java.lang.Object containing the class name, an @ sign and the hexadeci- male representation of the object's hash code.
To implement your own toString method, it must be redefined the. For example, the Hello class can be expanded to include the following method definition added:
override def toString = "Ready to say" + greeting
When redefining methods, the modifier override [4] is mandatory. written. If it is omitted, the Scala compiler will do this with the following Message acknowledged:
<console>: 13: error: overriding method toString in class
Object of type () java.lang.String;
method toString needs 'override' modifier
def toString = "Ready to say" + greeting
The toString method can now be called explicitly or it is used with Output of the object with println carried out automatically. Only in the Scala Shell it is used automatically when the constructor is called. The following This session is an example of this:
scala> val say = new Hello
say: Hello = Ready to say Hello
scala> println (say)
Ready to say Hello
scala> say.greeting = "Hi"
scala> println (say)
Ready to say hi
Now let's look again at the greeting field. Currently it can through simple assignment can be changed as required. In order not to allow any change, we just replace the var by a val in the definition. In many cases but a middle way between no and any change is what is desired.
The field is hidden for this in many object-oriented programming languages and access to it is only permitted via so-called getter and setter methods.
Scala takes a route that is easier for the programmer: each field that starts with the Keyword var is defined directly as a pair of getter and setter method interpreted. That is, the field is automatically hidden and a Getter method with the same name and a setter method with the same name supplemented by the characters _ =. Read access to the field then carries out the getter method, write access the setter method. To still the usual Syntax < varname > . Keeping < fieldname > = < value > becomes this automatically < varname > . < fieldname > _ = (< value >) made.
For example, if the greeting field is accessed for reading, the get Term method greeting executed. For example, if the greeting field is
say.greeting = "Hi"
assigned a value, the setter method greeting_ = is assigned the right Side of the equal sign as an argument, ie so
say.greeting _ = ("Hi")
executed.
Getter and setter methods can of course also be implemented yourself. Listing 4.3 shows an example. In this case, the actual field is called greet and is hidden with the modifier private [this] [5] . Access to the field takes place using the greeting and greeting_ = methods. The examples shown so far in the Scala shell continue to run unchanged.

Listing 4.3: The Hello class

```
class Hello {
private [this] var greet = "Hello"
def greeting = greet
def greeting _ = (greeting: String) {
if (greet == greeting)
println ("greeting is already set to \" "+ greet +" \ "")
else {
greet = greeting
println (this)
}
}
// ... the rest goes here
}
```

If greeting is now accessed for reading, the current value of the field greet returned. With write access, it is checked whether the current elle value of greet already matches the greeting parameter. Is if this is the case, this is output. Otherwise, the value passed is used by the Assigned the greet field and output the object with println. To do this To clarify, the following is another example session with the Scala shell specified:

```
scala> val say = new Hello
say: Hello = Ready to say Hello
scala> println (say.greeting)
Hello
scala> say.greeting = "Hi"
Ready to say hi
scala> say.greeting = "Hi"
greeting is already set to "Hi"
```

Since Scala fields and methods share a namespace, this can hidden field not also called greeting. Local variables and parameters however, as can be seen in Listing 4.3, the same names as members can be used. Zen. In order to still be able to access the shadowed member in such a case the object must be explicitly referenced with this. For example could instead of the line

```
if (greet == greeting)
```

in Listing 4.3 the line

```
if (this.greeting == greeting)
```

can be used and thus the getter method within the setter method can be used to access the greet field.

A pair of getter and setter methods is also known as a *property* - in based on the properties of C #, which however have a special syntax. Getter and setter methods can also be used without an associated variable. Listing 4.4 shows an example [6]. A euro field and a property are defined dollar.

Listing 4.4: The Currency Class

```
class Currency {
var exchangeRate = 2.0f
var euro
= 0.0f
def dollar = euro * exchange rate
```

```
def dollar_ = (m: float) {
euro = m / exchangeRate
}
override def toString = euro + "EUR /" + dollar + "USD"
}
```

Instead of explicitly assigning the value 0.0f to the variable euro, we can do this, because it corresponds to the standard value for the data type float, also automatically let sit. To do this, however, it is necessary in Scala to add an underscore. point. However, after a type can no longer be locally inferred, this must be specified. That said, we could use the second line in the class Replace Currency with the following line:

var euro: float = _

Without assigning the underscore, euro would correspond to an abstract variable blen and currency to an abstract class (see Section 4.1.6). The Standard values for the various data types are 0 for the numeric data types, false for the Boolean data type, () for the Unit type and null for all reference types.

For the user of the Currency class, it now looks as if the class has two fields: euro and dollar. In reality there is only one value in the euro field saved and converted every time when accessed via dollar. An example session looks like this:

```
scala> val m1, m2 = new currency
m1: Currency = 0.0 EUR / 0.0 USD
m2: Currency = 0.0 EUR / 0.0 USD
scale> m1.euro = 20
scale> m1
res0: Currency = 20.0 EUR / 40.0 USD
scala> m2.dollar = 20
scala> m2
res1: Currency = 10.0 EUR / 20.0 USD
```

First, two values m1 and m2 are defined and each of the two values assigned its own Currency object. Scala leaves a abbreviated spelling too. The euro value of 20 is then assigned to object m1 assigned and both values are returned. Conversely, the Dollar value set.

The class Currency contains another field in which the current rate is held becomes. In Listing 4.4 we defined the field as var, so it can be externally can be changed at will. A change in course in this case means a Change in dollar value, but no change in euro value. If we had If a dollar field and a euro property were returned, the dollar value would remain stable. If we think about it further, the rate must of course for all Currency objects have the same value. If it changes, it must be used in all existing objects be changed, and new objects must go directly to the new market value be generated.

The solution would be not to save the course in each object, but once to keep in a central location. Such a central point for objects of a class se is the so-called *companion object* . The companion object has the same Names like the class and must be together with the class in a source code File stand. This singleton object replaces the static fields and methods of Java and other object-oriented programming languages in favor of one uniform object model.

A revised version of the Currency class with a companion object is available shown in Listing 4.5.

Listing 4.5: The Currency Class and the Currency Object

```
object Currency {
var exchangeRate = 2.0f
}
class Currency {
var euro
= 0.0f
def dollar = euro * Currency.exchangeRate
def dollar_ = (m: float) {
euro = m / Currency.exchangeRate
}
override def toString = euro + "EUR /" + dollar + "USD"
}
```

The course in the companion object can now be accessed with Currency.exchangeRate can be accessed. If the course is changed in the companion object, this has like desired effects on all existing and all new objects, such as the the following session shows:

```
scala> val m1 = new currency
m1: Currency = 0.0 EUR / 0.0 USD
scale> m1.euro = 20
scale> m1
res0: Currency = 20.0 EUR / 40.0 USD
scala> Currency.exchangeRate = 4
scale> m1
res1: Currency = 20.0 EUR / 80.0 USD
scala> val m2 = new currency
m2: Currency = 0.0 EUR / 0.0 USD
scala> m2.dollar = 20
scala> m2
res2: Currency = 5.0 EUR / 20.0 USD
```

After changing course to 4.0, the dollar value of m1 is from 40 to $ 80 up. For the object m2 created after the course change applies immediately the new course.

We now return to the methods and consider the Class Hello. For the sake of clarity, we will start again with the first Version of the class from Listing 4.2 on page 48, with a greeting and a a method hello, which prints the greeting text using println, at.

We want to expand the class so that we are greeted by name can. A first approach would be to assign the class to a helloName method which would look like this:

```
def helloName (name: String) {
println (greeting + "" + name)
}
```

So we could say Hello and Hello Oliver, like the following Session shows:

```
scala> val say = new Hello
say: Hello = Hello @ 54373e38
scala> say.hello ()
Hello
scala> say.helloName ("Oliver")
```

Hello Oliver
It would of course be nicer if we didn't just hello and the other time helloName, but simply the same name in both cases hello could use. This is also possible and is called *overloading Methods* . When overloading methods, make sure that the pa- Parameter lists of all methods with the same name in terms of number or type distinguish. The methods can also have different types of results. However, this alone is not enough to differentiate and is used by the compiler not accepted.

Listing 4.6. The Hello class with two methods hello

```
class Hello {
var greeting = "Hello"
def hello () {
println (greeting)
}
def hello (name: String) {
println (greeting + "" + name)
}
}
```

Listing 4.6 shows the Hello class, which loads two methods with the name hello sits. The first method has no parameter of the type, the second method one String. This means that when the method is called, the argument list can be used. which of the two will be executed. If the argument list is empty, executed the first method. Does the argument list contain exactly one string or an expression that can be evaluated to a string, the two- th method executed. In all other cases the compiler finds an error and the program is not translated.
So far we have shown all members of a class without a *visibility* modifier. give. This means that the members are all public, that is, from every other class visible and usable.
An essential feature of object-oriented programming is the *information tion hiding* , *i.e. hiding* the implementation of a class. Of course not, because it is a secret, but rather in order to to be able to change implementation without running the risk that applications that use the class, are no longer compilable. The aim is to *develop* the *application To keep the gramming interface* (API) of a class stable, and automatically all belong to public members.
Scala offers the modifiers to limit the visibility of members private and protected. These are placed in front of the corresponding key words tern specified, e.g.

```
private var x = ...
protected class helper {...}
```

If a member of a class or an object is marked with private, in this way it can only be accessed within the class or the object.
Since Scala also allows the nesting of classes, the access protection for inner classes too. It applies here that from a further inside Class to the members further outside protected with private can be grasped. The reverse, however, does not apply and thus gives way to Example from Java, where basically all members of an inner Class are visible.
For members protected with protected applies that they are beyond a class only are visible in derived classes and not in all classes of the package like

in Java. Derived classes are discussed in Section 4.1.5.
It is also possible to reduce the visibility to an even more fine-grained to define se. There are also so-called qualifiers that follow in square brackets private or protected, for example private [X] or protected [Y]. X and Y stand for packages, classes or singleton objects. With the mode fier private [this] it is possible to restrict access to a member in this way. know that only within the object itself and not from other objects of the same class can be accessed as with private.
The companion object shown in Listing 4.5 on page 54 would have stellation can be any other singleton object. Then would have to from the currency class to the exchange rate just not with the expression Currency.exchangeRate, but via the name of the other object. be grasped.
Companion objects become interesting when it comes to access protection. It applies namely, for a class and its companion object: From the class can access all members of the companion with the private modifier Object can be accessed and vice versa.

Listing 4.7: SharedCounter.scala

```
class SharedCounter {
private [this] var counted = 0
def count () {
SharedCounter.increment ()
counted + = 1
}
override def toString =
"Current shared value is" + SharedCounter.value +
". Incremented shared counter" + counted + "times."
}
object SharedCounter {
private [this] var count = 0
private def value = count
private def increment () {
count + = 1
}
}
```

Listing 4.7 shows a class SharedCounter with the associated companion object 7 . The count variable count is located in Companion object and is only visible there due to private [this] bar. The two methods value and increment are also in the class se SharedCounter visible. A SharedCounter instance can share the common men counter with SharedCounter.increment () and count up to the current access the current status using SharedCounter.value. In addition, each has SharedCounter instance an object-private field counted in which held how often this instance has incremented the common counter. On this Field can only be accessed within the corresponding instance.
Due to the limitations of the Scala shell, the code from Listing 4.7 neither enter it in the shell nor load it as a file. It has to be compiled and can for example with a simple application as shown in Listing 4.8 getting tested.

Listing 4.8: The CounterTest application for testing the SharedCounter

```
object CounterTest extends Application {
val sc1 = new SharedCounter
val sc2 = new SharedCounter
for (i <- 1 to 10) {
```

```
sc1.count
println (sc1)
sc2.count
println (sc2)
}
}
```

Another special feature of Scala is shown in Listing 4.7 when looking at the two Methods value and increment visible. Both methods have no parameters meter, but only after increment there is an empty pair of brackets. The method value is a *parameterless method* and is written without an empty pair of parentheses. ben. The increment method, on the other hand, is an *empty-paren method* .

The difference becomes significant through a convention: If a method de has no parameters and only reads changeable data takes effect, it should be defined as a parameterless method. Has a method de side effects such as input / output or changing a variable blen, the method should be written with empty brackets.

With the option to leave out the empty pair of brackets, *uniform access principle* [8] , according to which it is transparent for the use of a class must be whether an attribute is implemented as a field or a method.

Since brackets always have to be written in Java methods and Scala interoperates very well with Java, empty brackets in Scala can be very liberal can be used or omitted. So it is basically also possible instead println () to print a line break println without parentheses write. However, this should not be done due to the side effect of the method will.

Conversely, if a parameterless method is defined, the compiler ensures that it is always used without an empty pair of brackets. Otherwise a later changing the method in a field will cause an error because on a Field must of course never be accessed with an empty pair of brackets.

Like many other languages, Scala does not differentiate between methods and Operators. What looks like an operator is actually simple too only one method. For example, if two numbers are added, we write in almost all languages 1 + 2. In Scala this corresponds to a method call of the Method + of object 1, actually (1). + (2) [9] . In Chapter 3 on page 31 the permitted identifiers are listed that are also used for method names can be.

Since operators are nothing special, the so-called infix operator Notation, i.e. the notation < object > < operator > < argument > , too not restricted to operators. Any method with one argument can be written in infix operator notation and thus becomes a Operator, eg "Hello World" substring 6. Has the method more than one Argument, the brackets around the argument list must be retained, e.g. at "Hello World" substring (6,7). Methods without an argument can written in postfix operator notation, e.g. "Hello" toUpperCase.

Does the method have side effects and therefore becomes the bracket by convention written, the Postfix operator notation should of course not be used.

For the prefix operator notation, i.e. specifying the method before the object, there are restrictions. In prefix notation, only the operators +, -,! and ˜ are written. These operators are so-called *unary* operators, so they only have one operand. The name of the The method belonging to the prefix operator < op > is unary_ < op > . So that means, the expression -3 corresponds to the expression (3) .unary_-. Had the method the name - without the unary_ prefix, it should be in postfix operator notation be used.

In Scala, arrays do not receive any special treatment as in most C-similar languages. Arrays are normal objects and have methods for assigning grabbed their elements. Read access to individual elements is provided by the Apply method, write access through update, e.g.

```
scala> val array = new Array [String] (2)
array: Array [String] = Array (zero, zero)
scala> array.update (0, "World")
scala> array.update (1, "Reader")
scale> for (i <- 0 to 1)
|
println ("Hello" + array.apply (i))
Hello World
Hello Reader
```

However, a more catchy syntax is also supported. On the element te can be accessed with array (i). Values can be in the array with array (i) = < value > . That is, the above session can-also look like this:

```
scala> val array = new Array [String] (2)
array: Array [String] = Array (zero, zero)
scala> array (0) = "World"
scala> array (1) = "Reader"
scale> for (i <- 0 to 1)
|
println ("Hello" + array (i))
Hello World
Hello Reader
```

However, this is not a special treatment of arrays either, it works basically for any object.

The rule for apply is: Follow an object name with 10 brackets with a or several values, the compiler transforms this into a call to the method apply with the values in the argument list. So it's enough in one class or to define the appropriate method apply for an object in order to to use wisely.

The rule for update is: If a variable is enclosed in brackets with an or If several arguments follow, a value is assigned, the compiler transforms this in a call to the update method with the arguments of the variable and the value to the right of the assignment operator. This means, For this notation, too, it is sufficient to define the update method.

4.1.2 What else classes can contain

In addition to fields and methods, classes can also be classes, objects and type synonyms included. The same of course also applies to objects. Let's start with the type synonyms. With the keyword type an existing type a new name will be given. Let's turn to the Hello class again to. Listing 4.9 defines a type synonym Greeting.

Listing 4.9: The Hello class with the type synonym Greeting

```
class Hello {
type Greeting = String
var greeting: Greeting = "Hello"
def hello () {
println (greeting)
}
}
```

If we then create an object say of the type Hello, the field has greeting the type say.Greeting, as shown below:

```
scala> val say = new Hello
say: Hello = Hello @ 1497b7b1
scala> say.greeting
res0: say.Greeting = Hello
```

Do we want an inner class or an object for a class or an object we just need to define it inside the curly braces.
An example for clarification is given in Listing 4.10.

Listing 4.10: Nested Classes and Objects

```
class A {
object B {
val c = 5
}
class D {
object E {
val c = 7
}
val c = 9
}
val f = new D
}
```

Class A from Listing 4.10 could then be used, for example, as follows-so:

```
scala> val x = new A
x: A = A @ 1c7b0f4d
scala> xBc
res1: Int = 5
scala> xfc
res2: Int = 9
scala> xfEc
res3: Int = 7
```

Nesting classes and objects usually makes sense when
if a class or an object contains several members that work well together.
can be included, but not required outside. An example is in listing 4.11 specified.

Listing 4.11. The Customer Class, which contains an Address object

```
class Customer {
var customerID: Int = _
object Address {
var street: String = _
var postcode: String = _
var city: String = _
var country: String = _
}
}
```

The Customer class contains an Address object in which the address of the customer which is encapsulated. In the following section we finally learn the constructive with which we can use the fields when creating the object be able to prove.

4.1.3 Constructors

New objects are constructed with the keyword new, which precedes the class name is written, e.g. new Hello. Of course, like both e.g. new Hello () can be written in Java. Both are in Scala equivalent and in this case has of course nothing to do with the Uniform Access Principle ple to do. Usually in Scala are in favor of tighter and better the brackets are omitted in readable code.

If an object is created with new, a constructor is executed. To- we didn't specify a constructor, but instead used the automatic one generated constructor.

In the case of the Hello class, we want to create the possibility directly at Generate a Hello object to pass your own welcome text. In Scala works with so-called *class parameters* , which are placed directly after the Class names are given.

Listing 4.12. The Hello class with the greeting class parameter

```
class Hello (greeting: String) {
def hello () {
println (greeting)
}
}
```

Listing 4.12 defines the Hello class with the class parameter greeting. If an object is now created with new Hello ("Hello"), it behaves the same way like the object previously created with the class from Listing 4.2 and new Hello. The The main difference is that greeting is not used outside of the class. can be accessed because the class parameter does not automatically create a field greeting was defined. Scala automatically generates from the class parameters table a constructor with exactly these parameters, which is used as the *primary constructor* referred to as. Without parameters, i.e. with new Hello, no object can more to be constructed.

If a field with the same name is to be created automatically for a class parameter the parameter must be declared as val or var. It can Visibility modifiers can also be placed in front of them.

Listing 4.13. The Hello class with the greeting class parameter and the greeting field

```
class Hello (var greeting: String) {
def hello () {
println (greeting)
}
}
```

If the Hello class is defined as shown in Listing 4.13, a Hello object can be changed after generating the welcome text as before den, e.g.

```
scala> val say = new Hello ("Hello")
say: Hello = Hello @ 63d12a6
scala> say.hello ()
Hello
scala> say.greeting = "Hi"
scala> say.hello ()
Hi
```

Anything that the primary constructor should do beyond that is immediately written in cash in class. For example, the require n check whether a condition is met. In Listing 4.14, when the witnessing an object checks that the passed string is not empty. The The exclamation mark stands for the logical negation, ie “the passed String is empty, does not apply ”.

Listing 4.14: The Hello class with the class parameter check

```
class Hello (greeting: String) {
require (! greeting.isEmpty)
def hello () {
println (greeting)
}
}
```

It is often desirable to have more than one constructor to create objects available to create objects with different parameter lists to be able to procreate. The other constructors are called *auxiliary constructors* and defined using def this (...). Each additional construct tor must first call another constructor with this (...). the goal is it to ensure that when creating an object the instructions of the primary constructor before the instructions of the additional constructor ren are executed and thus there is a single entry point into the class gives.

Listing 4.15: The Hello class with an additional constructor

```
class Hello (greeting: String) {
require (! greeting.isEmpty)
def this () = this ("Hello")
def hello () {
println (greeting)
}
}
```

Listing 4.15 defines a parameterless constructor in addition to the primary one, which sets the welcome text to the value Hello. A generated with new Hello The object then responds to hello with Hello. The empty pair of brackets may be cannot be omitted from the definition of the constructor. Will be an additional Constructor but only needed to set a default value, can do this since Scala 2.8.0 can also be implemented directly using a default argument.

Listing 4.16: The Hello class with class parameters and default argument

```
class Hello (greeting: String = "Hello") {
require (! greeting.isEmpty)
def hello () {
println (greeting)
}
}
```

If the class Hello is defined as shown in Listing 4.16, then other closing objects with new Hello ("Hi"), but also with new Hello without an additional constructor. The primary construct tor can also use an empty argument list due to the default argument be called.

Scala also offers the option of creating objects without new witness. For example, List (1,2,3) creates a list of the elements 1, 2 and 3. This is not special for classes in the standard library, but can also be easily adapted for your own classes.

This is because the expression List (1,2,3) is expanded by the compiler to List.apply (1,2,3). That is, apply is a method of companion Object. If the method is used to create an object of the associated class to generate and return, we call this the *factory method* .

Listing 4.17: The Hello class with factory methods in the companion object

```
class Hello (greeting: String = "Hello") {
require (! greeting.isEmpty)
def hello () {
println (greeting)
}
}
object Hello {
def apply () = new Hello
def apply (greeting: String) = new Hello (greeting)
}
```

The Hello class is used with the two apply methods in the Companion object as defined in Listing 4.17, Hello objects can then be can be generated with Hello () as well as Hello (< greeting >). Would If the empty pair of brackets are omitted in the first case, the expression would be that Designate the companion object itself, ie after evaluating the line

val say = Hello

say is not a Hello object, but a reference to the Singleton object Hello. So say doesn't understand the message hello. Instead, then but a Hello object can be created with the expression say (), because say () is transformed to say.apply ().

Let us now look again at the extension of the application trait in order to make multiple programs executable. As shown in section 3.3 on page 43 all code that is directly in the defined object and not within of a member, executed at startup. This is a fundamental feature from Scala, since this code was included in the primary constructor and at Initialization of an object is carried out. Starting an object initia-lize it first. Then the main function of the application trait executed and the program ended.

4.1.4 Enumerations

So far we have represented the welcome text as a string. Have with it we have chosen a very flexible implementation, but which can leaves. For example, a user of the Hello class with new Hello ("Gas station") create a Hello object that responds to the message hello with Gas station answers.

A simple possibility would be to allow the class parameter with a list. Compare siger values as shown in Listing 4.18. In the companion object a list of permitted values for greeting is defined and in the primary context checked structure as argument to require.

Listing 4.18: Comparison of the class parameter with a list of permissible values

```
class Hello (greeting: String = "Hello") {
require (Hello.acceptableGreetings contains greeting)
}
object Hello {
private val acceptableGreetings =
List ("Hello", "Hi", "Howdy")
}
```

Now, in an application, a Hello object with an illegal value

generated, e.g. new Hello ("Salve"), the source text can be used without an error message
be translated 12 . Only when the program is executed does the running
time environment with
java.lang.ExceptionInInitializerError
at HelloTest.main (HelloRuntimeError.scala)
...
Caused by: java.lang.IllegalArgumentException:
requirement failed
at scala.Predef $ .require (Predef.scala: 135)
...
So it would be better to check the permissible values when translating
can. Many programming languages offer so-called *enumeration types* for this
or in English *enumerations* , with which a finite number of values
can be laid. List types can also be defined in Scala,
however, according to the Scala philosophy, again not in any special language syntax, rather than normal objects.

Listing 4.19: Enumeration for welcome texts

```
object Greeting extends Enumeration {
val Hello, Hi, Howdy = Value
}
```

Listing 4.19 defines the Greeting object for an enumeration type.
ned. For this purpose the class Enumeration is extended. The values have the type Greeting.Value. Each call of the Value method creates a new value,
which becomes part of the enumeration. Overloaded versions of the Value method enable
make it possible to display an integer or a special string representation of the value.
eg the default value of the welcome text could be val Default
= Value ("Hello").

Listing 4.20: Hello class with enumeration for welcome texts

```
class Hello (greeting: Greeting.Value = Greeting.Hello) {
def hello () {
println (greeting)
}
}
```

If the Hello class should now use the enumeration type, the class
Parameter greeting the corresponding type Greeting.Value and the default value is set to Greeting.Hello, see Listing 4.20. By defini-
tion of a type synonym, the default value and an import statement 13 in front of the Hello class, as in Listing 4.21, the source code is even easier to read.

Listing 4.21: Hello class with enumeration for welcome texts, type synonym and Default value

```
object Greeting extends Enumeration {
type Greeting = Value
val Default = Value ("Hello")
val Hi, Howdy = Value
}
import Greeting._
class Hello (greeting: Greeting = Default) {
def hello () {
println (greeting)
}
}
```

Type Greeting = Value defines a type synonym. This means, the type Greeting.Value now also has the name Greeting.Greeting. After the import the prefix Greeting can be omitted. the. If, for example, an attempt is now made to translate program code, the new Hello (Huhu), it fails with the following message:
error: not found: value Huhu

4.1.5 Inheritance and subtyping

Another essential feature of object-oriented programming is that Deriving one class from another. The derived class is used as a *sub-class* , the class from which it was derived, as a *base class* or *super class* designated. When deriving , the subclass *inherits* all non-private members of the sisclass, ie the members are part of the subclass as if they were only in it been defined.
So far we have not specified a base class in our class definitions.
This means that the base class is automatically the scala.AnyRef class, which is based on the
Java platform corresponds to the java.lang.Object class. The defined in AnyRef ned methods are therefore also available in all classes, e.g. two Hello objects can be compared with the == method without using this method has been explicitly defined in the Hello class.
If another class is to inherit it, this must be done with the keyword extends can be specified when defining a class.

Listing 4.22: HelloAndGoodbye class as a subclass of Hello

```
class HelloAndGoodbye extends Hello {
def goodbye () = println ("Goodbye")
}
```

The HelloAndGoodbye class defined in Listing 4.22 inherits the hello method from the class Hello. Therefore, a HelloAndGoodbye object understands both the Message goodbye as well as hello. The following session illustrates this.

```
scala> val say = new HelloAndGoodbye
say: HelloAndGoodbye = HelloAndGoodbye @ 4e836869
scala> say.hello ()
Hello
scala> say.goodbye ()
Goodbye
```

When using the methods, we don't see any difference whether the method is in defined in the class or inherited from a base class.
Since every class also defines a data type, the question arises whether the data types of the sub- and base class are related in some way.
In fact, the type of the subclass is what is known as a *subtype of* the type the base class is. The subclass is a specialization of the base class, and on the other hand, we speak of a generalization.
After the class Hello has a class parameter for setting the greeting has text, we want to use it in the HelloAndGoodbye class as well and extend HelloAndGoodbye by two class parameters.

Listing 4.23: HelloAndGoodbye class with class parameters

```
class HelloAndGoodbye (
greeting: String = "Hi",
farewell: String = "Goodbye"
) extends Hello (greeting) {
def goodbye () {
println (farewell)
```

```
}
}
```

Listing 4.23 shows an implementation of the HelloAndGoodbye class with the two class parameters greeting and goodbye including default arguments th. The class parameter greeting is sent as a parameter to the base class Hello passed. This corresponds to calling the constructor of the base class se, which is done in Java with the keyword super, for example. In Scala can the call of the constructor of the base class exclusively on the ones in Listing 4.23 shown manner.

The keyword super is still there in Scala, and that for calling a method of the base class. This is useful, for example, when the inherited Method is redefined and at one point the method of the base class should be used or in stackable traits, which are explained in section 4.3.2 the.

If a HelloAndGoodbye object is created without arguments, the greeting text to the default value Hi specified in HelloAndGoodbye puts. The default value of greeting comes from the Hello class, like the two classes implemented are no longer applicable, since always the Default value used by greeting from the definition of HelloAndGoodbye becomes. If this default value is simply left out, it is no longer possible to create a HelloAndGoodbye object with no arguments, since the call of the constructor in the class HelloAndGoodbye without the greeting-Argument can be called.

Listing 4.24: Class parameters in Hello and HelloAndGoodbye use the same Default value.

```
object Hello {
val defaultGreeting = "Hello"
}
class Hello (greeting: String = Hello.defaultGreeting) {
def hello () {
println (greeting)
}
}
class HelloAndGoodbye (
greeting: String = Hello.defaultGreeting,
farewell: String = "Goodbye"
) extends Hello (greeting) {
def goodbye () {
println (farewell)
}
}
```

If the default value from Hello is to be used, this can be, for example, like in Listing 4.24. The default value is there in the default-Greeting of the Hello object and can be used in both classes Hello and HelloAndGoodbye can be used.

Listing 4.25: Incorrect redefinition of a field

```
class Hello (var greeting: String) {
def hello () {
println (greeting)
}
}
class HelloAndGoodbye (
var greeting: String, // does not compile
var farewell: String
) extends Hello (greeting) {
```

```
def goodbye () {
println (farewell)
}
}
```

If you have fields generated from the class parameters, you have to be on it make sure that the fields are inherited as long as they are not private.
In the source code in Listing 4.25, the generated greeting field is replaced by Hello redefined the greeting field in HelloAndGoodbye. But after there a override, the compilation fails with the following message:

```
HelloAndGoodbye.scala: 7: error: overriding variable
greeting in class Hello of type String;
variable greeting needs 'override' modifier
var greeting: String, // does not compile
^
one error found
```

Redefining the field is superfluous in Listing 4.25, since the field greeting inherited from Hello and is therefore already available anyway. A to-given a somewhat constructed application case would be in Lis-ting 4.26. First a HelloDefault class is defined with a immutable field greeting, which is not specified by a class parameter can be set. To set this value in the Hello subclass with a class To be able to set parameters, it must be redefined there. If this is not makes, an object created with new Hello ("Hi") is also added to the message hello print the string Hello and not Hi.

Listing 4.26: Redefining a field with a class parameter

```
class HelloDefault {
val greeting = "Hello"
def hello () {
println (greeting)
}
}
class Hello (override val greeting: String)
extends HelloDefault
```

Listing 4.26 shows another feature of Scala: If the body of a Class is empty as with the class Hello, the curly braces can be removed-be left.
By the way, the redefinition can also be prevented by adding the member in the base class is given the final modifier. Listing 4.27 shows an example play for it.

Listing 4.27: Preventing the redefinition of a field by the final modifier

```
class AlwaysHello {
final val greeting = "Hello"
def hello () {
println (greeting)
}
}
```

Attempting to redefine greeting in a derived class will result in a acknowledged with an error message, as can be seen in the following session:

```
scale> class Hi extends AlwaysHello {
|
override val greeting = "Hi"
| }
<console>: 7: error: overriding value greeting in class
AlwaysHello of type java.lang.String ("Hello");
```

value greeting cannot override final member
override val greeting = "Hi"
If there is an inheritance relation between two classes, an object of the Subclass can be assigned to a variable of the type of the base class. It can e.g. be written:

```
scala> val sayG: Hello = new HelloAndGoodbye ("Hi", "CU")
sayG: Hello = HelloAndGoodbye @ 1c0693a5
```

Although the created object would understand the goodbye message, the The goodbye method cannot be executed via the sayG variable:

```
scala> sayG.goodbye ()
<console>: 9: error: value goodbye is not a member of
Hello
sayG.goodbye
```

Calling the hello method works as expected:

```
scala> sayG.hello ()
Hi
```

Now let's consider another HelloTwice class, the shown in Listing 4.28.

Listing 4.28: HelloTwice class derived from the Hello class

```
class HelloTwice (greeting: String)
extends Hello (greeting) {
override def hello () {
println (greeting + "," + greeting)
}
}
```

In the HelloTwice class, the hello speech method inherited from Hello is used. finishes. Instead of outputting the welcome text once, it is now displayed twice with separated by a comma. Now let's create a HelloTwice object and assign it to a Hello variable, happens when calling hello fol- the following:

```
scala> val sayT: Hello = new HelloTwice ("Salut")
sayT: Hello = HelloTwice @ 65c94b8f
scala> sayT.hello ()
Salute, salute
```

Although sayT is of type Hello, the hello method is derived from HelloTwice executed and salute, salute issued. These phenomena let through Explain *polymorphism* and *dynamic binding* .
The sayT variable is of the Hello type. As such it can refer to an object that is of the Hello type. This also includes subtypes as there are is a so-called *specialization* , i.e. it is a HelloTwice object a special Hello object. The variable sayT is polymorphic, too German diverse. The same applies, of course, to the sayG variable.
When calling methods of the variables sayG and sayT, the Com- piler now only consider methods that have been defined in the Hello class. who are. Therefore, trying to use say.goodbye () already fails with the Compile fails. There is no goodbye method in the Hello class.
To understand that sayT.hello () is now the method from HelloTwice takes, it helps to formally call the method again as sending forwarding judge to look at. If the message hello is sent to the variable sayT det, the compiler checks whether an object that is referenced by sayT has the Message at all. After sayT has the type Hello and If the Hello class contains the hello method, this is allowed.
At runtime, the message is actually sent to the referenced by sayT Object sent. The HelloTwice object reacts to this with the execution

its hello method. So that means the permissibility of the method call is checked statically, but the actual method call is dynamically bound.

In derived classes, not only methods, but basically all members inherited from the base class can be redefined. Every time there is the prepend override modifier to the new definition.

On page 58 we already explained the Uniform Access Principle after it for the use of a class it must be transparent whether an attribute is used as a field or method is implemented. This approach applies to inheritance as well expanded. If a class contains a parameterless method, this can be carried out by a val can be redefined. This is particularly interesting in context with abstract classes discussed in the next section.

4.1.6 Abstract classes

A class is called abstract if it contains at least one member that is abstract is. A member is called abstract when it does not have a complete definition. Development

If a class does not hold an abstract member, it is called concrete. This in most object-oriented programming language defines the existing being a member in a class and thus demands concrete from everyone Subclasses that it will be implemented there. To clarify, we select one Example used in many programming books. We want dogs, cats and modeling cows. A first approach would be direct and independent de-definition of the corresponding classes, see Listing 4.29.

Listing 4.29: The Dog, Cat and Cow classes

```
class Dog {
def makeNoise () {
println ("woof, woof")
}
}
class Cat {
def makeNoise () {
println ("miaow")
}
}
class cow {
def makeNoise () {
println ("moo")
}
}
```

With the definitions of the Dog, Cat and Cow classes, dogs, cats and cows are created and make a noise with makeNoise:

```
scala> val lassie = new dog
lassie: Dog = Dog @ 1b9f9088
scala> lassie.makeNoise ()
woof, woof
scala> val meowth = new Cat
meowth: Cat = Cat @ 25d3e3f3
scala> mauzi.makeNoise ()
miaow
scala> val emma = new cow
emma: Cow = Cow @ 645b56c4
scala> emma.makeNoise ()
moo
```

Although every animal has a makeNoise method, it is not possible to Simply save the animals in a list and attach them to each one with a for loop to send the message makeNoise:

```
scala> val animals = List (lassie, meowth, emma)
animals: List [ScalaObject] = List (Dog @ 1b9f9088,
Cat @ 25d3e3f3, Cow @ 645b56c4)
scala> for (animal <- animals) animal.makeNoise ()
<console>: 10: error: value makeNoise is not a member of
ScalaObject
animal.makeNoise ()
```

To understand the problem, let's take a look at the types: lassie hat the dog type, mauzi is the cat type and emma is the cow type. Let's add the three in a list, the type parameter of the list type can be determined. The type you are looking for must be a super type of dog, cat and cow. The compiler inf The most special super type is ScalaObject and thus defines the type of the list animals as List [ScalaObject]. So have all elements at the same time of the list, if they are referenced via the list, the type ScalaObject. The compiler now checks whether the makeNoise method call in the for-Loop is allowed for a ScalaObject. But after makingNoise is not in ScalaObject is present, the compilation of the program section fails. But in order to be able to work with the list and makeNoise, we have to introduce a common base class containing the makeNoise method. The The next approach would be the one shown in Listing 4.30.

Listing 4.30: The Animal class and the Dog, Cat and Cow classes derived from it

```
class Animal {
def makeNoise () {
println ("?")
}
}
class Dog extends Animal {
override def makeNoise () {
println ("woof, woof")
}
}
class Cat extends Animal {
override def makeNoise () {
println ("miaow")
}
}
class Cow extends Animal {
override def makeNoise () {
println ("moo")
}
}
```

With the approach in Listing 4.30, our for loop now works, but there is two more things that we would rather not have had. First, animal Objects are created. But we really only want dogs, cats and cows allow. Second, we had to use the makeNoise method in the Animal implement, but don't really know what to output there. We get both problems with the solution shown in Listing 4.31 in the handle.

Listing 4.31: The abstract class Animal and derived classes Dog, Cat and Cow

```
abstract class Animal {
```

```
def makeNoise (): Unit
}
class Dog extends Animal {
def makeNoise () {
println ("woof, woof")
}
}
class Cat extends Animal {
def makeNoise () {
println ("miaow")
}
}
class Cow extends Animal {
def makeNoise () {
println ("moo")
}
}
```

The Animal class implemented in Listing 4.31 is abstract because it is a method without implementation. In addition, the keyword class the keyword abstract, which marks the class as an abstract class kiert. If it wasn't there, the class would try to translate canceled after an error message:

```
Animal.scala: 1: class Animal needs to be abstract, since
method make Noise is not defined
class Animal {
^
```

The makeNoise method is no longer used in the Dog, Cat and Cow classes redefined, but implemented for the first time. Therefore the modifier can override omitted. But it can also stop at this point. Like the following sit- shows, a dog, a cat and a cow can now be combined in one Be a list and make a sound using a for loop:

```
scala> for (animal <- List (new Dog, new Cat, new Cow))
|
animal.makeNoise ()
woof, woof
miaow
moo
```

In addition to abstract methods, abstract classes can also contain abstract vars, vals and types, but also contain concrete members. An extended animal class could look like Listing 4.32.

Listing 4.32. The abstract Animal class

```
import java.util.Calendar
abstract class Animal (val dateOfBirth: Calendar) {
var name: String
def makeNoise (): Unit
def age = {
val today = Calendar.getInstance
val age = today.get (Calendar.YEAR) -
dateOfBirth.get (Calendar.YEAR)
today.get (Calendar.YEAR,
dateOfBirth.get (Calendar.YEAR))
if (today before dateOfBirth)
age-1
else
```

age
}
override def toString =
name + "" + age + "year" + (if (age! = 1) "s" else "") + "old"
}
The Animal class defines an abstract field name [14] , a class parameter dateOfBirth, which can also be used externally as val, is an abstract method de makeNoise and a concrete method age. Also, the method toString redefined.
After we use the Java code for the date of birth and the calculation of the age Use the Calendar class from the java.util package, but not on everyone If you want to write java.util.Calendar in detail, we import with the first line and can simply write Calendar from now on.
A concrete subclass of Animal must then name and makeNoise plan and set the class parameter dateOfBirth. Becomes one of the

[14] We support the possibility that small children can rename their pet every day.
nen.

Member not implemented, the derived class is also abstract. In listing 4.33 the concrete class Dog is shown.

Listing 4.33: The Dog class

```
import java.util.Calendar
class Dog (
var name: String,
dateOfBirth: Calendar = Calendar.getInstance // today
) extends Animal (dateOfBirth) {
def makeNoise () {
println ("woof, woof")
}
}
```

The following session shows the use of the Dog class and the implementation tion of trixi, a bird:

```
scala> import java.util. {Calendar, GregorianCalendar}
import java.util. {Calendar, GregorianCalendar}
scala> val lassie = new Dog ("Lassie",
|
new GregorianCalendar (1999, Calendar.APRIL, 12))
lassie: Dog = Lassie 11 years old
scala> val hugo = new Dog ("Hugo")
hugo: Dog = Hugo 0 years old
scala> val trixi = new Animal (Calendar.getInstance) {
|
var name = "Trixi"
|
def makeNoise () {
|
println ("chirp, chirp")
|
}
| }
trixi: Animal = Trixi 0 years old
scala> trixi.makeNoise ()
chirp, chirp
```

It is also possible to use an import statement in the Scala shell. With Calendar and GregorianCalendar are selected from the specified statement java.util and can then be used without the prefix java.util.

be used. Imports are discussed in detail in Section 4.2.
The definition of trixi gives the impression that the Animal class can te be instantiated, especially since the Scala shell also has the Animal type inferred for trixi. But this is not the case. Through new Animal (...) {...} defines an *anonymous class* that extends Animal. After the class does not have a name of its own, it does not define a new type. Hence gets trixi the Animal type.

4.2 Code organization

At the latest as soon as we work with several classes and inheritance, it is important ting to organize the code as clearly as possible. In Scala, the source group code into *packages* . Since we have not yet explicitly specified a package ben, everything was in the *unnamed* package.
The definition of named packages is explained in section 4.2.1. An innovation in Scala 2.8 represent the package objects discussed in Section 4.2.2, with to which other elements besides classes and objects are added to packages. can be added. Not always the fully qualified name of a class or having to write an object, there are also import clauses in Scala (see Section 4.2.3), with which a lot more is possible.

4.2.1 Packages

If a *package clause is* specified at the beginning of a file , the all source code of this file in the specified package. A package clause begins with the keyword package, followed by the package name. Packages can be arranged hierarchically. The levels are separated with a at a point. For example, specifying the
package org.obraun.scalabook
the entire source code of the file in the package scalabook in the package obraun assigned in the org package. In Scala this can also be done by three consecutive The following package clauses must be specified:
package org
package obraun
package scalabook
As this notation already suggests, Scala packages can also be used their packages included. Therefore, what is in an outer package must ge is not addressed with the fully qualifying package name must become. For example, if we are in a class within the Packages scalabook, so we can use the org.obraun.misc.Other class Reference misc.Other.
Since Scala 2.8 there is one in the two notations given above Difference: If, as in the first case, the packages are directly are written together separately, is not included in the intermediate packages seeks, but only top level. Are the packages individually with one Package clause specified, a search is also made between what was in both the versions was the case.
In order to only search for top levels prior to version 2.8, the string _root_ placed in front of the top package during an import. Of course read The two approaches can be combined as desired. For example, the Clauses
package org
package obraun.scalabook
first searched in the org package, then top level searched.
Scala packages can not only be specified for an entire source code file.

but also for parts of it. In addition, it is possible to should belong to a package, after the package clause in curly brackets to border. That makes it possible to have different parts of a file different Assign packages. Listing 4.34 shows an example.

Listing 4.34: Source code file with code for several packages

```
package org {
class Org
package obraun {
class OrgObrown
}
package scale {
class OrgScala
}
}
package org.obraun.scalabook {
object OrgObraunScalabook
}
```

After compiling the source code file defined in Listing 4.34, we find present the following directories and class files in the structure shown:

```
org
+ - dark brown
|
+ - OrgObrown.class
|
+ - scalabook
|
+ - OrgObrownScalabook.class
|
+ - OrgObrownScalabook $ .class
+ - Org.class
+ - scale
+ - OrgScala.class
```

4.2.2 Package Objects

With Scala 2.8, the collection framework (see section 6.2) reorganized. As a result, classes migrated from one package to another deres. In order to ensure the smoothest possible migration for existing Scala software guarantee, the idea is obvious in the packages from which the class has disappeared, simply a type synonym for the new class and a value, that references the new companion object. For example, the List from the package scala into the package scala.collection.immutable has been postponed. Therefore, only the following should be included in the package scala added to make the list available as scala.List as before. len:

```
type List [+ A] = scala.collection.immutable.List [A]
val List = scala.collection.immutable.List
```

Unfortunately, it doesn't work that simple, because although Scala has different con Structures can be nested in almost any way, packages contain only classes and objects, but no type synonyms and values. The Lö- solution was found with the so-called *package objects* .

An object becomes a package object by firstly using the key word package is prepended to the keyword object *and* saved in a Source code file with the name package.scala in the directory of the

speaking packages is saved. Everything that is de-
is defined, becomes part of the corresponding package.
That means, in the example given above with the list, the two lines
in the package object scala in the file package.scala in the directory scala
must be included (see Listing 4.35).

Listing 4.35: The package object scala

```
package object scale {
type List [+ A] = scala.collection.immutable.List [A]
val List = scala.collection.immutable.List
// lots more
}
```

4.2.3 Imports

With import clauses it is possible to add packages or their components via their
make simple names usable without qualifying packages. Example
becomes wise after the line

```
import java.io.File
```

with the simple identifier File referred to this java.io.File.
Such imports can be anywhere in Scala. Is the
Import, for example, within a function such as

```
def fun = {
import java.io.File
// do something with file
}
```

is the simple name File up to the closing curly bracket possible. Then java.io.File must be written again, except
there is also an import clause there. All members can also be imported by using the underscore
the. For example, with import java.io._
all members of the package java.io imported. It is also possible with the same Syntax to import the members of an object. Listing 4.36 shows an example in which after the import [15] to the field noOfM of the companion object with the
simple identifier noOfM can be accessed. Without the import would have to
we write Mountain.noOfM. Of course, this works for any
ge objects [16] .

Listing 4.36: The Mountain Class with Companion Object

```
class Mountain (val name: String,
val height: Int) {
import Mountain._
noOfM + = 1
}
object Mountain {
private var noOfM = 0
def numberOfMountains = noOfM
}
```

Instead of importing just one member or all of them, individual members can be imported into
be summarized in an *import selector clause* . For example, with

```
import java.util. {Calendar, GregorianCalendar}
```

both java.util.Calendar and java.util.GregorianCalendar
imported. The import of java.util. {_} Is otherwise the same as the import
from java.util._. Within an import selector clause, individual elements
elements can also be renamed. For example, after the import

import java.util. {Calendar => Cal, GregorianCalendar}
java.util.Calendar under the identifier Cal and java.util.GregorianCalendar available under the name GregorianCalendar. Should a individual elements can be renamed, but all of them can still be imported we also specify this in a one-liner. For example, in the following example the undash for the "rest":
import java.util. {Calendar => Cal, _}
It is also possible to import everything except certain elements. This will be also used the syntax for renaming, but this time with the undash as a new name. The following clause gets everything from java.io imported except for the File class:
import java.io. {File => _, _}
Every Scala source code file already has three implicit imports, namely:
import java.lang._
import scala._
import Predef._
The peculiarity here in contrast to normal imports is that latere imports overshadow previous ones. For example, a class with the namemen StringBuilder included in both java.lang and scala.
The identifier then references StringBuilder through the above sequence scala.StringBuilder.

4.3 traits

Scala only supports single inheritance like many modern object-oriented proprogramming languages. That is, a class can only have exactly one base class. Of course, the base class can also extend another class. Moresubject inheritance, as is possible in C ++, for example, can lead to an impenetrable clear and complicated design and enables the appearance of the mentioned *Diamond problem* 17 .
The diamond problem arises when a class D is made up of two base classes B and C and these two in turn from class A. The name is thanks the problem of graphing the relationship between the four Classes that such a hash (Engl. *Diamond*) looks. Now A has a method that is redefined in both B and C, it is not clear which implementation should apply to D.
In order not to be restricted to a single base class, many have objector-oriented programming languages introduced the concept of interfaces. One Interface can be seen as a very special abstract class that does not have a single ge concrete implementation. But that means that every concrete class, that implements an interface, for all methods of the interface an implementation must contain.
The approach either leads to very lean interfaces, i.e. interfaces with very few methods whose implementations are often cumbersome to use, or to interfaces whose implementation involves a large number of methods that may look the same in many classes.
Scala has no interfaces, but so-called *traits* , which in addition to abstract metrics methods may also contain implementations of methods and fields.
Section 4.3.1 discusses traits as rich interfaces. Besides, it is possible to change a method with the help of traits. This is discussed in section 4.3.2.

4.3.1 Rich interfaces

First of all, the only differences between abstract classes and traits are, that the latter have no constructors, and the keyword used. The abstract class Animal from Listing 4.32 on page 76 could be used as a trait as in Listing 4.37 shown look like.

Listing 4.37: The Trait Animal

```
import java.util.Calendar
trait animal {
var name: String
val dateOfBirth: Calendar
def makeNoise (): Unit
def age = {
val today = Calendar.getInstance
val age = today.get (Calendar.YEAR) -
dateOfBirth.get (Calendar.YEAR)
today.set (Calendar.YEAR,
dateOfBirth.get (Calendar.YEAR))
if (today before dateOfBirth)
age-1
else
age
}
override def toString = {
name + "" + age + "year" + (if (age! = 1) "s" else "") + "old"
}
}
```

The differences between the trait animal (Listing 4.37) and the abstract one Class Animal (Listing 4.32) are therefore

Use of the keyword trait instead of abstract class and

Definition of the class parameter as a normal member.

In contrast to Dog from Listing 4.33 on page 77 the class parameter dateOfBirth is defined as val and not as Passing class parameters to Animal. The Dog class, which includes the Animal is shown in Listing 4.38.

Listing 4.38: The Dog class

```
import java.util.Calendar
class Dog (
var name: String,
val dateOfBirth: Calendar = Calendar.getInstance
) extends Animal {
def makeNoise () {
println ("woof, woof")
}
}
```

Even if Dog now uses the Animal trait and does not inherit from the class, it will continues to use the extends keyword. A trait is a special form the so-called *mixin* . A mixin contains reusable, related All functionalities are combined into a unit that is mixed into a class can be. The name comes from the English *mix in* (to *mix in* , to stir mix in). The specialty of the trait is that a class that has a trait mixes in, but does not specify a base class with extends, the base class of the trait takes over. In our example, the Trait Animal has the base class AnyRef, which so that it also becomes the base class of Dog.

After the presented approach of imposing Animal as a trait and not as a class If something is constructed, let's change the example slightly build up. First, let's define an abstract Animal class for our animals (see Listing 4.39).

Listing 4.39: The abstract class Animal without dateOfBirth and age

```
abstract class Animal {
var name: String
def makeNoise (): Unit
}
```

However, we now define the Animal class without dateOfBirth and age, since this is a functionality that is certainly not only needed in animals can. Instead, we define a HasAge trait (see Listing 4.40).

Listing 4.40: The HasAge trait

```
trait HasAge {
import java.util.Calendar
val dateOfBirth: Calendar
def age = {
val today = Calendar.getInstance
val age = today.get (Calendar.YEAR) -
dateOfBirth.get (Calendar.YEAR)
today.set (Calendar.YEAR,
dateOfBirth.get (Calendar.YEAR))
if (today before dateOfBirth)
age-1
else
age
}
}
```

If we now want to implement the Dog class in such a way that it performs the same function
nality as before, we need to extend the Animal class and add the Trait Mix in HasAge. If a trait is added to a base class or to a mixed into another trait, this follows the keyword with. Further Traits then follow each other with their own with.

Listing 4.41: The Dog class with the Animal base class and the HasAge trait

```
import java.util.Calendar
class Dog (
var name: String,
val dateOfBirth: Calendar = Calendar.getInstance
) extends Animal with HasAge {
def makeNoise () {
println ("woof, woof")
}
override def toString = {
name + "" + age + "year" + (if (age! = 1) "s" else "") + "old"
}
}
```

The Dog class is shown in Listing 4.41. The main change is that Specification of with HasAge. However, according to this design, the toString Method in Dog, and similarly in Cat and Cow, can be redefined, since in the age method is not known to the Animal class and only through the trait HasAge is introduced.

But the way out is very simple. Not in the Dog class, but in the class Class Animal should be mixed in with the HasAge trait. The Animal class with the HasAge trait is shown in Listing 4.42. The Dog class can then can be used again in the version from Listing 4.38 on page 84.

Listing 4.42: The abstract class Animal with the trait HasAge

```
abstract class Animal extends HasAge {
```

```
var name: String
def makeNoise (): Unit
override def toString = {
name + "" + age + "year" + (if (age! = 1) "s" else "") + "old"
}
}
```

It is also possible to add an anonymous class that uses a trait define. However, since a trait does not allow class or "trait" variables, abstract members of the trait must be defined accordingly. Consider we use the trait PositiveNumber defined in Listing 4.43.

Listing 4.43: The PositiveNumber trait

```
trait PositiveNumber {
val value: Int
require (value> 0)
}
```

An abstract val of the Int type is defined in the PositiveNumber trait. Au- The require also ensures that the value of value does not is less than or equal to zero. Now if we have an anonymous class that contains the Trait contains, want to define, the obvious approach would be to use the val value as in the following session:

```
scala> val n = new PositiveNumber {
|
val value = 12
| }
java.lang.IllegalArgumentException: requirement failed
at scala.Predef $ .require (Predef.scala: 134)
...
```

As you can see, this leads to an exception. This is because the Creating an object first assigned the default value for Int and with require is checked. Only then would the value be set to 12 the. By removing the line require (value> 0) we can do this easily check:

```
scala> trait PositiveNumber {
|
val value: Int
| }
defined trait PositiveNumber
scala> val n = new PositiveNumber {
|
val value = 12
| }
n: java.lang.Object with PositiveNumber =
$ anon $ 1 @ 40914272
scala> n.value
res0: Int = 12
```

But we want to keep the require in the trait and therefore have to look for a look for another way out. There are basically two of them: *pre-initialization te fields* and *lazy vals* . Lazy vals are discussed in Section 5.1. A field is pre-initialized if it is defined in curly brackets in front of the trait becomes. That is, if we put our positive number n as shown in the following listing define give, the require sees the correct value 12:

```
scale> val n = new {
|
val value = 12
```

| } with PositiveNumber
A very useful trait included in the Scala distribution is Ordered. The Trait Ordered is shown in Listing 4.44.

Listing 4.44: The Ordered Trait

```
trait Ordered [A] extends java.lang.Comparable [A] {
def compare (that: A): Int
def <(that: A): Boolean = (this compare that) <0
def> (that: A): Boolean = (this compare that)> 0
def <= (that: A): Boolean = (this compare that) <= 0
def> = (that: A): Boolean = (this compare that)> = 0
def compareTo (that: A): Int = compare (that)
}
```

Objects of a class that implements the trait can be assigned with <,>, <= and> = be like. For this only the abstract method compare has to be implemented that compares the object (this) with another object (that) and returns an x as the result, for which applies:

x < 0
exactly when
this < that
x == 0
exactly when
this == that
x > 0
exactly when
this > that

For example, if we now want the feature for the HasAge trait from Listing 4.40 to add that to be able to compare all of them according to age, we must use the trait as shown in Listing 4.45.

Listing 4.45: The HasAge trait implements the Ordered trait.

```
trait HasAge extends Ordered [HasAge] {
import java.util.Calendar
val dateOfBirth: Calendar
def age = {
val today = Calendar.getInstance
val age = today.get (Calendar.YEAR) -
dateOfBirth.get (Calendar.YEAR)
today.set (Calendar.YEAR,
dateOfBirth.get (Calendar.YEAR))
if (today before dateOfBirth)
age-1
else
age
}
def compare (that: HasAge) = this.age compare that.age
}
```

The only two digits that are opposite the original trait from listing 4.40 are different, the extends Ordered [HasAge] and the single-line definition of compare, which simply refers to the one in the Int defined compare.

4.3.2 Stackable modifications

With traits it is possible to check different modifications one after the other. teln. We want to do this with the following simple use case for entering

Make strings clear:
1. A character string should be returned as the result of a get function the.
2. A character string should be able to come from different sources, for example from from user input or from a file.
3. When entering the user interface, it should be possible to optionally display a prompt. ben.
4. It should be possible to read in the character string, e.g. for error look in the program to output to the console.
5. It should be possible to add the character strings in a list save and thus at any point in time to all previously read to access a string again.
6. It should be possible to manage a blacklist with character strings. If the string that has been read is in the blacklist, it should be marked with seven asterisks (*******) be replaced.
7. Points 4, 5 and 6 should be freely combinable, eg with blacklisting and output to console.

The first two points can be represented by an abstract base class or a trait and concrete implementations are solved. In Listing 4.46, the abstract Base class Input and the two derived classes ReadLineInput and FileInput.

Listing 4.46: The abstract class Input and the derived classes ReadLine-Input and FileInput

```
abstract class input {
def get (): String
}
class ReadLineInput extends Input {
def get () = readLine ()
}
class FileInput (filename: String) extends Input {
import scala.io.Source
import java.io.File
private [this] val contents =
Source fromFile (new File (filename)) getLines
def get () = {
if (contents.hasNext) contents.next () else ""
}
}
```

The abstract class Input contains an abstract method get. The derived The fourth class ReadLineInput implemented get through readline. The derived Class FileInput defines a class parameter for the file name. The The content of the file is then used when initializing a FileInput object of the source companion object. The fromFile method is required a java.io.File object as an argument and returns a Source object. With the getLines method, an iterator is finally generated which, for each Access with next returns a line from the file. This is then in the method de get used. If all lines of the file are "used up", hasNext returns the value false back. In that case the result of get is the empty string.

The third point, the optional prompt, is also usefully represented by a Another derived class implemented, in this case derived from the class ReadLineInput. The ReadLineInputPrompt class is again in Listing 4.47. given

Listing 4.47: The ReadLineInputPrompt class

```
class ReadLineInputPrompt (prompt: String)
```

```
extends ReadLineInput {
override def get () = {
print (prompt + "")
super.get ()
}
}
```

The ReadLineInputPrompt class has the prompt as a class parameter. The Method get is inherited from ReadLineInput and redefined so that first the prompt and a space are output and then the get method of the base class is called with the expression super.get ().
The remaining points 4 to 7 from the list on page 88 can be used with the approach of deriving more specific classes from the previous ones, of course. ren, but the number of classes becomes very large after all conceivable com- combinations are to be realized.
Scala offers a very elegant way out with the help of traits. With traits you can namely, methods of classes can also be modified. These modifications can then be connected in series. Hence we speak of *stackable modifications* (stackable modifications).
To implement point 4, we define a trait echo that contains the get- Modified method so that it *also* outputs the entered character string. The trait echo is shown in Listing 4.48.
Listing 4.48: The Echo Trait

```
trait echo extends input {
abstract override def get () = {
val input = super.get ()
println (input)
input
}
}
```

The Trait Echo has two special features. First, the trait expands a class se, namely the abstract class Input, and secondly the get method calls with super.get () the abstract method get from input. This seems like at first make little sense, since the super call then fails in the input class. gen would.
By marking the method as abstract override, the
The construct now has the following meaning: The extends input means that the Trait Echo can only be mixed into a class if this class *is before* another trait or a class implements the get method.
So the call super.get () also makes sense, because with it the get- Method called in the form as it was before the trait was mixed in. In The application from Listing 4.49 contains some examples for clarification. th.
Listing 4.49: The StackableTraits1 Object

```
object StackableTraits1 extends Application {
println ("ReadLineInput")
(new ReadLineInput) .get ()
println ("ReadLineInput with echo")
(new ReadLineInput with Echo) .get ()
println ("ReadLineInputPrompt")
(new ReadLineInputPrompt (">")). get ()
println ("ReadLineInputPrompt with echo")
(new ReadLineInputPrompt (">") with Echo) .get ()
}
```

Listing 4.49 also shows that a trait into an object with with can be mixed in. The following listing shows the execution of the object StackableTraits1 after compilation. The comments ← *input* and ← *Echo* were added later to make it clear where the user is has entered something and where the method changed by the Echo-Trait the Input has returned.

```
$ scala StackableTraits1
ReadLineInput
Hello
← input
ReadLineInput with echo
Hello
← input
Hello
← echo
ReadLineInputPrompt
> Hello
← input
ReadLineInputPrompt with echo
> Hello
← input
Hello
← echo
```

The next required modification is the saving and the possibility of the later retrieval of all entries. The collect trait (see Listing 4.50) sets this around.

Listing 4.50: The Trait Collect

```
trait Collect extends Input {
import scala.collection.mutable.ListBuffer
private [this] var inputs = new ListBuffer [String]
def inputList = inputs.toList
abstract override def get () = {
val input = super.get ()
inputs + = input
input
}
}
```

The entries are saved in an object-private ListBuffer and made available as an immutable list via the inputList method. The ListBuffer class must be imported explicitly. The next one Read strings can be added to the ListBuffer with the + = method will. In the Trait Collect, too, the get method must again be abstract override so that an already implemented measurement method to be able to change.

The trait collect can now be used to define the class My-Input can be used as follows:

```
class MyInput extends ReadLineInputPrompt (">")
with Collect
```

The MyInput class extends the ReadLineInput class and then adds add the trait collect.

Listing 4.51. The StackableTraits2 Object

```
object StackableTraits2 extends Application {
val in = new MyInput
in.get ()
in.get ()
```

```
println (in.inputList)
}
```

If the application from Listing 4.51 is now compiled and started, the result look like this:

```
$ scala StackableTraits2
> Hello world
> Hello readers
List (hello world, hello reader)
```

What is particularly interesting is the series connection of the two Echo and Collect traits. Let's define MyInput as

```
class MyInput extends ReadLineInputPrompt (">")
with Collect with Echo
```

so the renewed execution of StackableTraits2 looks like this:

```
$ scala StackableTraits2
> Hello world
Hello World
> Hello readers
Hello readers
List (hello world, hello reader)
```

The get method of the MyInput class is called by both echo and changed by Collect. The entry is displayed again on the screen. and stored in the ListBuffer.

The last variant that we want to implement is the blacklist trait (she-he Listing 4.52).

Listing 4.52: The blacklist trait

```
trait blacklist extends input {
val blacklist: List [String]
abstract override def get () = {
val input = super.get ()
if (blacklist contains (input trim))
"******"
else
input
}
}
```

The trait blacklist first declares an abstract val with the designation-a blacklist as a list of strings. The modified get method behaves so that a read-in string is checked to see whether it is in the blacklist is included. If this is the case, the character string, as on page 88 under point 6 given, replaced by seven asterisks. With the trim method, removed all spaces at the beginning and end of the string.

Listing 4.53. The StackableTraits3 Object

```
object StackableTraits3 extends Application {
val inBEC = new ReadLineInputPrompt ("BEC>")
with Blacklist with Echo with Collect {
val blacklist = List ("Hello World")
}
inBEC.get ()
println (inBEC.inputList)
val inCBE = new ReadLineInputPrompt ("CBE>")
with Collect with Blacklist with Echo {
val blacklist = List ("Hello World")
}
```

```
inCBE.get ()
println (inCBE.inputList)
}
```

Now let's define the StackableTraits3 object shown in Listing 4.53 and run it, this is what happens:

```
$ scala StackableTraits3
BEC> Hello World
******
List (******)
CBE> Hello World
******
List (Hello World)
```

When first entered, Hello World became both output and in the List replaced by asterisks. For the second input, however, only for output. In the list contains the unchanged entry.

This example is very nice to see that the order is important in to which the modifications are applied. InBCE's get method in Listing 4.53 was first blacklisted by the trait, then by Echo and modified at the end by Collect. That is, first the character chain te Hello World replaced by the asterisks, then output and then to the List saved.

The order at inCBE is different. Hello World is there first in the list is saved, then replaced by asterisks and finally output ben. By changing the order to with Echo with Blacklist with Collect, for example, the character string could first be output unchanged. and then replaced by asterisks in the list.

Let's look again at the object inCBE from Listing 4.53:

```
val inCBE = new ReadLineInputPrompt ("CBE>")
with Collect with Blacklist with Echo {
val blacklist = List ("Hello World")
}
```

The right side of the equal sign makes an object an anonymous Generates a class that extends the ReadLineInputPrompt class. The class ReadLineInputPrompt in turn extends ReadLineInput and this extends the abstract class input. In addition, the three traits Collect, Blacklist and echo mixed in.

After all three traits and the ReadLineInput and ReadLine-InputPrompt define the get method, the question arises as to which method de is executed by the expression inCBE.get (). For classes that inherit from each other, the question is easy to answer. But it is interesting how the traits are classified, especially since their get methods all have one super call included.

Scala's answer to this question is *linearization* . Through linearization all classes and traits are brought into a well-defined, linear order. A super call then simply flows into the method of the next class or of the next trait in the linear chain.

The linear order is calculated from back to front. The last links in the chain are the base class and its linear order. In our example is this the chain ReadLineInputPrompt → ReadLineInput → Input → AnyRef → Any.

Then the traits are processed from left to right. All classes, which are already present in the linearization are transferred when the Chain of traits omitted, ie with Collect the chain is extended tert to Collect → ReadLineInputPrompt → ReadLineInput → Input →

AnyRef → Any.
With the blacklist and echo traits, the linearization result is echo → Blacklist → Collect → ReadLineInputPrompt → ReadLineInput → Input → AnyRef → Any.
This means that the get method from echo is called up for the expression inCBE.get (). call. This first calls the method from Blacklist with super.get ().
This in turn get from Collect etc. This makes it clear that the entered Hello World value first lands in the list and only after return of the method de from Collect is replaced by an asterisk.
The linearization of

```
val inBEC = new ReadLineInputPrompt ("BEC>")
with Blacklist with Echo with Collect {
val blacklist = List ("Hello World")
}
```

is therefore Collect → Echo → Blacklist → ReadLineInputPrompt → ReadLineInput → Input → AnyRef → Any. Hence, the asterisks in in this case both output and saved in the list.
By changing the order in which the traits are mixed in, it is so it is also possible to output the unchanged input, but as an asterisk save.

4.4 Implicits and rich wrappers

Scala uses a number of Java types. For example, the string has the type java.lang.String. In Scala a part of a string can be entered with return the method drop, e.g.

```
scala> val str = "Hello World"
str: java.lang.String = Hello World
scale> str drop 6
res0: String = World
```

When looking at the Java API documentation, however, it becomes apparent that a method
drop is not defined at all in the java.lang.String class. At a su-
In the Scala API documentation, we find the drop method in the class se StringOps. However, the type of str is not StringOps. 18th
The solution lies in the so-called *implicit conversions* just *Implicits* . There- with can automatically transfer an object to another object of another if necessary Class to be converted. This approach makes it possible in Scala to Enrich existing classes with additional methods. The "other" classes are therefore also called *rich wrappers* .
In the example, the String object must automatically be converted into a StringOps object
can be converted to use the drop method. The method drop returns a string as the result.

18 Before Scala 2.8, a string was converted into a RichString. In the RichString class the collection methods such as drop and map were then defined. The disadvantage of the approach was that the result of the methods in RichString was also a RichString and not a String. To-
In addition to StringOps, Scala 2.8 also has the WrappedString class and its methods return a WrappedString.

The automatic conversion works with perfectly normal functions that marked with implicit for the compiler. For our example this is the method

```
implicit def augmentString (x: String): StringOps
```

from the PreDef object. This means that the expression str drop 6 becomes the

String Hello World through augmentString into a StringOps object converted. This then understands the message drop with the argument 6 and returns the value World of type String as the result.
The conversion functions are performed by the compiler before compiling inserted into the code. So str drop 6 is not translated, but rather augmentString (str) drop 6
The compiler is allowed to insert implicit conversions to avoid type errors. those that would otherwise occur. There are three places where implicits are used will:

1. Conversion of the recipient of a message.

In the above example, this led to the use of augmentString.

2. Conversion to the expected type.

For example, if we had

```
val str2: scala.collection.immutable.WrappedString =
str drop 6
```

written, the string would be written with the implicit method wrapString in converted to a WrappedString.

3. Implicit parameters.

These are described from page 98 onwards.
The exact rules are:
Only the functions that are available with the Keyword implicit are highlighted.
The definition must be visible as a simple identifier, ie in the scope. are e.g. contain implicit conversion functions in an object Sample, they are used as simple names after the import clause import Sample._ ner faded in and applicable.
The compiler also searches the companion objects of the source and Target type. These conversions do not have to be seen as simple identifiers. be cash.
The conversion must be unique. There are several functions that the Correct type errors, neither is applied, but the type error reported.
Only one implicit transformation is used at one point. When a Type A exists and B is needed only after direct conversions searched from A to B. There is a conversion from A to C and another from C to B, the two are *not* automatically applied one after the other. det.
Implicit casts can simplify your code in many places. We want to illustrate this with an example. Listing 4.54 shows two classes defined to represent bands and their records.

Listing 4.54. The Record and **Tape** classes

```
class Record (title: String) {
override def toString = title
}
class Band (name: String) {
private var records: List [Record] = List ()
def addRecord (record: Record) {
records :: = record
}
override def toString = name + ":" + records
}
```

With these classes you can now create bands and records, e.g.

```
scala> val jl = new band ("The Jesus Lizard")
jl: Band = The Jesus Lizard: List ()
```

```
scala> jl.addRecord (new Record ("Goat"))
scala> println (jl)
The Jesus Lizard: List (Goat)
```

Instead of jl.addRecord (new Record ("Goat")) it would be more pleasant to if we just had to write jl.addRecord ("Goat"). A possibility would be to add a method addRecord (title: String) to the Band class continue. Sometimes this is not desirable or not possible at all, for example, if the classes Tape and Record are part of a library. Instead, let's define an implicit conversion of a string to a Record object, we achieve the same result, as the following session shows:

```
scala> implicit def stringToRecord (title: String) =
|
new record (title)
stringToRecord: (title: String) Record
scala> jl.addRecord ("Pure")
scala> println (jl)
The Jesus Lizard: List (Pure, Goat)
```

Implicits are also a great way to simulate new syntax. A map can yes, for example

```
Map ("A" -> "Augsburg", "B" -> "Berlin")
```

be generated. This notation is not a special syntax. The string in front the arrow is converted into an ArrowAssoc, and its method -> gives returns a tuple that can be inserted into the map.

Another application for implicit are the *implicit parameters* , i.e. parameter of a function that do not have to be specified when calling, but can be supplemented by the compiler.

To illustrate, we want to refer to the input example from Section 4.3.2 Entering our record collection build up. For simplification, the plate collection of a map, consisting of the name of the band and the list of name. Listing 4.55 shows the RecordLibrary class.

Listing 4.55. The RecordLibrary class

```
class RecordLibrary {
private var records = Map [String, List [String]] ()
def addInteractive (input: Input) = {
print ("band name:")
val bandname = input.get ()
print ("Recordtitle:")
val recordtitle = input.get ()
records + = bandname -> (records get bandname match {
case None
=> List (recordtitle)
case Some (rs) => (recordtitle :: rs)
})
}
override def toString = records.toString
}
```

The last four lines of the addInteractive method already give a small one Foretaste of the *pattern matching* , which is explained in section 5.4. The Code in this example does the following: The Map get method gets the Value for key rebond name determined. There is no corresponding entry in the Map, None is returned. In this case, the tuple is derived from the band name men and the list with the disk name. If there is already an entry den, the disk list rs is returned as Some (rs). In this case it will with the band name and the previously available list supplemented by the entered

A new tuple is created with the same plate name. The generated entry ends up finally with + = in the record collection.
The input can be made using the input parameter as described in section 4.3.2 the approach presented. For example, with the following
a record collection is created for the lines and a new one is prompted
Line tape and disk name are queried:

```
val myRecords = new RecordLibrary
myRecords.addInteractive (new ReadLineInputPrompt ("\ n>"))
```

The disadvantage of this approach is that each time addInteractive the input object has to be passed over and over again. An association
The implicit parameters provide the increase. The parameter of addInteractive must first be marked with implicit:

```
...
def addInteractive (implicit input: Input) = {
...
```

This means that the method can be used with the input parameter as before. In addition, it is now possible to add a variable of the type Input with the key word implicit. Here, too, it applies again that the variable is
cher identifier must be visible. For example, according to the definition of

```
implicit val myPreferredInput = new ReadLineInput
```

and, if necessary, the corresponding import statement, the addInter-
active can be called without parameters.
Implicit parameters are not restricted to a single parameter, but rather
The keyword implicit refers to the entire parameter list.
To use implicit and explicit parameters together, we must first
know that in Scala it is possible to have functions with more than one parameter list define. The underlying concept of *currying* comes from the functional programming and is therefore only explained in Chapter 5.
For example, we can change addInteractive so that we have an explicit
zite and have an implicit parameter list, as shown in Listing 4.56.

Listing 4.56: Tape Name Input, RecordtitleInput, and RecordLibrary

```
class reel name Input (val input: Input)
class RecordtitleInput (val input: Input)
class RecordLibrary {
private var records = Map [String, List [String]] ()
def addInteractive (overrideEntry: Boolean = false)
(implicit bandIn: BandnameInput,
recordIn: RecordtitleInput) = {
print ("band name:")
val bandname = bandIn.input.get ()
print ("Recordtitle:")
val recordtitle = recordIn.input.get ()
records + = bandname -> (records get bandname match {
case None
=> List (recordtitle)
case Some (rs) =>
if (overrideEntry) List (recordtitle)
else (recordtitle :: rs)
})
}
override def toString = records.toString
}
```

The implicit parameter list contains a flag as the only parameter that states whether the old entry for the band, if any, has been replaced by the new entry.

should be written or not. Having given a default value for it the parameter can also be omitted. But it cannot be implicit be passed, but is determined by the definition. That is, the pro The method's programmer dictates what to do if there is no argument for the Parameter is present.

The implicit parameter list contains two entries: an input object for the tape input and one for entering the record title. After the compiler has completed the ziten parameter only selects according to the type, it makes sense to use as rare as possible

Types to use. If the two implicit parameters were of the type Input, then could not be distinguished. So here we have two simple wrapper Classes BandnameInput and RecordtitleInput defined. So defined the user of the RecordLibrary class, what if there is no argument for the implicit parameter list is passed.

Let us now define two suitable values, such as

implicit val bandInput = new bandnameInput (new ReadLineInput)

implicit val recordInput = new RecordtitleInput (new ReadLineInputPrompt (">"))

we can use the method by the expression myRecords.addInteractive () use.

You have now got to know everything that is more object-oriented Programming is to be assigned. In the next chapter we will continue with the functional programming continued.

Chapter 5

Functional programming

As a hybrid language, Scala combines object-oriented programming with the functional programming 1 . Object-oriented programming can Most people can imagine something concrete. But what is functional Programming language? Whether a programming language has the label "functional" is allowed, has been and is much discussed. Recently one also flared up Discussion whether Scala can call itself that. Martin Odersky, the creator of Scala, Instead, Scala names one in the blog post [Ode10a] from January 2010 *post-functional* language.

Just for the question of what a functional programming language is there are different answers. There is agreement on the core of the functional programming: the calculation by evaluating mathematical Functions and the avoidance of status and changeable data. The means that if we use val instead of var in Scala, we are a bit fun- more functional.

Functional programming is accompanied by a variety of concepts that implementation in Scala are the subject of this chapter. In the first section we will present you with the needs evaluation, with which the calculation of a val performed the first time it is accessed. In from- Section 5.2 discusses functions and recursions. An essential one The features of functional programming are the higher-order functions (see section 5.3), which can have a function as argument or result- nen.

Many functional programming languages support pattern matching, a generalization of the switch-case-construct. Pattern matching and the so-called We introduce the case classes in Section 5.4. That on the American niche mathematician and logician Haskell B. Curry declining concept the currying makes it possible to define your own control structures in Scala. ren (see section 5.5). Then we will go into section 5.6 again come back to the keyword for to show you that more than one ne loop behind it. Last but not least, we'll throw another one in Section 5.7 View of the very sophisticated type system from Scala.

5.1 Lazy evaluation

By default, all fields of a class are used in Scala when creating an object project calculated. We speak of the so-called *eager evaluation* . In one In some cases, however, it does not necessarily make sense to carry out complex calculations

This may not even lead to a higher result during the entire existence of an object required to be carried out immediately. The key to this is *lazy evaluation* , which can also be translated with *needs evaluation* . This becomes the value of a Field calculated exactly when it is accessed for the first time. in the In contrast to a method, this value is then evaluated in an evaluated form saved. This means that if the field is accessed again, there is no need to repeat it be calculated.

Scala defines the modifier lazy for this purpose, which is only permitted for vals is. Such lazy vals are allowed everywhere and not just as fields of objects.

With the following session we want to demonstrate the behavior of lazy vals:

```
scala> val x = {
|
```

```
print ("Please enter a number:")
|
readInt
| }
Enter a number: 12
x: Int = 12
scale> lazy val y = {
|
print ("Please enter a number:")
|
readInt
| }
y: Int = <lazy>
scala> print (y)
Enter a number: 13
13
scala> print (x)
12
scala> print (y)
13
```

In Listing 4.43 on page 86, we defined the PositiveNumber trait. Around To save you having to scroll back, we want to state it here again:

```
trait PositiveNumber {
val value: Int
require (value> 0)
}
```

While creating an anonymous class, we noticed that a val in a subclass is only initialized after calling the constructor of the base class. We had solved the problem with the predefined fields. A second possibility ability to solve this are lazy vals. However, only concrete vals can be lazy his. Therefore it is not possible to assign the val value with the modifier lazy see.

Listing 5.1: The PositiveNumber trait with a lazy val

```
trait PositiveNumber {
val inValue: Int
lazy val value = {
require (inValue> 0)
inValue
}
}
```

The admittedly somewhat cumbersome version of the positiveNumber traits now allow a definition of the following form:

```
scala> val n = new PositiveNumber {
|
val inValue = 12
| }
n: java.lang.Object with PositiveNumber =
$ anon $ 1 @ 409a44d6
```

Note, however, that an object with the value 0 for the inValue can now be generated successfully. The exception thrown by require is then only thrown when value is accessed for the first time. The following example site This should make this clear:

```
scala> val m = new PositiveNumber {
|
val inValue = 0
| }
m: java.lang.Object with PositiveNumber =
$ anon $ 1 @ 2754de0b
scala> m.value
java.lang.IllegalArgumentException: requirement failed
at scala.Predef $ .require (Predef.scala: 134)
...
```

For a lazy val x to make sense, all other vals in their Calculation access x, be lazy. Otherwise the value of x would be immediate required and thus calculated. Since vars cannot be lazy, the-se don't need the value of x for their calculations, or x shouldn't be lazy his.

5.2 Functions and recursions

An essential feature of functional programming is support of functions as *first class values* . This means that functions are values and can as such, just like numbers or strings, for example in lists. saves or even parameters or results from other functions his.
Functions can not only be used as functional equations, as discussed so far, but can also be defined as a *function* literal . For example, the function
def inc (i: Int) = i + 1
also as a function literal
(i: Int) => i + 1
to be written. 2 After a value is defined by (i: Int) => i + 1
it can be assigned to a variable. So we can write
val inc = (i: Int) => i + 1
Because there is a function behind inc, we can refer to inc to a number apply:

```
scala> val inc = (i: Int) => i + 1
inc: (Int) => Int = <function1>
scala> inc (2)
res0: Int = 3
```

We also see the type of the function (Int) => Int, i.e. in the above session a function with a parameter list containing an int and the result styp Int. For functions with 0 to 22 parameters are in the Scala distribution Defined traits. The output < function1 > after the type is the result of the toString method of the Trait Function1. This also means in particular that every function in Scala is an object.
It is also possible to define a function literal that has free variables, e.g.
val adder = (i: Int) => i + a

The variable i is a *formal parameter* , but the variable a is a reference to a variable in the enclosing scope. Therefore a variable with the identifier a in the definition of adder. The compl-ler generated for adder then a so-called *closure* , the variable a *captured* . Since the values of variables can change in Scala, the current value of a, but a reference to the variable in the closure a bound. Changes in a have an effect according to the definition of adder immediately, as the following session is designed to illustrate:

```
scale> var a = 10
a: Int = 10
scala> val adder = (i: Int) => i + a
adder: (Int) => Int = <function1>
scala> adder (2)
res0: Int = 12
scale> a = 20
a: Int = 20
scala> adder (2)
res1: Int = 22
```

The variable a initially has the value 10. Consequently, the application of the tion adder evaluated to the value 2 to 12. If a is then set to 20, the result of adder (2) changes accordingly.

Since according to the concept of functional programming there are no changeable There are variables, i.e. only vals, if we program purely functionally, not possible to calculate values by grinding. For example, the code is in Listing 5.2 for calculating the sum of the numbers in the list list imperative, since he does the calculation by changing the state, here the value of the variable sum.

Listing 5.2: imperative calculation of the sum of the numbers in a list

```
def sum (list: List [Int]) = {
var sum = 0
for (elem <- list) sum + = elem
sum
}
```

Such a programming task is used in functional programming solved by *recursion* . 3 A functional version of sum is shown in Listing 5.3. posed. After the function contains a recursive call, the result nest type cannot be determined and must therefore be specified.

Listing 5.3: Recursive calculation of the sum of the numbers in a list

```
def sum (list: List [Int]): Int = {
if (list.isEmpty) 0
else list.head + sum (list.tail)
}
```

Recursion means that the function calls itself again. The function sum in Listing 5.3 adds the first element to the sum of the remainder of the list. The me- method isEmtpy returns true if the list is empty, head returns the first Element and tail back the remaining list. If the list is empty, the result is 0. for brevity and clarity and to avoid changes in status the recursive version of sum is preferable. But unfortunately, recursion is gel less efficient than an imperative approach. This is also one of the reasons why the language designers at Scala decided to use imperatives Allowing programming: Because it can lead to more efficient solutions.

This disadvantage of the recursive approach can be explained in a certain case by the Optimize compiler away. And then when the function is *end recursive* (*tail recursive*), i.e. if the last thing computed in the function is the re italic call itself is. In this case the compiler can use the recursion replace a loop. The sum function in Listing 5.3 cannot be optimized because the result of the recursive call ends with the first element is added to the list. Listing 5.4 shows a function sum that is a terminal recursive Uses auxiliary function. This can be optimized by the compiler. The auxiliary function, the value calculated so far and the remaining list are transferred so that the Addition is calculated before the recursive call and thus the recursive up-call is the final calculation of sumHelper.

Listing 5.4: Final recursive calculation of the sum of the numbers in a list

```
def sum (list: List [Int]) = {
def sumHelper (x: Int, list: List [Int]): Int = {
if (list.isEmpty) x
else sumHelper (x + list.head, list.tail)
}
sumHelper (0, list)
}
```

Before the release of Scala 2.8.0, the common way to test whether the Final recursion has been optimized by a loop in the event of the recursion being canceled throw an exception and then check the stack trace to see if the function called himself or not.

Listing 5.5: Recursive calculation of the sum of the numbers in a list with a @ tailrec-Annotation

```
import scala.annotation.tailrec
// is not compiled because it is not final recursive
@tailrec def sum (list: List [Int]): Int = {
if (list.isEmpty) 0
else list.head + sum (list.tail)
}
```

Since Scala 2.8.0 there is an annotation for this: @tailrec. For example, if we wisely, as can be seen in Listing 5.5, the non-end recursive function sum from Listing 5.3 with the @ tailrec annotation, the translation attempt leads to the following the mistake

```
<console>: 6: error: could not optimize @tailrec annotated
method: it contains a recursive call not in tail
position
@tailrec def sum (list: List [Int]): Int = {
^
```

On the other hand, the function sum from Listing 5.4 is preceded by a @tailrec sumHelper function compiled without error message, that is, sumHel could be optimized by.

As the following session shows, a terminal recursive function cannot always be optimized:

```
scala> import scala.annotation.tailrec
import scala.annotation.tailrec
scale> class Tailrec {
|
@tailrec def g (i: Int): Int = if (i == 0) 0
|
else g (i-1)
| }
<console>: 7: error: could not optimize @tailrec annotated
method: it is neither private nor final so can be
overridden
@tailrec def g (i: Int): Int = if (i == 0) 0
```

As can be seen from the error message, a method that is in a sub-great can be redefined, not optimized

The core of the problem of recursive functions is that the stack has to deal with every function call grows, which ultimately depends on the memory size and number of re course steps to an overflow and thus a crash of the program can lead. So-called *trampolines* [4] are a means of avoiding this . There the functions are implemented in such a way that they are a function instead of a value return with which the next step can be calculated. That is, the recursive call does not take place in the function itself, but the trampoline Function performs one step at a time. With Scala 2.8.0 such Trampoline functions through the scala.util.control.TailCalls object directly supported.

Trampolining is particularly interesting with reciprocal recursion, that is if two or more functions call each other, which is not automatic table can be optimized. The classics are the two functions isEven and isOdd, which calculate whether a number is even or odd and which (as from Listing 5.6) are mutually recursively defined 5 .

Listing 5.6: Mutually recursive functions isEven and isOdd

```
def isEven (n: Int): Boolean =
if (n == 0) true else isOdd (n-1)
def isOdd (n: Int): Boolean =
if (n == 0) false else isEven (n-1)
```

The two functions cannot be optimized and resulted in one Test computer at isEven (100000) to a StackOverflowError. Through the Trampoline approach, shown in Listing 5.7, is still used for any number between the entered and 0 the function isEven or isOdd called, but now one after the other.

Listing 5.7: Mutually recursive functions using isEven and isOdd of the tramponline approach

```
import scala.util.control.TailCalls._
def isEven (n: Int): TailRec [Boolean] =
if (n == 0) done (true) else tailcall (isOdd (n-1))
def isOdd (n: Int): TailRec [Boolean] =
if (n == 0) done (false) else tailcall (isEven (n-1))
```

Instead of a Boolean, these two functions give a TailRec [Boolean] back. To end the embedded recursion, the done, for the recursion step is the tailcall function. The expression isEven (100000) thus returns a function that can be evaluated with result. The Expression isEven (100000) .result calculates the value without stack overflow true.

5.3 Higher order functions

Functions that have functions as parameters or return functions, are called *higher-order* functions. These are an immediate consequence from the fact that functions are *first class values* , i.e. equal to others Values stand. Higher order functions are a very practical means of Abstraction, as we want to show you in the following example.

Let us consider a function incList that increments all the numbers in a list. animals. We could define this function recursively, for example as in Listing 5.8.

Listing 5.8: The incList function for recursively incrementing all elements of a list

```
def incList (list: List [Int]): List [Int] = {
if (list.isEmpty) List ()
else list.head + 1 :: incList (list.tail)
}
```

Furthermore, we could perhaps also need a function that includes all elements of one doubled a list. The corresponding function is shown in Listing 5.9.

Listing 5.9: The doubleList function for recursively doubling all elements of a list

```
def doubleList (list: List [Int]): List [Int] = {
if (list.isEmpty) List ()
else list.head * 2 :: doubleList (list.tail)
}
```

The two functions incList and doubleList are only very different little. Where the expression list.head + 1 appears in incList, it says in double-List instead is list.head * 2, and of course the recursive call contains once incList and once doubleList.

Let's define two functions:

```
def inc (x: Int) = x + 1
def double (x: Int) = x * 2
```

and if you use them, as shown in Listing 5.10, the functions still see each other a bit more similar.

Listing 5.10: The incList and doubleList functions using the functions inc and double

```
def incList (list: List [Int]): List [Int] = {
if (list.isEmpty) List ()
else inc (list.head) :: incList (list.tail)
}
def doubleList (list: List [Int]): List [Int] = {
if (list.isEmpty) List ()
else double (list.head) :: doubleList (list.tail)
}
```

With a higher order function we could use the inc or double function passed as an argument. That is, instead of the two almost identical functions We can use the funList function (see listing 5.11), which expects a function as a parameter with which the list items elements should be changed.

Listing 5.11: The funList functions with a function for changing the individual Elements as parameters

```
def funList (fun: Int => Int, list: List [Int])
: List [Int] = {
if (list.isEmpty) List ()
else fun (list.head) :: funList (fun, list.tail)
}
```

With the funList function as well as inc and double we are able to generate the Define functions incList and doubleList as follows:

```
def incList
(list: List [Int]) = funList (inc
, list)
def doubleList (list: List [Int]) = funList (double, list)
```

In fact, this approach of *mapping* a function over a list is *used* as a method already made available. Instead of defining funList yourself, you can we use the higher-order function map:

```
def incList
(list: List [Int]) = list map inc
def doubleList (list: List [Int]) = list map double
```

As a next step we can save ourselves the definition of inc and double, by passing function literals instead:

```
def incList
(list: List [Int]) = list map (i => i + 1)
def doubleList (list: List [Int]) = list map (i => i * 2)
```

And finally, we can even add the bound variable i in the expression replace to the right of the arrow with a placeholder and write:

def incList
(list: List [Int]) = list map (_ + 1)
def doubleList (list: List [Int]) = list map (_ * 2)
The compiler then places the respective element in place of the underscore. This saves us from introducing a name for the variable. With the We define a so-called *partially applied function* (*partially applied function*). This also works with multiple variables and multiple Underlined. For example, we define through
scala> val add = (_: Int) + (_: Int)
add: (Int, Int) => Int = <function2>
a function add that expects a parameter list with two arguments. The Type inference mechanism cannot type for the two arguments of add so we need to add type information. We wouldn't have Type, it would look like this in the Scala shell:
scala> val add = _ + _
<console>: 5: error: missing parameter type for expanded
function ((x $ 1, x $ 2) => x $ 1. $ plus (x $ 2))
val add = _ + _
^
<console>: 5: error: missing parameter type for expanded
function ((x $ 1: <error>, x $ 2) => x $ 1. $ plus (x $ 2))
val add = _ + _
^
The correctly defined function add can refer to an argument list consisting of two ints, are used:
scale> add (2,3)
What looks like a function call here actually corresponds to add. apply (2,3), i.e. the object with the name add reacts to the message apply with an argument list that contains two ints.
In functional programming, the list dominates as a data structure. For they are usually defined in order to a variety of higher order functions transform the list into a new one. The new collection framework (see Section 6.2) of Scala 2.8 defines many of these functions for all collections. We explain some of the functions below using the list as an example.
In addition to the already presented map, which shows all elements of a list with the transferred
function and returns the new list, there is also the function on foreach, which has a function of type A => Unit as argument and this with all elements. For example, with
list.foreach (e => println (e))
all elements of a list list are output line by line. Here too can the bound variable e can be replaced by the underscore:
list.foreach (println (_))
Instead of println (_) you can also write println _ [6] . So stands the Placeholder no longer for one parameter, but for the entire parameter terlist, which in this case contains a parameter. Becomes a function in context expected, a placeholder for the entire parameter list can even be omitted like for example
list.foreach (println)
The following can then also be written in infix operator notation:
list foreach println
A whole series of higher-order functions have predicates, i.e. functions with the result type Boolean as a parameter. This allows for example a Find part of a list for which a predicate applies or not. With list filter

(_ <3) a new list is calculated that contains all elements that are less than 3
are. The filterNot function inverts the predicate. dropWhile removes the
Elements as long as a condition applies, takeWhile only takes this, span divides
the list according to the predicate in two sub-lists. For each predicate p and each
List l applies:
l span p ≡ (l takeWhile p, l dropWhile p)
as the following listing should clarify:
scala> val list = List (1,2,3,4,5)
list: List [Int] = List (1, 2, 3, 4, 5)
scala> list span (_% 2 == 1)
res0: (List [Int], List [Int]) = (List (1), List (2, 3, 4, 5))
scala> list takeWhile (_% 2 == 1)
res1: List [Int] = List (1)
scala> list dropWhile (_% 2 == 1)
res2: List [Int] = List (2, 3, 4, 5)
The partition function divides the list into two lists with all elements
the first list fulfills the predicate and all of the second list do not, e.g.
scala> list partition (_% 2 == 1)
res3: (List [Int], List [Int]) = (List (1, 3, 5), List (2, 4))
Other useful functions are forall and exists, which determine whether a pre-
dikat is fulfilled for all or for at least one element of the list, e.g.
scala> list forall (_ <3)
res4: Boolean = false
scale> list exists (_ <3)
res5: Boolean = true
A typical application for lists is to display the elements using an operational
on to a single value, e.g. the addition of all elements. This
Combining is called *folding* because the list is combined into one value-
is folded. Like many functional programming languages, Scala also provides
ready for functions, starting from the left by folding a list
foldLeft and, starting from the right, foldRight. Usually the case
no consideration was given to whether the list was empty or not
acts. Therefore, in addition to the operation, a value is required as a parameter that
one is the result of applying the convolution function to the empty list
and on the other hand at the end or at the beginning of the convolution using the
operation
linked to the rest.
The expression
list.foldLeft (0) (_ + _)
calculates the sum of the elements of the list list with the starting value 0 by adding
successively all elements are linked with the + operation.
In Scala, instead of the functions foldLeft and foldRight, the operators
/: and: \ are used. The two operators correspond to the two functions
nen, whereby according to the rule for operators ending with:, at /: die
List on the right and the start value on the left. So that looks the typical application
natural and easier to understand, such as with
(list: \ 0) (_ + _)
or
(0 /: list) (_ + _)
In the first case, the number 0 on the right of the operator becomes the remainder from
the right
added and in the second case accordingly from the left. With the following session
it becomes a little clearer.
scala> ("Beginning ->" /: list) (_ + _)

```
res6: java.lang.String = beginning -> 12345
scala> (list: \ "<- end") (_ + _)
res7: java.lang.String = 12345 <- end
```

The use of foldLeft or foldRight leads to the same result nis, but the expression is less catchy:

```
scala> (list foldLeft "start ->") (_ + _)
res8: java.lang.String = beginning -> 12345
scala> (list foldRight "<- end") (_ + _)
res9: java.lang.String = 12345 <- end
```

For non-empty lists there are also the variants reduceLeft and reduceRight which do not need a start parameter. The functions scanLeft and scanRight calculate the list of all intermediate results, as shown in the following listing:

```
scala> (list scanLeft "Start ->") (_ + _)
res10: List [java.lang.String] = List (beginning ->, beginning
-> 1, beginning -> 12, beginning -> 123, beginning -> 1234,
Beginning -> 12345)
scala> (list scanRight "<- end") (_ + _)
res11: List [java.lang.String] = List (<- end, 5 <- end,
45 <- end, 345 <- end, 2345 <- end, 12345 <- end)
```

Even if we haven't got all of the higher functions available as standard Have mentioned order, we will now stop and refer for further Further information on studying the Scala API.

Higher-order functions can have functions not only as parameters, but also return as a result. For example, we can use

```
def mkAdder (x: Int) = (y: Int) => x + y
```

define a function mkAdder that is applied to a parameter x a Returns a function that adds x to the relevant parameter, for example:

```
scala> val plus2 = mkAdder (2)
plus2: (Int) => Int = <function1>
scale> plus2 (5)
res12: Int = 7
```

To conclude this section, to give you an idea of how programming with higher-order functions can be powerful, consider ten the following expression:

```
(1 to 10) .toList map (x => x + (_: Int)) map (_ (3))
```

The first part, (1 to 10) .toList map (x => x + (_: Int)), generated from the List of numbers 1 to 10 functions corresponding to the mkAdder function (see above). The part map (_ (3)) then applies every function from the list to the Number 3, i.e. the result of the expression is List (4, 5, 6, 7, 8, 9, 10, 11, 12, 13). In the partial expression _ (3) is the placeholder for the function there. The argument, the number 3, is already in brackets.

5.4 Case classes and pattern matching

The *pattern matching* , the comparison with a pattern, a sort of generalized nertes switch-case, as it is known from the C-like languages. How with switch and case, a variable can be checked for different values, e.g.

```
number match {
case 1 => println ("one one")
case 2 => println ("one two")
```

```
case _ => println ("something else")
}
```

Here the value of the variable number is first compared with the value 1. If the comparison is successful, the code after the double arrow => is executed. This means that a one is output for the value 1. Then the entire th block finished. If number is 2, the value does not match pattern 1. Therefore, next checked that it fits pattern 2. After it does, will issued a two. Does another value neither pay attention to pattern 1 nor 2, is matched with the third pattern, the underscore. The underscore is the *wildcard pattern* that everything fits.
Scala checks when compiling whether there are cases that cannot be reached-nen. If we put the wildcard pattern at the beginning, this would mean that for any value of number the first case fits and therefore always something else is issued. However, even the attempt fails translate this expression, as the following session shows:

```
scala> number match {
|
case _ => println ("something else")
|
case 1 => println ("one one")
|
case 2 => println ("one two")
| }
<console>: 9: error: unreachable code
case 1 => println ("one one")
^
<console>: 10: error: unreachable code
case 2 => println ("one two")
^
```

If we want to define a function that uses pattern matching its arguments differs, we can do it as in Listing 5.12.

Listing 5.12: Definition of the checkNumber function with pattern matching

```
def checkNumber (number: Int) = number match {
case 1 => println ("one one")
case 2 => println ("one two")
case _ => println ("something else")
}
```

It is of course also possible to specify the expression as a function literal (see Listing 5.13).

Listing 5.13: checkNumber with pattern matching as a function literal

```
val checkNumber = (number: Int) => number match {
case 1 => println ("one one")
case 2 => println ("one two")
case _ => println ("something else")
}
```

Scala allows an even more concise notation, corresponding to the partially applied functions (see page 110), in which we use the term saving the variable number. The shorter form is in Listing 5.14 shown.

Listing 5.14: checkNumber with pattern matching as a function literal without explicit parameter display

```
val checkNumber: Int => Unit = {
case 1 => println ("one one")
```

```
case 2 => println ("one two")
case _ => println ("something else")
}
```

If we want to output the passed number in the latter case, we can too match to a variable. Anything can be done on a variable as on the underscore be matched. In the third case in Listing 5.15, the variable number matched. This newly introduced variable can then be found on the right of the double arrow.

Listing 5.15: checkNumber with pattern matching on a variable

```
val checkNumber: Int => Unit = {
case 1
=> println ("one one")
case 2
=> println ("one two")
case number => println ("something else:" + number)
}
```

Listing 5.16 shows the possibility of using pattern matching to match the type of a value determine. The checkValue function has a parameter of the type Any. In order to checkValue can, for example, refer to an Int, a Double, a String or anything else. The pattern i: Int then fits for any value of type Int.

Listing 5.16: checkValue with pattern matching on types

```
val checkValue: Any => Unit = {
case i: Int
=> println ("an int:" + i)
case d: Double => println ("a double:" + d)
case _
=> println ("something else")
}
```

Of course we can also mix the different patterns in one Use the function as shown in Listing 5.17.

Listing 5.17: checkValue with pattern matching for a value and for types

```
val checkValue: Any => Unit = {
case 1
=> println ("one one")
case _: Int
=> println ("any int (no one)")
case d: Double => println ("any double:" + d)
case any
=> println ("something else:" + any)
}
```

The previously used representation of sequences such as lists as lists (1, 2, 3) or 1 :: 2 :: Nil [7] is also available as a pattern. So can but not only on the entire list, but also on lists with specific ones Values can be matched (see Listing 5.18).

Listing 5.18. checkValue with pattern matching for a value and for types

```
val checkLists: List [Any] => Unit = {
case Nil =>
println ("an empty list")
case List (_, 2, _) =>
println ("a three-element list" +
"with a 2 in position 2")
case List (_, _, _) =>
println ("a three-element list")
```

```
case _ :: _ :: Nil =>
println ("a two-element list")
case _ :: _ =>
println ("a non-empty list")
}
```

Since type parameters in Scala are removed during compilation just as in Java den, it is not possible to use a pattern regarding the type parameter match. [8] Listing 5.19 attempts to do something different with lists of strings output as with lists from Ints.

Listing 5.19: Example of pattern matching that occurs unexpectedly due to type erasure behaves

```
// Attention : Type Erasure
val doesNotWorkAsExpected: List [Any] => Unit = {
case _: List [String] =>
println ("a list of strings")
case _: List [Int] =>
println ("a list of ints")
}
```

As the following session shows, the second case is never reached because the type Parameter is no longer available at runtime and both patterns then apply to each any list fit:

```
scala> val listOfInts = List (1,2,3)
listOfInts: List [Int] = List (1, 2, 3)
scala> doesNotWorkAsExpected (listOfInts)
a list of strings
```

If the Scala shell is started with the -unchecked flag, we also see the talking warnings:

```
<console>: 6: warning: non variable type-argument String
in type pattern List [String] is unchecked since it is
eliminated by erasure
case _: List [String] =>
^

<console>: 8: warning: non variable type argument Int in
type pattern List [Int] is unchecked since it is
eliminated by erasure
case _: List [Int] =>
^
```

If it is only important to know whether the first element is a string, that can Pattern can be structured as in the first case of Listing 5.4. However, that fits Pattern then, for example, on the List list ("Hello", 1, true, 3.4): List [Any].

```
val worksAsExpected: List [Any] => Unit = {
case (x: String) :: _ =>
println (
"a list with a string as the first element"
)
case _ => println ("another list")
}
```

Of course, tuples can also be matched, like the following Listing 5.20 shows.

Listing 5.20: checkValue with pattern matching on tuples

```
val checkValue: Any => Unit = {
case (1, "Hello") =>
println ("a tuple with a 1 and \" hello \ "")
```

```
case (_, 1.2)
=> println ("A tuple with the value" +
"1.2 second")
case (_, _, _)
=> println ("A triple")
case i: Int
=> println ("an int:" + i)
case _
=> println ("something else")
}
```

In addition to the pattern, so-called *guards* can also be specified. One Guard is a Boolean expression that is introduced with if. If the patient tern fits, the associated guard is evaluated. Only if its result is true, the code behind the arrow is executed.

Listing 5.21: Pattern matching with guards

```
val checkValue: Any => Unit = {
case (x: Int, y: Int) if x * y> 0 =>
println ("same sign")
case (_: Int, _: Int) =>
println ("different signs")
case _ => println ("no int tuple")
}
```

In Listing 5.21, a guard is used to check whether the two com-components of the tuple have the same sign. Before that, the pattern ensures that both components are Ints.

5.4.1 Case classes

So far we have only used patterns with predefined types. Pattern Mat-But ching is also possible with objects of self-defined classes and even with very little additional effort. We only have to pass a *case class* through Define the key word case. Listing 5.22 shows a simple example game.

Listing 5.22: Definition of the Case class Movie

```
case class Movie (title: String, fsk: Int)
```

By defining the Movie class as a case class, it is possible to refer to a mus-ter of the form Movie (t, f) with a string t and an Int f.

Listing 5.23 shows the printAllowedAtAgeOf function that uses Pattern matching is broken down into its components and distinguishes whether the FSK number is 0 or not.

Listing 5.23: The printAllowedAtAgeOf function with pattern matching for movie Objects

```
val printAllowedAtAgeOf: Movie => Unit = {
case Movie (t, 0) =>
println (t + "(no age restriction)")
case Movie (t, i) => println (t + "(free from" + i + ")")
}
```

The usage then looks like this:

```
scala> val movie = Movie ("At the Limit", 0)
movie: Movie = Movie (At the limit, 0)
scala> printAllowedAtAgeOf (movie)
At the limit (no age limit)
```

scala> printAllowedAtAgeOf (new Movie ("Matrix", 16))
Matrix (free from 16)
The function printAllowedAtAgeOf works as expected. Throw
But let's take another look at the first two lines of the above session,
so we notice two things: firstly we created the movie without new,
and the output on the second line doesn't look like it usually does.
We owe all of this to the case keyword in front of the class definition
from Movie. The compiler not only enables pattern matching, but also
dern also generates canonical implementations of toString, equals
and hashCode. In addition, the class parameters are automatically converted to val-
Fields. If necessary, however, var can be prepended explicitly. That means we
can do a lot with the movie straight away, as the following session shows:
scala> println (movie.title)
At the limit
scala> if (movie == Movie ("At the Limit", 0))
|
println ("the same movie")
the same movie
scala> print (movie)
Movie (At the Limit, 0)
In addition, the compiler automatically creates a companion object with
an apply and an unapply method. The factory method apply
is it possible to use Movie ("At Limit", 0) instead of new Movie ("At Limit", 0)
write. The unapply method is a so-called *extractor method* and will
required for pattern matching in Scala. Unapply becomes a movie object
broken down into its components in the form of a tuple of the class parameters:
scala> Movie.unapply (movie)
res8: Option [(String, Int)] = Some ((At Limit, 0))
Attention: The automatically generated methods all refer to the
Class parameters. It is of course still possible to add further fields and additional
add some constructors to a Case class.
In the above session a new data type appears: Option [(String, Int)]
with the value Some ((At Limit, 0)). This option type is always used in Scala
used when the result is an optional value, ie if also something
can go wrong. 9 In general, option [T] has two possible values Some (x),
where x is a value of type T and represents the successful case, and the
Value None, which corresponds to the error.
The option type is used, for example, in the Scala Collections library.
det, as the following session should exemplify:
scala> val cities =
|
Map ("A" -> "Augsburg", "B" -> "Berlin")
cities: scala.collection.immutable.Map [java.lang.String,
java.lang.String] = Map ((A, Augsburg), (B, Berlin))
scala> cities get "A"
res0: Option [java.lang.String] = Some (Augsburg)
scala> cities get "C"
res1: Option [java.lang.String] = None
After we have created a map, we have access to the pair with the
Key "A" returns the value "Augsburg" embedded in some. Who tried
Access to the pair with the key "C", which does not exist, leads to the
Result None.
As of Scala 2.8.0, a copy method is also generated for case classes with which
a copy of an object can be created, e.g.

```
scala> val movie2 = movie.copy ()
movie2: Movie = Movie (At Limit, 0)
```

Thanks to the *named* and *default arguments* introduced with Scala 2.8 (see page 36) individual fields, again limited to the class parameters, elegantly assigned another value, e.g.

```
scala> val movie3 = movie.copy (title = "Maya the Bee")
movie3: Movie = Movie (Maya the Bee, 0)
```

To avoid runtime errors, it is important to use all possible patterns during pattern matching.
special cases to be observed. If a case is not dealt with, data types are turned off the Scala standard library issues a corresponding warning:

```
scala> val errorOnEmptyList: (List [Any]) => Any = {
|
case x :: _ => x
| }
<console>: 6: warning: match is not exhaustive!
missing combination
Nile
errorOnEmptyList: (List [Any]) => Any = <function1>
```

Of course, this helpful warning does not appear as soon as a default case occurs is defined by the underscore:

```
scala> val throwExceptionOnEmptyList
| : (List [Any]) => Any = {
|
case x :: _ => x
|
case _ => throw new exception
| }
throwExceptionOnEmptyList: (List [Any]) => Any =
<function1>
```

In the following section we will show you how we can issue such a warning for can get self-defined classes.

5.4.2 Sealed Classes

First we define an abstract class Lecture for courses.
When it comes to courses, we differentiate between lectures and exercises and tutorials given by students. To use pattern matching, define
Let's rename the three subclasses Course, Exercise and Tutorial as case classes. The implementation of the four classes is shown in Listing 5.24.

Listing 5.24: The Lecture, Course, Exercise and Tutorial classes

```
abstract class lecture
case class Course (title: String) extends Lecture
case class Exercise (belongsTo: Course) extends Lecture
case class tutorial (belongsTo: Course) extends Lecture
```

Then we can use the courseTitle function (as shown in Listing 5.25 shows) with pattern matching.

Listing 5.25: The courseTitle function

```
def courseTitle (lecture: Lecture) = {
lecture match {
case Course (title) => title
case Exercise (Course (title)) => title
case Tutorial (Course (title)) => title
}
}
```

If we only define patterns for course and exercise, the function can still be translated without an error message:

```
scala> def courseTitle (lecture: Lecture) = {
|
lecture match {
|
case Course (title) => title
|
case Exercise (Course (title)) => title
|
}
| }
courseTitle: (lecture: Lecture) String
```

Applying the function to a tutorial then leads to a MatchError, as the following session shows:

```
scala> courseTitle (Tutorial (Course (
|
"Advanced functional programming")))
scala.MatchError: Tutorial (Course (advanced
functional programming))
at .courseTitle (<console>: 11)
...
```

Without additional information, the Scala compiler cannot warn that a case was probably forgotten during matching in the courseTitle function de, since it is basically possible in an object-oriented language to lower class of lecture.

The creation of further subclasses of Lecture can, however, be prevented the. This enables the compiler to issue the required warning. To do this must we *seal* the class Lecture with the keyword sealed . For a *Sealed Class means* that all classes derived from it are in the same source code file as the sealed class must stand. So we define the four classes as in 5.26 shown in a file.

Listing 5.26: The sealed class Lecture and the case classes derived from it Course, Exercise and Tutorial

```
// in a common source code file
sealed abstract class lecture
case class Course (title: String) extends Lecture
case class Exercise (belongsTo: Course) extends Lecture
case class tutorial (belongsTo: Course) extends Lecture
```

The subsequent definition of courseTitle for course and exercise only then delivers the desired warning:

```
scala> def courseTitle (lecture: Lecture) = {
|
lecture match {
|
case Course (title) => title
|
case Exercise (Course (title)) => title
|
}
| }
<console>: 11: warning: match is not exhaustive!
missing combination
Tutorial
lecture match {
```

```
^
courseTitle: (lecture: Lecture) String
```
However, the compiler's capabilities are only limited to sealed classes restricts the directly derived case classes. Let's define courseTitle, as seen in the following session, we can get no warning but still cause a MatchError:
```
scala> def courseTitle (lecture: Lecture) = {
|
lecture match {
|
case Course (title) => title
|
case Exercise (Course (title)) => title
|
case Tutorial (Course ("Prog 2")) => "Prog 2"
|
}
| }
courseTitle: (lecture: Lecture) String
scala> courseTitle (Tutorial (Course ("Prog 1")))
scala.MatchError: Tutorial (Course (Prog 1))
at .courseTitle (<console>: 13)
...
```
We use a sealed class, but we consciously want individual cases leave out, for example because we know that they cannot occur, we can inform the compiler of this with the @unchecked annotation. We get in that case no more warning. For example, we would do the following Function without the @ unchecked annotation receive a warning that the Nile case is missing. With the annotation we can override the function without warning. put:
```
def nonEmptyListMatch (l: List [Any]) =
(l: @unchecked) match {
case 1 :: _ => println ("List begins with the 1")
case _ :: _ => println ("List does not start with 1")
}
```

5.4.3 Partial functions

If, as shown in the previous section, we cover all case classes, but not all cases within the classes, so we can use courseTitle as *par-Define functional function* 10 , as shown in Listing 5.27.

Listing 5.27: The partial function courseTitle
```
def courseTitle: PartialFunction [Lecture, String] = {
case Course (title) => title
case Exercise (Course (title)) => title
case Tutorial (Course ("Prog 2")) => "Prog 2"
}
```
The PartialFunction has two type parameters: the argument type and the Batch type. In the above listing, a partial function from Lecture to String defined. Let's use the partial function like the one previously defined Function courseTitle, so we can still get a MatchError produce:
```
scala> courseTitle (Tutorial (Course ("Prog 1")))
scala.MatchError: Tutorial (Course (Prog 1))
at .courseTitle (<console>: 13)
```

...
However, it is possible to use the isDefinedAt method dynamically (i.e. for running time) to check whether the partial function is defi-
is defined, *before* we walk unknowingly into the match Error:
scala> courseTitle.isDefinedAt (
|
Tutorial (Course ("Prog 1")))
res5: Boolean = false
The PartialFunction trait defines a few other useful methods:
andThen composes the partial function with a function that
result transformed, e.g.
scala> (courseTitle andThen (_.map (_. toUpper))) (
|
Course ("Programming 2"))
res6: String = PROGRAMMING 2
orElse composes the partial function with a function that calculates
if the partial function is not defined for the argument, e.g.
scala> val unknown: PartialFunction [Lecture, String] = {
|
case _ => "unknown title"
| }
unknown: PartialFunction [Lecture, String] = <function1>
scala> (courseTitle orElse unknown) (
|
Course ("Programming 2"))
res7: String = programming 2
scala> (courseTitle orElse unknown) (
|
Tutorial (Course ("Programming 2")))
res8: String = unknown title
lift turns the partial function into a total function that is defined for
Values x the result Some (x) and for undefined values the result
Returns None, e.g.
scala> (courseTitle lift) (Course ("Prog 1"))
res9: Option [String] = Some (Prog 1)
scala> (courseTitle lift) (Tutorial (Course ("Prog 1")))
res10: Option [String] = None

5.4.4 Variable names for (partial) patterns

In some cases, an object with a pattern is broken down, but the whole
Object on the right side of the double arrow used again. To not something like that as
case Tutorial (Course ("Prog 2")) =>
"This semester: tutorial for the lecture" +
Course ("Prog2")
having to write where the course ("Prog 2") is on the left
is repeated on the right side, you can use the Pattern Tutorial (course @ Course ("Prog 2")) the name course is assigned for the partial pattern,
so that instead of the above line
case Tutorial (course @ Course ("Prog 2")) =>
"This semester: tutorial for the lecture" + course
can be written.

5.4.5 Exception handling

Although *exception handling* (*exception handling*) is not the functional product programming, it fits nicely in the section on pattern matching.
Do we have to expect that an exception will be thrown in a code block e.g. because we are trying to open a file, we enclose the Block with try and react in the subsequent catch block to the possible certain exceptions. Unlike other programming languages like Java, the provide several catch blocks for different exceptions, in Scala they are a single catch block using pattern matching between the exceptions and differed.
Listing 5.28 shows an example in which a number is entered from the command line. should be read. If the user enters a string that is not in a Converts Int, an exception is thrown. This is then in the Catch block caught.

Listing 5.28: Exception handling in the readIntOption function

```
def readIntOption () = {
try {
Some (readInt)
} catch {
case _: NumberFormatException => None
}
}
```

In the try block we can assume that everything will go well and the value the readInt reads into a Some object. If something goes wrong, will leave the block and enter the catch block. In this the exception examined with pattern. If the pattern applies, the corresponding Code executed. If no pattern fits, the exception is not handled and thrown further. In Listing 5.28 there is only one pattern that can be ne NumberFormatException fits. All other exceptions remain from the ReadIntOption function untreated.
For the handling of different exceptions, no additional catch-Blocks needed. Using pattern matching, several exceptions can be be treated in a block. Listing 5.29 shows an alternative implementation tion of the readIntOption function, in which all exceptions except the NumberFormatException a previously self-defined ReadIntException is thrown.

Listing 5.29: Different handling of exceptions in readIntOption

```
case object ReadIntException extends
Exception ("unexpected error in readIntOption")
def readIntOption () = {
try {
Some (readInt)
} catch {
case _: NumberFormatException => None
case _ => throw ReadIntException
}
}
```

After the ReadIntException object has been defined as a Case object, be matched by the caller. There is also a finally Block that is always executed, regardless of whether the try block is processed could be switched or an exception was thrown. With the exception it is regardless of whether it was caught in a catch block or not. The Finally block follows the catch block with the finally keyword or, if not available, to the try block. A try without a catch with a finally makes sense if no exception is to be handled, but one or more instructions such as closing a filehandle unrelated should be executed before the function is terminated.

Listing 5.30: The readIntOption function with try, catch and finally

```
def readIntOption () = {
try {
Some (readInt)
} catch {
case _: NumberFormatException => None
case _ => throw ReadIntException
} finally {
println ("readIntOption finished")
}
}
```

Listing 5.30 shows an example in which at the end of the function always on the console readIntOption is output *before* Some, None or the exception is passed.

Scala knows no difference between so-called *checked* and *unchecked exceptions* . Java makes this distinction and requires the Checked Exceptions in the signature of a method. Again, this is in Scala not possible at first. But if a Scala method is used in Java, which can throw a checked exception, and does the Java method have a catch Blocking this, the Java compiler will display an error stating that the Exception is not thrown at all - otherwise it would be in the signature. The way out in Scala is the @throws annotation, which is the class of the exception has as an argument, e.g.

```
class Reader (fname: String) {
private val in = new BufferedReader (new FileReader (
fname))
@throws (classOf [IOException])
def read () = in.read ()
}
```

If there is a chance that your Scala code will be used out of Java you should get into the habit of using the @throws annotation. Within from Scala it is unnecessary.

5.4.6 Extractors

In Section 5.4.1 we explained case classes and their numerous advantages. But case classes also have a disadvantage: They make their specific data representation explicit. If it's all about the elegance of pattern matching, we don't have to use a case class. We can instead use an object with a Implement a unapply method. An object with an unapply method we call it an *extractor* .

Listing 5.31 shows the HeaderField extractor object, which is a key-value Pair extracted from an email header field, e.g. from the string From: scala@obraun.net the tuple (From, scala @ obraun.net).

Listing 5.31: The HeaderField Extractor

```
object HeaderField {
def unapply (s: String) = {
val (key, value) = s.span (_! = ':')
if (key.isEmpty || value.isEmpty)
else
Some ((key, value.tail trim))
}
```

}
The unapply method tries to retrieve the string on the first occurrence of the Sign: to be divided into two parts. If one of the two parts is empty, it was Colon was the first or last character on the line or did not come at all in front. Otherwise, the second part will contain the first character, the colon, and then removed all spaces at the beginning and at the end.

Listing 5.32 shows the Email class. An email object consists of a map with pairs of the name of a header field and the associated rigen value and from a string that represents the text of the email. The toString method has been redefined for demonstration purposes (see Scala Shell Session below).

Listing 5.32. The Email Class

```
class Email (val header: Map [String, String],
val body: String) {
override def toString: String = header + "\ n" + body
}
```

The stringToEmail function (see Listing 5.33) uses the extractor header Field to use pattern matching to break down a header line into its components. lay. To do this, the parameter s is first converted into a list of Lines broken down. Then the list is broken down into two parts. The empty line The chain serves as a separator, because between the header and body of an email is a blank line.

With the header and body list we create a new email object, where we the two lists still have to be converted into a map or a string. The We edit the list of header fields with a fold from right to left an empty map as a starting value. The function of folding takes one line and the previously calculated map. Can the line with the HeaderField extractor in a Key-value pair are decomposed, the pair and the map with the map Method + creates a new 11 map. The list that represents the email body still contains the leading blank line. This is removed 12 , and from the list of Lines a single string with line breaks is generated again.

Listing 5.33. The stringToEmail function

```
implicit def stringToEmail (s: String) = {
val (headLines, body) = s.lines.toList span (_! = "")
new Email (
(headLines: \ Map [String, String] ()) (
(field, map) =>
field match {
case HeaderField (k, v) => (map + (k -> v))
case _ => map
}
),
body.tail mkString "\ n"
)
}
```

After the function stringToEmail with the keyword implicit mar-we don't even have to use the function explicitly, we have to can assign a string to a variable of the type Email. After this leads to a type error, the compiler may check all implicit functions. whether exactly one of them is able to transform the string into an email mate. The following session shows this in the example:

```
scala> val email: Email = "" "From: scala@obraun.net
|
| Subject: Hello readers
```

```
|
|
|
| Have fun with Scala.
|
|
|
| Greetings
|
| Oliver Braun "" ". StripMargin
email: Email =
Map (Subject -> Hello readers, From -> scala@obraun.net)
Have fun with Scala.
Greeting
Oliver Braun
```

5.4.7 Pattern matching with regular expressions

Like many modern programming languages, Scala also supports regular training press. Strings can be broken down with regular expressions. A re gular expression matches a character string or it does not match. To that extent he is very similar to the previous patterns. Therefore, regular expressions in Scala exactly how patterns are used.

To create a regular expression, the class scala.util. matching.Regex can be used. This is not above the Predef object available, but must be imported explicitly. In the following sit- tion becomes a regular expression for a date in the form day.month.year generated, whereby the day and the month can be one or two digits and the Year must be two or four digits:

```
scala> import scala.util.matching.Regex
import scala.util.matching.Regex
scala> val dateRegex = new Regex (
|
"" "(\ d {1,2}) \. (\ d {1,2}). (\ d {2} | \ d {4})" "")
dateRegex: scala.util.matching.Regex = (\ d {1,2}) \. (\ d
{1,2}). (\ D {2} | \ d {4})
```

The syntax for the regular expression corresponds to the Java syntax and the re- derum the Perl syntax for regular expressions. A regular expression can can also be generated directly from a string using the r method. This means, instead of the above session you can also write:

```
scala> val dateRegex =
|
"" "(\ d {1,2}) \. (\ d {1,2}). (\ d {2} | \ d {4})" "". r
dateRegex: scala.util.matching.Regex = (\ d {1,2}) \. (\ d
{1,2}). (\ D {2} | \ d {4})
```

The string for the regular expression must have three double characters, otherwise \ d, for example, as a control character is interpreted. Of course it is also possible to mask everything accordingly and just take a few quotes. This will make the string but a bit more confusing:

```
scala> val dateRegex =
|
"(\\ d {1,2}) \\. (\\ d {1,2}). (\\ d {2} | \\ d {4})". r
dateRegex: scala.util.matching.Regex = (\ d {1,2}) \. (\ d
{1,2}). (\ D {2} | \ d {4})
```

The dateRegex groups the numbers for the day, month and year with the round brackets. So there are three groups in the regular expression, that can be used for the pattern. Listing 5.34 shows an example of a Function specified that checks whether a character string corresponds to a date. If this is the case, a tuple is returned which consists of day, month and year stands. In order to be able to react appropriately in the event of an error, the function uses the type option for the result.

Listing 5.34: The extractDate function for decomposing a character string with a pattern Matching and a regular expression

```
def extractDate (str: String): Option [(Int, Int, Int)] = {
val dateRegex =
"" "(\ d {1,2}) \. (\ d {1,2}). (\ d {2} | \ d {4})" "". r
str match {
case dateRegex (d, m, y) =>
Some ((d.toInt, m.toInt, y.toInt))
case _ => None
}
}
```

5.5 Currying and own control structures

We have already discussed the implicit parameters on page 98 addressed the *currying* . Currying is the transformation of a function on with several parameters in a chain of functions with one parameter each ter. The currying is named after the logician and mathematician Haskell Brooks Curry, after whose first name the purely functional programming language Haskell was named.

We first want to use the classic example to explain the curry Use sizing: the add function to add two whole numbers. The The uncured version of add might look like Listing 5.35.

Listing 5.35. The uncurled function add

```
def add (x: Int, y: Int) = x + y
```

A possible use of the add function would be, for example:

```
scale> add (1,2)
res0: Int = 3
```

If we now curry add, it becomes a function with only one parameter, as shown in Listing 5.36.

Listing 5.36. The curryed function add

```
def add (x: Int) = (y: Int) => x + y
```

If we now apply the curry version to a number, we get a radio tion that we can then apply to a second number:

```
scala> val add1 = add (1)
add1: (Int) => Int = <function1>
scala> add1 (2)
res1: Int = 3
```

The curryed function add does not have to end with a function literal on the right th page can be defined. Scala allows the specification of several parameter lists. This means that the function is then usually implemented as in Listing 5.37. animals.

Listing 5.37: The curryed function add with two parameter lists

```
def add (x: Int) (y: Int) = x + y
```

The application of the function shown in Listing 5.37 is then exactly like the the function from Listing 5.36. It is also possible with both, immediately specify both parameter lists, e.g.
scala> add (1) (2)
res2: Int = 3
Curryed functions can also be generated from non-curryed ones. There-there is the method curried in all function n traits for $n \geq 2$. Consider Let's repeat the uncurled function add from Listing 5.35. Then can we define the curryed function by:
def addCurried = (add _). curried
The addCurried function defined in this way can now be displayed on two parameter lists.
be turned:
scala> addCurried (2) (3)
res3: Int = 5
Such curryed functions are interesting, for example, when using tion in higher order functions, as shown in the following session:
scala> val add1 = addCurried (1)
add1: (Int) => Int = <function1>
scala> (1 to 10) .toList map add1
res4: List [Int] = List (2, 3, 4, 5, 6, 7, 8, 9, 10, 11)
This means that no placeholders have to be specified for the parameters here, but only the identifier of the function itself. This also works for the complete parameter list of not curryed functions. The following expression calculates the sum of all elements of a list with the non-curryed func-tion add from Listing 5.35:
scala> ((1 to 10) .toList: \ 0) (add)
res5: Int = 55
The add function has the type (Int, Int) => Int. That suggests that currying is not about individual parameters, but whole pa-parameter lists goes. But if we look at a parameter list as a single parameter, so it is simply a tuple. Thus, the implementation in Scala fits back to theory. So currying is not just for individual parameters, but also possible for parameter lists. Listing 5.38 shows the definition of the Function addTuple, which adds two tuples component by component.

Listing 5.38: The addTuple function with two two-element parameter lists
def addTuple (a: Int, b: Int) (c: Int, d: Int) = (a + c, b + d)
The function addTuple can then be adapted to two "tuples" as follows.
turn:
scala> addTuple (1,2) (3,5)
res6: (Int, Int) = (4.7)
The word tuple is in quotation marks in the preceding sentence because it is it is not a tuple, but two parameter lists. An application the function addTuple on two real tuples is not possible:
scale> val t1 = (1,2)
t1: (Int, Int) = (1,2)
scale> val t2 = (3.5)
t2: (Int, Int) = (3.5)
scala> addTuple (t1) (t2)
<console>: 9: error: not enough arguments for method
addTuple: (a: Int, b: Int) (c: Int, d: Int) (Int, Int).
Unspecified value parameter b.
addTuple (t1) (t2)

^

We could either "unpack" the tuples when using the function:
scala> addTuple (t1._1, t1._2) (t2._1, t2._2)
res7: (Int, Int) = (4.7)
which doesn't make the code any clearer either. Or else we define addTuple with two parameter lists, each containing a tuple, as shown in Listing 5.39.

Listing 5.39: The addTuple function with two parameter lists with one tuple each

```
def addTuple (t1: (Int, Int)) (t2: (Int, Int)) =
(t1._1 + t2._1, t1._2 + t2._2)
```

The components of the two tuples are used with the methods _1 and _2. seized. It is also possible to use pattern matching to convert the tuples into their To disassemble the components (see Listing 5.40).

Listing 5.40: The addTuple function with two parameter lists, each with a tuple and Decomposition through pattern matching

```
def addTuple: ((Int, Int)) => ((Int, Int)) => (Int, Int) = {
case (a, b) => {
case (c, d) => (a + c, b + d)
}
}
```

The addTuple function defined for tuples can then really be applied to tuples. as the following session is intended to illustrate:

```
scale> val t1 = (1,2)
t1: (Int, Int) = (1,2)
scale> val t2 = (3.5)
t2: (Int, Int) = (3.5)
scala> addTuple (t1) (t2)
res8: (Int, Int) = (4.7)
scala> addTuple ((5,3)) ((8,3))
res9: (Int, Int) = (13.6)
scala> addTuple (5.3) (8.3)
res10: (Int, Int) = (13.6)
```

As can be seen above, when applying the function to two tuples the double pairs of brackets, one pair for the tuple formation and one pair for the Parameter list, not to be written. A pair of brackets is enough. At the definition of the function in Listing 5.40, the double brackets in the type must be specified, otherwise it would be a parameter list consisting of two ints and not from a tuple.

What we have shown so far with regard to currying can be explained with the solve a stroke almost as elegantly, e.g.

```
scala> def add (x: Int, y: Int) = x + y
add: (x: Int, y: Int) Int
scala> def add1 = add (1, _: Int)
add1: (Int) => Int
scala> (1 to 10) .toList map add1
res11: List [Int] = List (2, 3, 4, 5, 6, 7, 8, 9, 10, 11)
```

If a function is expected in the context, the underscore can even be omitted. as can be seen in the last input line of the above session.

Currying has one more decisive factor for the scalable language Scala. dend property: it can be used to define control structures, that look like built-in control structures.

One more detail you need to know about this is the ability to list parameters with exactly one parameter enclosed in curly instead of round brackets to be able to eat. So we can write:

```
scala> addTuple {(5,3)} {(8,3)}
```

```
res12: (Int, Int) = (13.6)
```

but not

```
scale> add {1, 2}
<console>: 1: error: ';' expected but ',' found.
add {1, 2}
^
```

Let us now consider the printTupleAddedTo function defined in Listing 5.41 to output the component-wise sum of two tuples.

Listing 5.41: Definition of the printTupleAddedTo control structure

```
def printTupleAddedTo (t1: (Int, Int)) (t2: (Int, Int)) =
println (t1 + "+" + t2 + "=" +
(t1._1 + t2._1, t1._2 + t2._2))
```

We can then use this function as, for example, as shown in Listing 5.42 Use control structure. It is important that in the second parameter list on The end actually returning a tuple. Hence the final instruction in this case (x, y).

Listing 5.42: Script to read in two numbers and output after adding them with a Tuple with the self-defined printTupleAddedTo control structure

```
printTupleAddedTo (1,2) {
print ("Enter the first component:")
val x = readInt
print ("Enter the second component:")
val y = readInt
(x, y)
}
```

By replacing the round brackets with curly braces, we can't just pass a value as a second argument, but a block of code that consists of several statements. We use instead of the curly round one Parentheses, this leads to the following error:

```
scala> printTupleAddedTo (1,2) (
| print ("Enter the first component:")
| val x = readInt
<console>: 3: error: ')' expected but 'val' found.
val x = readInt
^
```

With the support of higher-order functions it is also possible Define control structures that have functions as parameters. In listing 5.43 defines a function that has a predicate [13] and a number as parameters. If the number fulfills the predicate, correct is output, otherwise incorrect.

Listing 5.43: The guessNumber function

```
def guessNumber (predicate: Int => Boolean) (number: Int) =
if (predicate (number)) println ("correct") else
println ("wrong")
```

The use of the guessNumber function as a control structure could then look as shown in 5.44. The predicate is rounded off as a function literal Pass parentheses, the number is then in a code block from the command line read.

Listing 5.44: Reading in a number and comparing it with a predicate

```
guessNumber (_ == 5) {
print ("What number are we looking for?")
readInt
}
```

As a further example, we want to use the Email class from Section 5.1.6 again use. In Listing 5.32 on page 129, we defined the class. With the radio tion stringToEmail (see Listing 5.33 on page 130) and the HeaderField-

Extractor (see Listing 5.31 on page 128) we have put a string in an email Object transformed.
We now want to define our own control structure email with which we create an email object. The code following the identifier email Block should only set the header fields. We also want a second one Code block with the body can be passed. The identifier stand withBody. This means that an email with an empty body should be created by

```
email {
// Define header fields
}
```

An email with header and body

```
email {
// Define header fields
} withBody {
// Define body
}
```

The control structure email is defined in Listing 5.45 by the companion Object of the class Email with the method email.

Listing 5.45. The email object with the email method

```
object email {
def email (header: Map [String, String]) =
new email (header, "")
}
```

The extension of the email control structure to email-withBody-control structure is defined in Listing 5.46. The method gets a body and returns a new email object.

Listing 5.46. The Email class with the withBody method

```
class Email (val header: Map [String, String],
val body: String) {
override def toString: String = header + "\ n" + body
def withBody (body: String) = new Email (header, body)
}
```

To be able to write email instead of Email.email, the method simply has to be can only be imported. Listing 5.47 shows the definition of the function as an example stringToEmail with the self-defined control structure.

Listing 5.47: Implementation of the stringToEmail function with the self-defined email-withBody control structure

```
implicit def stringToEmail (s: String) = {
import Email.email
val (headLines, body) = s.lines.toList span (_! = "")
email {
(headLines: \ Map [String, String] ()) (
(field, map) =>
field match {
case HeaderField (k, v) => (map + (k -> v))
case _ => map
}
)
} withBody {
body.tail mkString "\ n"
}
}
```

Instead of using it as a control structure, email. email (...). withBody (...), since it is an ordinary

methods.
The functional approach with the methods email and withBody has the following part that two objects are created: the first by the companion object for the method email and the second of this object itself in the method withBody. This is a typical example in which it is necessary to weigh up whether performance
For reasons of mance, the data structure should or should not be changeable.
A possible deviation from the functional approach is shown in Listing 5.48. represents.

Listing 5.48: Definition of the Email class with a variable field

```
class Email (val header: Map [String, String],
private [this] var b: String) {
def body = b
override def toString: String = header + "\ n" + b
def withBody (body: String) = {
b = body
this
}
}
```

Besides the need to be more careful with the changeable email object body can no longer be used as a named parameter.
be used. If the class parameter were named body, no method can with the same name to access the body.
Since control abstractions are often used to implement functions in-within the control structure, we still need a mechanism
Must to execute functions in the control structure. Let's look at in the following a function that encapsulates the evaluation of an expression in such a way that
that it returns None on any exception. Is the evaluation
If no exception is thrown, the calculated value f is assigned as Some (f). returned. For example, optionCatch (8/2) should have the value Some (4) and optionCatch (8/0) due to the ArithmeticException the value None calculate.
A first approach is presented in the following session:

```
scala> def optionCatch (f: Any) = {
|
try {
|
Some (f)
|
} catch {
|
case _ => None
|
}
| }
optionCatch: (f: Any) Option [Any]
scala> optionCatch (8/2)
res0: Option [Any] = Some (4)
scala> optionCatch (8/0)
java.lang.ArithmeticException: / by zero
at. <init> (<console>: 7)
...
```

As can be seen, the exception is not generated in the optionCatch function, but rather

thrown outside. This is also evident, because in Scala all
le function arguments are always evaluated *before* the function is called.
This behavior is called *call-by-value* .
A simple trick would be to pass a function instead of the expression f.
This is expressed by specifying the type () => Any. The
The function is then passed and only in the optionCatch function
Application evaluated on the empty parameter list. The following session shows
this approach:

```
scala> def optionCatch (f: () => Any) = {
|
try {
|
Some (f ())
|
} catch {
|
case _ => None
|
}
| }
optionCatch: (f: () => Any) Option [Any]
scala> optionCatch (() => 8/2)
res1: Option [Any] = Some (4)
scala> optionCatch (() => 8/0)
res2: Option [Any] = None
```

If desired, the optionCatch function calculates the value Some (4) for 8/2
and for 8/0 the value None. The exception is caught in optionCatch and
does not penetrate outside. What is extremely ugly, however, is the need to
ment as a function literal.
However, this can also be remedied with the *by-name* parameters. It will
Compared to the definition above, the empty parameter list is simply left out.
A parameter defined in this way is transferred via *call-by-name* . That means un-
evaluated! The following session shows the finished optionCatch function with
a by-name parameter and the application of the function to the expressions
8/2 and 8/0:

```
scala> def optionCatch (f: => Any) = {
|
try {
|
Some (f)
|
} catch {
|
case _ => None
|
}
| }

optionCatch: (f: => Any) Option [Any]
scala> optionCatch (8/2)
res3: Option [Any] = Some (4)
scala> optionCatch (8/0)
res4: Option [Any] = None
```

With this version of optionCatch, the following code, for example to be written:

```
optionCatch {
print ("Numerator?")
val n = readInt
print ("Denominator?")
val d = readInt
n / d
} match {
case Some (x) => println ("Result is" + x)
case None => println ("An error occurred")
}
```

Regardless of whether the input threw an exception or one as a denominator If zero was entered, An error occurred is displayed.

5.6 For expressions

Even if the keyword for is usually imperative for loops are introduced, these are based on a more powerful construct in Scala, the has its roots in functional programming: *comprehension* . Comprehension means to traverse something that includes (*to comprehend*) what we find and calculate something new from it. The expressions with the keyword for are therefore used in Scala as *for-comprehensions* or *for-Expressions* called. For example, a simple for expression is the following de:

```
for (x <- 1 to 10) println (x)
```

This expression prints the numbers 1 to 10 each on a separate line. The sub-expression in brackets is called *generator* because it contains the individual elements generated that are used during the run. A generator always has the shape < variablename > <- < collection > . The locally introduced variant ble corresponds to a val and is therefore unchangeable. The partial expression 1 to 10 creates the collection range (1,2,3,4,5,6,7,8,9,10), which run through becomes.

Even if it is no different than a for loop in any imperative ven programming language looks like 14 , it is more of a mathematical one Expression $\forall x \in \{ 1 , 2 , 3 , 4 , 5 , 6 , 7 , 8 , 9 , 10 \}$ • println (x).

Scala's for-comprehensions also allow the direct specification of so-called ter *filter* too. For example, in the following expression, only the odd Numbers between 1 and 10 output:

```
for (x <- 1 to 10; if (x% 2 == 1)) println (x)
```

Generator and filter can each be specified on a separate line the. The semicolon can be omitted:

```
for (
x <- 1 to 10
if (x% 2 == 1)
) println (x)
```

If several conditions are necessary, these can of course be set in the filter with booclear operators. But it is also possible and mostly more clearly to indicate several separate filters. In the following example only the odd numbers between 1 and 100 divisible by 5 give:

```
for (
x <- 1 to 100
if (x% 2 == 1)
```

```
if (x% 5 == 0)
) println (x)
```

The use of Scala in a version before 2.8 makes it necessary to switch between the Filter to write a semicolon even if we put the filter on two lines to distribute. You can do this by using curly braces bypass.

You can also specify multiple generators. These must be in round brackets mern are also separated by semicolons in 2.8. Therefore we use the following example curly brackets:

```
for {
x <- 1 to 10
t <- 2 to x-1
if (x% t == 0)
} println (t + "divides" + x)
```

The above expression acts like two nested for loops. The two te generator corresponds to the head of the inner loop. The identifier x thus assumes the values 1 to 10 one after the other. For any value of x, t takes the values 2 to x-1. If x-1 is less than 2, the calculated range is empty. Is t divisor of x, which is given by the filter, then t divides x given. Overall, when evaluating the above-mentioned form Comprehension the following on the console:

```
2 divides 4
2 divides 6
3 divides 6
2 divides 8
4 divides 8
3 divides 9
2 divides 10
5 divides 10
```

In addition to specifying generators and filters, the first part of the for-Expression variables can be defined that are valid within the second part. In the following example the string t divided x is assigned to the variable str that can then be used for println. A variable introduced in this way corresponds again to a val.

```
for {
x <- 1 to 10
t <- 2 to x-1
if (x% t == 0)
str = t + "divides" + x
} println (str)
```

If you use round brackets, there must also be a gap between the filter and the finition of str a semicolon. Of course, as a second part of the for expression is a block of code and not just a single line such as the following expression:

```
for {
x <- 1 to 10
t <- 2 to x-1
if (x% t == 0)
} {
print (t)
print ("shares")
println (x)
}
```

A for-comprehension becomes particularly interesting through the keyword yield 15 , with which the results of each step are stored in a new collection. can be collected. The keyword yield is used between the first th and second part of the for expression. With the following for-Comprehension is a vector of pairs, consisting of the respective part ler t and the number x produces:

```
val pairs = for {
x <- 1 to 10
t <- 2 to x-1
if (x% t == 0)
} yield (t, x)
```

A println (pairs) executed afterwards gives

```
Vector ((2.4), (2.6), (3.6), (2.8), (4.8), (3.9), (2.10),
(5.10))
```

out. We could also get the same result with the higher-order functions map, For example, program filter and flatMap 16 like this:

```
(1 to 10) flatMap (x => (2 to x-1) map (t => (t, x)))
filter {case (t, x) => x% t == 0}
```

In fact, the compiler will convert a for-comprehension into a Expression transformed before it is translated into bytecode. Already on that still quite simple example, it becomes clear that the notation with for min-at least for the inexperienced functional programmer much easier to learn sen and is to be understood.

A for-comprehension is possible for all collections, for example also for a map, as we illustrate with the following, somewhat more extensive example want. First we define case classes for lectures and in Listing 5.49 for a study.

Listing 5.49: The case classes Course and Study

```
case class Course (name: String,
passed: Boolean,
creditPoints: Int)
case class study (semester: Map [Int, List [Course]])
```

A lecture has a name and a number of credit points. also our lecture class contains a flag indicating whether the lecture was passed or Not. Holger's two-semester studies with his previous achievements is given as an example in Listing 5.50.

Listing 5.50: Holger's previous studies

```
val holgersStudy = Study (
Map (1 -> List (Course ("Prog 1",
true, 5),
Course ("OS 1",
false, 3),
Course ("Networks 1", true, 3)),
2 -> List (Course ("Prog 2",
true, 5),
Course ("OS 2",
false, 3),
Course ("Networks 2", false, 3))))
```

For example, we can now use the for-Comprehension calculate the list of lectures that Holger has successfully completed Has. To do this, we use pattern matching in the first generator to convert the pairs Extract the second component from the map. The second generator is running about the lectures, and with the filter we check whether the "passed" - Flag is not. Finally, we add the name of the lecture to the ending collection.

Listing 5.51: Calculation of the names of the lectures successfully completed by Holger

```
val coursesPassed = for {
(_, courses) <- (holgersStudy semester)
c <- courses
if c.passed
} yield c.name
```

The value of coursesPassed is List (Prog 1, Networks 1, Prog 2).
In the next step, instead of the simple list of lectures, we want a pel, consisting of the total number of credit points achieved so far and the List of lectures, calculate. The obvious approach is to start with the list te of the pairs consisting of the score and name with a for-expression, too calculate and with a foldRight to sum the points and add the list as shown in Listing 5.52.

Listing 5.52: Calculation of pairs from the credit points and the names of Holger's successfully completed lectures - incorrect

```
val coursesPassedWithPoints = for {
(_, courses) <- (holgersStudy semester)
c <- courses
if c.passed
n = c.name
p = c.creditPoints
} yield (p, n)
val creditPointsAndCoursesPassed =
(coursesPassedWithPoints: \ (0, List [String] ())) {
case ((p, n), (sum, ns)) => (p + sum, n :: ns)}
```

Interestingly, creditPointsAndCoursesPassed has the value:
(8, List (Prog 2, Networks 1)
The result of the passed Prog 1 lecture has disappeared. She dives The one in the list still contributes to the total of the credit points. But where is the mistake? Even on closer inspection, we seem to have done everything right to have.
If we look at the intermediate result, the end result becomes clear, because the The value of coursesPassedWithPoints is Map ((5, Prog 2), (3, Networks 1)). After Prog 2 and Prog 1 both have 5 credit points, only one dives of the two values with the "key" 5 in the map, namely the last one calculated value.
The only question that remains to be answered is why the result of courses PassedWithPoints is a map and not a list of tuples. This is entirely simply because we use a map in the first generator and the for-Comprehension, if possible, creates the same Art Collection. In Listing 5.51 we only gave a single value after the yield. So could the result will not be a map. In Listing 5.52, however, it is a tuple and can be used as a Key-value pairs are interpreted.
A correct solution to the problem, a pair consisting of the overall number of credit points and the list of passed lectures is in Listing 5.53 shown.

Listing 5.53: Calculating pairs from the credit points and the names of Holger's successfully completed lectures - correct

```
val coursesPassedWithPoints = for {
(_, courses) <- ((holgersStudy semester) toList)
c <- courses
if c.passed
n = c.name
p = c.creditPoints
} yield (p, n)
val creditPointsAndCoursesPassed =
```

(coursesPassedWithPoints: \ (0, List [String] ())) {
case ((p, n), (sum, ns)) => (p + sum, n :: ns)}
The only difference to the code in Listing 5.52 is the conversion of the map into a list of tuples *before* use in the first generator with the method de toList. As expected, creditPointsAndCoursesPassed has the Value:
(13, List (Prog 1, Networks 1, Prog 2))
The value of coursesPassedWithPoints is now actually List ((5, Prog 1), (3, Networks 1), (5, Prog 2)), i.e. a list of tuples and not a map more.

5.7 Type system

Scala is statically typed. In other words, type checks are used for translation time and not just at runtime instead of as with dynamically typed Languages. Nevertheless, the typical disadvantage of static typing applies (i.e. the emergency
flexibility to indicate types everywhere) for Scala. Scala has a typinfe- mechanism with which the type of an expression is in most cases can be determined automatically. The places where a type is indicated we have already discussed in Section 3.1.
Without going into the conflict, which sometimes escalates into a religious war, static vs. Wanting to start dynamic typing remains yet find that a large number of programming errors type errors which are used by the programmer for static typing and dynamic under certain circumstances can only be discovered by a user.

5.7.1 Standard types

Even if the Scala standard library is only introduced in Chapter 6, At this point, let's get some information about the types in Scala hold tight. At the top of the type hierarchy in Scala is the type Any. The two Any subtypes are AnyVal and AnyRef.
The AnyVal type, which stands for the so-called *primitive Scala types* , has flat side by side the subtypes Boolean, Byte, Short, Char, Int, Long, Float, Double and Unit. 17th
The AnyRef type is the basic type of all other types, including self-defined ones, and speaks on the Java platform java.lang.Object, on .NET System.Object. Between AnyRef and the Scala reference types there is still the type ScalaOb- ject, which serves as a marker to distinguish Scala classes from Java classes the.
In addition, so-called *bottom types are* defined in Scala . The type zero with the value zero is a subtype of all AnyRef subtypes. The type is Nothing Subtype of all, including primitive types.
The non-existence of a searched value is indicated in Scala by the data type Option expressed. For example, consider finding a value for a key in a map. Can't have any for the key k Key-value pairs are found, this is indicated by the result None. shows. If a key-value pair (k, v) is found, the value v must now also embedded in the option type. Therefore, in this case Some (v) becomes- returned. Unlike in Java, for example, where a null reference renz is used to display the non-existence, already in the type of a function visible that a result is optional

5.7.2 Parametric polymorphism and variance

Scala supports *parametric data types* . These are data types that start with a Type parameters are defined. These types are in Java, for example, *overall called nerical types* . With a concrete value, the type parameter is then instantiated by a type. For example, lists are of type List [T] for a type T. A concrete list then has a concrete type, e.g.

```
scala> val list = List (1,2,3)
list: List [Int] = List (1, 2, 3)
```

Both the type parameter and the concrete type for the parameter are in square gen brackets. If a generic type has more than one type parameter, separated by commas, eg Map [A, B]. A parameterized type like eg List or Map is also referred to as *type constructor* .

Type constructors with two type parameters can also be written infix den, ie instead of Map [A, B] we could also write A Map B. It becomes interesting this notation in connection with names of types which, like Opera- foolish look, e.g. +. With so-called *type synonyms* we can use existing Give types new names. For example, we could use a synonym for Map like define as follows:

```
type -> [A, B] = Map [A, B]
```

With this type synonym and the infix spelling we can then use the type write a Map [Int, String] as

```
Int -> string
```

At this point, the note is certainly appropriate that code is understandable and good should be legible. The flexibility of Scala allows a lot. Whether this is in your projects is helpful or rather confusing, you have to decide for yourself in each case.

Functions can also be parameterized with type variables. For example creates the following function mkList from any number of elements ten of type A a list of type List [A].

```
def mkList [A] (xs: A *) = xs.toList
```

If we apply mkList to different elements, we can use the Scala- Shell look at the specific type. The following session should clarify this. lichen:

```
scala> mkList ()
res0: List [Nothing] = List ()
scala> mkList (1,2,3)
res1: List [Int] = List (1, 2, 3)
scala> mkList ("One", "Two", "Three")
res2: List [java.lang.String] = List (One, Two, Three)
scala> mkList (1, "Two", 3.0)
res3: List [Any] = List (1, Two, 3.0)
```

In the above session, what is known as *subtyping also becomes* clear. Will the empty List generated without information about the type parameter becomes the bottom type Taken nothing. As in the second case, three ints are used as arguments for the If the mkList function is passed, the result is of the List [Int] type. With strings according to List [String]. Do the arguments differ Type, so the most specific common super type is taken. In the case of a With an int, a string and a double, the common super type is Any. In this case we get a List [Any].

The following case, for example, is also interesting

```
scala> mkList (1, 2.0)
res4: List [Double] = List (1.0, 2.0)
```

In this case, a common supertype is not determined, but a implicit conversion made the int a double. Do we want the Int really keep it as an int in the list, we can explicitly use the type parameter

Instantiate AnyVal:

```
scala> mkList [AnyVal] (1, 2.0)
res4: List [AnyVal] = List (1, 2.0)
```

In Scala, generic types behave rigidly by default, ie *non-variant* . To
To illustrate, let's define a class MyClass with a type parameter:

```
class MyClass [T]
```

Even if a type A is a subtype of a type B, MyClass [A] and
MyClass [B] in no subtype relation to each other. Let's define for example
wise the function

```
def g (x: MyClass [AnyRef]) = x
```

this can only be set to a value of the type MyClass [AnyRef].
apply as the following session is intended to illustrate:

```
scala> val myAnyRef = new MyClass [AnyRef]
myAnyRef: MyClass [AnyRef] = MyClass @ 40442b95
scala> val myString = new MyClass [String]
myString: MyClass [String] = MyClass @ 4611dfe3
scala> g (myAnyRef)
res11: MyClass [AnyRef] = MyClass @ 40442b95
scale> g (myString)
<console>: 9: error: type mismatch;
found
: MyClass [String]
required: MyClass [AnyRef]
g (myString)
```

In order to make the data type flexible, i.e. *covariant* , the formal type parameter is
meter preceded by a +. So let's change the above definition class MyClass [T]
to

```
class MyClass [+ T]
```

so for every subtype A of a type B the following also applies: MyClass [A] is a subtype
of
MyClass [B]. Specifically, it means that we now also apply g to myString.
can:

```
scala> class MyClass [+ T]
defined class MyClass
scala> def g (x: MyClass [AnyRef]) = x
g: (x: MyClass [AnyRef]) MyClass [AnyRef]
scala> val myString = new MyClass [String]
myString: MyClass [String] = MyClass @ 3432a325
scale> g (myString)
res0: MyClass [AnyRef] = MyClass @ 3432a325
```

The opposite case is called *contravariant* and is annotated with -. Defini-
let's rename MyClass as

```
class MyClass [-T]
```

for example we can apply g to an object of type MyClass [Any],
but not on MyClass [String]. The characters used in this way are called + and -
Variance annotations .
Many Scala collections are covariant, e.g. List, Seq or Queue. The map is
for example, for the key non-variant and for the values covariant. she is
defined as Map [A, + B].
An illustrative example of the use of contravariance is the
Function traits. For example, is defined for one-digit functions

```
trait Function1 [-T1, + R]
```

This means that Function1 is contravariant in the first and covariant in the second
Type parameters. Let us define the following classes for illustration:

class person
class Woman extends Person
and the identity function:
def h (p: person) = p
so we can use a value of a subtype as an argument instead of a person
of Person, but not a supertype value. Conversely,
Let's use the result as the value of a supertype, but not the other way around.
In other words, this means: the argument can also be more specific, and the
result can be used as a value of a more general type. The following
This session should illustrate this with specific examples:
scala> h (new woman)
res0: Person = Woman @ 53601a4f
scala> h (new AnyRef)
<console>: 8: error: type mismatch;
found
: java.lang.Object
required: person
h (new AnyRef)
^
scala> h (new Woman): AnyRef
res2: AnyRef = Woman @ 733638d4
scala> h (new Woman): Woman
<console>: 9: error: type mismatch;
found
: Person
required: Woman
h (new Woman): Woman
^
The error message from h (new AnyRef) refers to the argument. The
Error message at h (new Woman): Woman on the result.
Covariance and contravariance are only for classes with immutable fields
permitted. Let us consider the mutable class
class MyMutableClass [T] (var a: T)
The setter for field a is a function from T to Unit. There T nonva
be riant or contravariant. The getter returns a value of type T. There
T should be non-variant or covariant. Overall, therefore, only the possibility remains
left of nonvariance. This always applies when reading and on a field
can be accessed for writing.

5.7.3 Upper and Lower Bounds

The generic types presented in the previous section accept everyone
any type parameter. With the variance annotations it is beyond that
possible to specify whether between two specific parameterized types such as
List [AnyRef] and List [String] have a subtype relationship. To man-
However, in some places it also makes sense to use the permissible type parameters from the start
to restrict.
To clarify, let's consider the classes given in Listing 5.54
Person, Woman and Man.
Listing 5.54: The Person, Woman, and Man classes
abstract class person
class Woman extends Person
class Man extends Person
We want to further define a class for a list of people. A first

Approach would be the following definition:

```
class ListOfPersons (persons: Person *) {
val list = persons.toList
override def toString = list.toString
}
```

With this we can generate the following lists of people:

```
scala> val listOfPersons =
|
new ListOfPersons (new Woman, new Man)
listOfPersons: ListOfPersons = List (Woman @ 2caee320,
Man @ dc160cb)
scala> val listOfWomen =
|
new ListOfPersons (new Woman, new Woman)
listOfWomen: ListOfPersons = List (Woman @ 409bad4f,
Woman @ 2c8f3eac)
scala> val listOfMen = new ListOfPersons (new Man, new Man)
listOfMen: ListOfPersons = List (Man @ 1a0283e, Man @ 39b1ff47
)
```

It would of course be nicer if the type could already tell whether it was a list of women, a list of men, or a mixed list.
To do this, we can modify the ListOfPersons class so that it has a type parameter which can then be instantiated with Woman, Man or Person.
The class would then look like this:

```
class ListOfPersons [T] (persons: T *) {
val list = persons.toList
override def toString = list.toString
}
```

If we repeat our inputs from before with the parameterized class, we see that the typing corresponds to our wishes:

```
scala> val listOfPersons =
|
new ListOfPersons (new Woman, new Man)
listOfPersons: ListOfPersons [Person] = List (
Woman @ 76eb2133, Man @ 46d0d843)
scala> val listOfWomen =
|
new ListOfPersons (new Woman, new Woman)
listOfWomen: ListOfPersons [Woman] = List (Woman @ 4c9549af,
Woman @ 5d18a770)
scala> val listOfMen = new ListOfPersons (new Man, new Man)
listOfMen: ListOfPersons [Man] = List (Man @ 448be1c9,
Man @ 3b947647)
```

Now the problem is: We can also do the following:

```
scala> val listOfInts = new ListOfPersons (1, 2, 3)
listOfInts: ListOfPersons [Int] = List (1, 2, 3)
```

and we don't really want that. The solution to our problem is an *upper bound* . This allows us to restrict the set of permissible type parameters know that these are values of the type Person or derived from it. One Upper Bound is specified directly with the type parameter with the operator <:.
The ListOfPersons class then looks like the one shown in Listing 5.55.

Listing 5.55: The ListOfPersons class with an upper bound

```
class ListOfPersons [T <: Person] (persons: T *) {
val list = persons.toList
```

```
override def toString = list.toString
}
```

The examples with women and men work as before, but the trying to use Ints now fails with an error message:

```
scala> val listOfInts = new ListOfPersons (1, 2, 3)
<console>: 6: error: inferred type arguments [Int] do not
conform to class ListOfPersons's type parameter bounds
[T <: person]
val listOfInts = new ListOfPersons (1, 2, 3)
^
```

Upper bounds are also of interest in connection with properties expressed by traits. A trait can also be used in an up-be specified by bound. For example, let's define a function following signature:

```
def sort [T <: Ordered [T]] (xs: List [T]): List [T]
```

so we can use the sort function on a list of any type that has the Trait Ordered mixed in. This allows the defined in the Trait Ordered Functions to implement sort can be used.
Analogous to the upper bounds, Scala also has lower bounds. These are used, for example, in the Queue class of the standard library. An un-variable queue is covariant, ie the definition begins with class Queue [+ A]. However, the class offers a method enqueue that an element in queue up. Of course, the old queue remains ge unchanged and a new one is returned. Nonetheless, one is Definition of the shape

```
def enqueue (elem: A) = ... // error
```

not possible because the argument is in a contravariant position [18] . Here the lower bound helps. Instead of an argument of type A, enqueue expects an argument of a type B, for which the following applies: B is a supertype of A, i.e. contravariant.
The lower bound is defined with the operator> :. So for the enqueue Method:

```
def enqueue [B>: A] (elem: B) = ...
```

We can also have a lower and an upper bound for one type at the same time specify. For example, the doit method is the one shown in Listing 5.56 Class MyClass is defined for all x: C, for which C is supertype of A and C is Subtype of B.

Listing 5.56: The MyClass class with the doit method, in which a Lower and Upper Bound is defined

```
class MyClass [A, B] {
def doit [C>: A <: B] (x: C) = ...
}
```

5.7.4 Views and View Bounds

In Section 4.4 we looked at implicits. These implicits are common to many Places used for the implicit conversion of one type to another. Such Conversions are also called *views* . That means: a type S view for type T is an implicit value with a function type S => T.
A function that uses such a view must have it as an implicit parameter to hand over. For example, let's write a function that has the maximum calculated from a list, the methods of the ordered-Traits will be available. If we use the following as a signature, the function is Can only be used with the element types that implement the ordered trait:

```
def maxList [T <: Ordered [T]] (elems: List [T]): T = ...
```

If we use a view, the element type does not have to implement the ordered trait.
ment, but an implicit conversion from T to Ordered [T]
be available. The definition with the view as an implicit parameter then sees
like this:
def maxList [T] (elems: List [T])
(implicit converter: T => Ordered [T]): T = ...
The converter does not have to be used explicitly in the body of the maxList function.
be det. It is available as an implicit conversion. Hence the introduced
Name converter is also unnecessary, and instead of the above signature, a shorter
be practiced:
def maxList [T <% Ordered [T]] (elems: List [T]): T = ...
The expression T <% Ordered [T] is a so-called *view bound* and says:
The maxList function can access a list of elements of any
Type T can be used as long as T is treated as Ordered [T], ie in a
Ordered [T] can be converted. Is a type T without conversion
If it is already an Ordered [T], the View Bound is of course also considered fulfilled.

5.7.5 Context Bounds

Version 2.8 introduces another construct at the type level: the *context bound* . A context bound for a type T would be, for example, T: Ordered. in the
In contrast to the View Bound T <% Ordered [T], this does not mean that a
ne conversion from T to Ordered [T] has to be available, just that
there must be a value of type Ordered [T]. A context is expanded
Bound of the form T: Ordered namely to an implicit parameter with the
Type Ordered [T]. An application example for the context bounds are the ma-
nifeste, which are presented in the following section.

5.7.6 Arrays and @specialized

Arrays in Scala are (not) a specialty. Arrays in Scala should not be particularly
learn how to handle them and work properly in the collection framework (see
Section 6.2), ie in particular the various higher-level functions
Orders such as map or foldRight should also be applicable to arrays.
On the other hand, Scala arrays are supposed to be fully interoperable with Java arrays
and, above all, use the efficient Java implementation.
The implementation of arrays has changed fundamentally with version 2.8.
Before 2.8 the values were automatically converted back and forth and a little *com piler magic* added. However, this sometimes led to poor performance
and other problems. The collection methods could be applied to arrays.
applied, but the result was then no longer an array and thus
the interoperability with Java there.
The same problem existed with strings, by the way. A Scala string is
speaks java.lang.String. Through an implicit conversion in one direction
String could use a variety of additional methods with a string
will. Here, too, the result was a RichString, which is no longer
was compatible with the Java string.
The solution for arrays and similarly for strings is that instead of one
There are now two implicit conversions: into an ArrayOps or StringOps
and into a WrappedArray or WrappedString. Define the Ops variants
the Collection methods, but return an array as a result. This order
Conversion from an array to an ArrayOps is so short-lived that it can be used by
modern virtual machines can even be optimized away. The Wrapped
Variants remain a Scala collection and are therefore no longer compatible with
the Java types.
A slightly modified procedure for determining a suitable im
For explicit conversions, the conversions can be prioritized so that
in the first place the Ops variant and in the second place the Wrapped variant

comes. In fact, the implicits for ArrayOps and StringOps in the Predef object and the implicits for WrappedArray and WrappedString in the LowPriorityImplicits class. Now the trick is that LowPriorityImplicits is the base class of the Predef object. With the mo- In differentiated procedures, the implicits in Predef have a higher priority like the inherited from LowPriorityImplicits. By the way, the approach can too can be used in own programs to prioritize implicits.
Another problem (solved) is the following: Scala has generic arrays, Java Not. There are nine different representations of an array in Java: eight for the various primitive data types 19 and one for reference types .
Scala does not make this difference, but unifies the object model.
But if an array [Int] is used in a Scala program, the-
It can of course be represented by the Java int array. To ensure this must be known at runtime which representation is to be selected. The however, generic types in Scala are based on *type erasure* . That is, the type parameters are checked at the time of compilation and after successful Exam removed. So there is basically no information about the Type parameters are no longer available.
The solution to this problem is called a manifest. A value of type Manifest [T] provides the complete information about Type T. One such manifest in most cases does not even have to be generated by yourself, but can generated by the compiler and is typically used as an implicit parameter meter passed. That is, the only place where we usually get that Encountered manifest is the signature of a function. Even that is enough for arrays weakened version, the ClassManifest, which has already been generated can if the top-level class of a type is known. With arrays you just have to determine whether it is a counterpart of a primitive Java type or some is any reference type.
If we now define a function listToArray 20 , for example , we have to Define ClassManifest as an implicit parameter (see Listing 5.57).

Listing 5.57: listToArray with an implicit ClassManifest parameter

```
def listToArray [T] (list: List [T])
(implicit m: ClassManifest [T]) = {
val xs = new Array [T] (list.length)
for (i <- 0 until list.length) xs (i) = list (i)
xs
}
```

After the parameter m in the entire function listToArray at all is not required, it can be anonymized by a *context bound* , as in Listing 5.58 is shown.

Listing 5.58: The listToArray function with a context bound

```
def listToArray [T: ClassManifest] (list: List [T]) = {
val xs = new Array [T] (list.length)
for (i <- 0 until list.length) xs (i) = list (i)
xs
}
```

In particular, it should be noted that functions that do not themselves have an array create, but call a function that does this, get a ClassManifest to necessitate. For example, let's define the function:

```
def mkArray [T: ClassManifest] (x: T *) =
listToArray (x.toList)
```

so this also needs a ClassManifest. To declare without a ClassManifest come, the GenericArray can be used, which is always on the representation sentation as a reference array.

A very similar problem is basically the use of primitive data types as type parameters. Because instead of direct use The primitive data type on the Java Virtual Machine is converted into a Object packed [21] . This process is called *boxing* . Programs that such *boxed primitive values* can be up to ten times slower than people who work directly with the primitive values. This leads to many Programmers do not use generic collections, but prefer specialized write te versions.

With Scala 2.8 the @specialized annotation is now found [22] . So can special versions for the primitive types are generated by the compiler. target it is also possible to generate specialized versions in the standard library. sen.

For example, consider the following class definition:

```
class Vector [@specialized A] {
def apply (i: Int): A = // ...
def map [@specialized (Int, Boolean) B]
(f: A => B) = // ...
}
```

Due to the @specialized annotation in front of the type parameter A, the Class Vector specialized for all primitive types. The second annotation @specialized (Int, Boolean) before the type parameter B in the definition of the map method means that the method also works for Int and Boolean as the result type of the function that is "mapped" over the vector becomes.

5.7.7 Generalized Type Constraints

Scala offers the possibility of using *generalized type constraints* to further restrict the parameters of a class or a trait. The three constraints are:

A =: = B means: Type A must be B.

A <: <B means: A must be a subtype of B (analogous to <:).

A <% <B means: A must be convertible into B (analogous to <%).

The three constraints each correspond to classes with two type parameters, i.e. =: = [A, B], <: <[A, B] and <% <[A, B], but are usually as above indicated written in infix notation.

The constraints are usually set using an implicit *evidence* parameter formulated. Listing 5.59 shows an example.

Listing 5.59: The Foo class with generalized type constraints

```
class Foo [A] (a: A) {
def stringLength (implicit evidence: A =: = String) =
a.length
def addIntToInt (x: Int)
(implicit evidence: A <: <Int): Int = a + x
def addDoubleToNumber (x: Double)
(implicit evidence: A <% <Double): Double = a + x
}
```

The class Foo has a type parameter A, which is not restricted. In the class There are three methods. The stringLength method can only be used if the type parameter is of type String. The addIntToInt method is only usable for those instances of Foo where the type parameter is is an int. Finally, the type must be addDoubleToNumber can be converted into a double.

Some of these methods could also be used with isInstanceOf and asInstanceOf

be formulated. The main advantage of generalized type constraints is that they are checked at compile time, not runtime. The the following session should illustrate this:

```
scala> val string = new Foo ("Hello World!")
string: Foo [java.lang.String] = Foo @ 781fb069
scala> val int = new Foo (1234)
int: Foo [Int] = Foo @ 2d791620
scala> val float = new Foo (1.23F)
float: Foo [float] = Foo @ 3479404a
scala> string stringLength
res0: Int = 12
scala> int stringLength
<console>: 8: error: could not find implicit value for
parameter evidence: =: = [Int, String]
int stringLength
^
scala> float stringLength
<console>: 8: error: could not find implicit value for
parameter evidence: =: = [Float, String]
float stringLength
^
scala> string addIntToInt 1
<console>: 8: error: could not find implicit value for
parameter evidence: <: <[java.lang.String, Int]
string addIntToInt 1
^
scala> int addIntToInt 1
res4: Int = 1235
scala> float addIntToInt 1
<console>: 8: error: could not find implicit value for
parameter evidence: <: <[Float, Int]
float addIntToInt 1
^
scala> string addDoubleToNumber 4.56
<console>: 8: error: could not find implicit value for
parameter evidence: <% <[java.lang.String, Double]
string addDoubleToNumber 4.56
^
scala> int addDoubleToNumber 4.56
res7: Double = 1238.56
scala> float addDoubleToNumber 4.56
res8: Double = 5.790000019073486
```

5.7.8 Self-type annotation

The type of the value this can be declared explicitly with a *self type annotation* will. Self-type annotations can also be used to be synonymous for defining this. The latter is helpful, for example, if from an in-A method of an outer class should be accessed. In listing An example is given in 5.60. A self-type annotation consists of one nem identifier immediately after the opening bracket of a class or of a trait is written, and the double arrow =>.

Listing 5.60: Nested classes A, B and C with the self-type annotations selfA and selfB

```
class A {selfA =>
```

```
def printIt (message: String) =
println ("A.printIt:" + message)
class B {selfB =>
def printIt (message: String) =
selfA.printIt ("B.printIt:" + message)
class C {
def printItA (message: String) =
selfA.printIt ("C.printItA:" + message)
def printItB (message: String) =
selfB.printIt ("C.printItB:" + message)
}
val c = new C
}
val b = new B
}
```

Immediately after the opening curly bracket the class A is used as a synonym the identifier selfA is defined for this. The same for class B is the identifier selfB. In class B, the this from class A is shadows. The identifier selfA (or any other) is still valid and can be used from B to create the object of type A, ches contains the type B object. It is analogous for class C. There selfA and selfB are valid. The following session presents this using a concrete example:

```
scala> val a = new A
a: A = A @ 56092666
scala> a.printIt ("Hello")
A.printIt: Hello
scala> abcprintItA ("Hello")
A.printIt: C.printItA: Hello
scala> abcprintItB ("Hello")
A.printIt: B.printIt: C.printItB: Hello
```

Explicitly declaring the type of this is even more powerful. Consider we see the three traits in Listing 5.61. Instead of the Trait Animal by trait Animal extends Noise with Food, only the type is changed accordingly. given. As a result, the two methods are just like an extends ... makeNoise and eat can be used in Animal. The version from Listing 5.61 appears but a bit more natural, because an animal is neither a noise nor a food. In other programming languages would probably have an animal with one field each for noise and food.

Listing 5.61: The Noise, Food and Animal traits with a self-type annotation

```
trait noise {
def makeNoise: Unit
}
trait food {
def eat: Unit
}
trait animal {
self: Noise with Food =>
def run = {
makeNoise
eat
makeNoise
|
}
```

Listing 5.62 shows the implementation of the Dog class. A dog is a Animal. However, since Animal has a self-type annotation, Dog still has a suitable noise and a suitable food implementation. Zen. This is ensured via the Bark and Gorge traits.

Listing 5.62: The Bark and Gorge traits and the Dog class

```
trait Bark extends Noise {
def makeNoise = println ("Woof, woof!")
}
trait Gorge extends Food {
def eat = println ("Gorge, gorge!")
}
class Dog extends Animal with Bark with Gorge
```

The implementation of the Bird class with the Tweet and Pick traits is in Listing 5.63.

Listing 5.63: The Tweet and Pick traits and the Bird class

```
trait Tweet extends Noise {
def makeNoise = println ("Chirp, chirp!")
}
trait Pick extends Food {
def eat = println ("Pick, pick!")
}
class Bird extends Animal with Tweet with Pick
```

We can then create a bird and a dog and both "ab-run ", as the following session shows:

```
scala> val birdie = new bird
birdie: Bird = Bird @ 36656758
scala> birdie.run
Chirp, chirp!
Pick, pick!
Chirp, chirp!
scala> val lassie = new dog
lassie: Dog = Dog @ 3798f5e7
scala> lassie.run
Woof, woof!
Gorge, gorge!
Woof, woof!
```

5.7.9 Structural and existential types

With a structural type (*structural type*) we can state that we have a Type that has a certain structure. Listing 5.64 is an example specified.

Listing 5.64: The RunWithTime Object and the RunMe Class

```
object RunWithTime {
type Something = {def run ()}
def runWithTime (f: Something) = {
import scala.compat.Platform.currentTime
val executionStart: Long = currentTime
f.run
val total = currentTime - executionStart
println ("[total" + total + "ms]")
}
}
class RunMe {
```

```
def run () {
println ("Starting")
Thread.sleep (1000)
println ("stopping")
}
}
```

A structural type Something is specified in the RunWithTime object. The Structure says it can be of any type, but the run method for the type must be defined. The RunMe class defines such a type. Therefore For example, it can do the following:

```
scala> RunWithTime.runWithTime (new RunMe)
Starting
Stopping
[total 1005ms]
```

This ultimately saves us from having to run a trait with the abstract method which the RunMe class then adds.

Existential types (*existential types*) can be used to transfer types abstract. For example, if pattern matching is done with a list, is The element type no longer exists at runtime due to Type Erasure. It can therefore be specified as an underscore, ie as List [_]. The ones in listing 5.65 uses this for pattern matching with lists and maps.

Listing 5.65: The matchOnCollections function, the existential types for the pattern Uses matching for lists and maps

```
val matchOnCollections: AnyRef => Unit = {
case _: List [_] => println ("A list")
case _: Map [_, _] => println ("One Map")
case _
=> println ("something else")
}
```

Specifically, existential types are meant to be Java's Wildcard and Raw To use types from Scala. In Java there is, for example, the type specification Iterator <?>, Which means something like an iterator of some type. This can written in Scala as an iterator [_]. Strictly speaking, this is the one Abbreviation for:

Iterator [T] forSome {type T}

Similarly, for the Java type Iterator < ? extends Component > write in Scala:

Iterator [T] forSome {type T <: Component}

This can also be written more compactly with the placeholder syntax as:

Iterator [_ <: Component]

Chapter 6
The Scala standard library

The Scala standard library consists of the package scala with a number of Modules and sub-packages. In section 6.1 we will first give you one

Overview and discuss the Predef object that is automatically generated for each Program is available. In Section 6.2 we discuss the collection Framework that was completely revised with Scala 2.8. Scala offers an ex-cellular XML support. Well-formed XML expressions can be used directly as literary le can be used in the source code (see Section 6.3). An approach that also comes from the functional programming has been adopted, the use of Parser combiners. We will go into this in Section 6.4. The chapter closes with a little look at the programming of graphical user interfaces with the scala.swing package in Section 6.5.

6.1 Overview and the Predef Object

The package scala contains a variety of types and values. Types are class sen, traits or type synonyms. Values are objects or vals. Many of them have we already treated or we will treat. The type synonyms and vals are defined by the package object scala, essentially, to the shifted with the 2.8 classes and objects ı additionally their original name.
As mentioned in Section 5.7, at the top of the class hierarchy is the Figure 6.1 shows the abstract class Any. The one for Any and thus Methods defined for any object are shown in Listing 6.1.
Any
AnyVal
Double
Float
Long
Int
Short
byte
Unit
Boolean
Char
AnyRef
ScalaObject
Cunning
option
. . . further Scala classes
String
. . . Further
Java classes
Nothing
zero
Figure 6.1: The Scala class hierarchy
Listing 6.1: The methods of the root class Any

```
def equals (that: Any): Boolean
final def == (that: Any): Boolean =
if (null eq this) null eq that else this equals that
final def! = (that: Any): Boolean =! (this == that)
def hashCode: Int
def toString: String
def isInstanceOf [A]: Boolean
def asInstanceOf [A]: A
```

In Scala, unlike in Java, objects are usually compared with == or! =. chen. The two methods are marked with the final modifier, so they

cannot be redefined. The equals method, which == and da-
with also! = is used to redefine equality as required. This
but should always be accompanied by a suitable redefinition of hashCode.
go because objects that are considered equal also have the same hash value
should have, but only this.

The toString method returns the representation of the object as a string and
should also be redefined in your own classes according to your ideas
the. The two methods isInstanceOf and asInstanceOf enable
check whether an object is an instance of a certain class or can be used for
Casting an object to be used on another class, e.g.

```
scala> "Hello" .isInstanceOf [AnyRef]
res0: Boolean = true
scala> "Hello" .isInstanceOf [ScalaObject]
res1: Boolean = false
scala> "Hello" .asInstanceOf [AnyRef]
res2: AnyRef = Hello
```

For numeric types S and T with x: S, x.asInstanceOf [T] can be added
can be used to convert x into a value of type T. This corresponds to that
Calling the method x.toT, e.g.

```
scala> 1.7.asInstanceOf [Int]
res3: Int = 1
scala> 1.7.toInt
res4: Int = 1
```

The Any class has two immediate subclasses: AnyVal and AnyRef. The class
se AnyVal is the base class for the values that are not implemented as objects in Java.
are mentored. The nine subclasses are shown in Figure 6.1. Objects
of the classes can only be accessed through the corresponding literals, but not with new
be generated. The classes are arranged flat under AnyVal, the values can
However, they can sometimes be implicitly converted into one another. From AnyVal
can
no further classes can be derived. Stand for AnyVal and all subtypes
of course the methods defined in Any are available.

The AnyRef class is the base class for all other classes: both all Scala-
Classes that are not subclasses of AnyVal, all Java classes that are created in Scala
used, as well as all self-defined classes. In addition there is
nor the trait ScalaObject, which automatically includes all Scala classes, including
defined, in contrast to Java classes marked as such. That means you can-
to find out via isInstanceOf [ScalaObject] whether it is a
Scala class or not, e.g.

```
scala> List (1,2,3) .isInstanceOf [ScalaObject]
res5: Boolean = true
scala> "Hello World" .isInstanceOf [ScalaObject]
res6: Boolean = false
```

As you can see above, the string in Scala is not a Scala class, but java.
lang.String and therefore not an instance of ScalaObject. The AnyRef class
Incidentally, corresponds to java.lang.Object on the Java platform. To avoid
misunderstandings
Preventing confessions: If you define a class in Scala, you have to
Specify neither AnyRef nor ScalaObject as base class or trait [2]. This
follows automatically.

In the class AnyRef, the abstract methods from Any and two more,
eq and ne, defined. The methods are listed in Listing 6.2.

Listing 6.2. The methods of the AnyRef class

```
def equals (that: Any): Boolean = this eq that
```

final def eq (that: AnyRef): Boolean = ...
final def ne (that: AnyRef): Boolean =! (this eq that)
def hashCode: Int = ...
def toString: String = ...

The method call this eq that returns true if and only if that this and that reference the same object 3 . The methods ne and equals are defined by eq 4 . The implementations of the method the hashCode and toString correspond to the implementations in java. lang.Object. That is, the hash value is taken from the one assigned to the object Memory address is calculated, and toString returns the class name, an @ sign and return the hash value. For many classes from the Scala standard library the three methods are already more sensibly defined. For your own classes, you should do that too.

There are some classes for which either a special syntax (*syntactic sugar*) is required. is offered or for which the compiler generates special code. Most we have already got to know:

the class String with the corresponding string literals,
the classes tuples n , for $1 \leq n \leq 22$, which are defined by the syntax (.., .., ...) can be generated, and
the classes Function n , for $1 \leq n \leq 22$, which are usually .. => .. => ... to be written.

The Array class is special for the compiler so that it does not have any special for the programmer (see Section 5.7.6). In addition there is There is also a special syntax for the Node class, which we will introduce in Section 6.3 will be 5 .

The Predef object is a specialty in a slightly different way The object and thus everything that is defined in it is automatically added to each scale File imported. In the following we want to give you a rough overview of give the content.

First, some type synonyms are defined in PreDef, e.g.

type string
= java.lang.String
type class [T]
= java.lang.Class [T]
type Map [A, + B] = collection.immutable.Map [A, B]
type set [A]
= collection.immutable.Set [A]

In addition, everything that was defined in the package object scala is also available in pre-
def visible. Various methods for errors or assurances are also gen (*assertions*) such as error, exit, assert, assume and require. That means we can later simply use our programs

assert (x> 0)

write without a keyword being reserved for it as in Java or a ne special syntax is necessary. assert just stands for Predef.assert and is a completely normal method. Assert is then implemented for example wise so:

```
def assert (assertion: Boolean) {
if (! assertion)
throw new java.lang.AssertionError ("assertion failed")
}
```

Of course there is an overloaded method that still has a message as a parameter ter has. Next, the type synonym Pair for Tuple2 and Triple introduced for Tuple3 with the corresponding companion objects.

We want to go back a bit more at ArrowAssoc. A map contains Key-value pairs. This means that we can create a map as follows, for example witness:
Map (Tuple2 (1, "one"), Tuple2 (2, "two"))
After the type synonym pair is available, also through:
Map (Pair (1, "One"), Pair (2, "Two"))
Since there is a special syntax for tuples, also through:
Map ((1, "one"), (2, "two"))
But usually we create a map in Scala with the following syntax:
Map (1 -> "One", 2 -> "Two")
This is not a special syntax; it has to do with the ArrowAssoc class. The ArrowAssoc class defines a method called -> which from the object to which the method is applied and the parameter Tuple makes. That is, from 1 -> "one" becomes, if 1 is an instance of the class ArrowAssoc would be the pair (1, "one"). And how does the 1 become a ArrowAssoc? Through the implicit conversion:
implicit def any2ArrowAssoc [A] (x: A): ArrowAssoc [A] =
new ArrowAssoc (x)
In this example we can once again see very nicely how we are in Scala introduce new syntax. It continues in the Predef object with functions for output and reading, e.g. println, print, readLine, readInt and many more. These functions are all defined in the Console object, and by being present in Predef we can use the
Just write an example:
val x = readLine ()
print (x)
Predef, of course, also includes a variety of implicit conversions for the primitive, numeric types, for the various array representations, for Autoboxing of the primitive types into the corresponding Java reference types, e.g. Int to java.lang.Integer and for strings.
Finally, in Predef, the implicit relationships discussed in 5.7.6 Versions with lower priority from the base class LowPriorityImplicits available.

6.2 The collection framework

With version 2.8 the Scala Collection Framework was redesigned and educated. All collection classes are now in the package scala.collec-tion.generic contains various classes and traits to create collections witness. Usually, these classes and traits are not directly from used by us and therefore not considered further here.
There are three versions of most collections: one in scala.collection, one in the sub-package immutable and one in the sub-package mutable. The class se in scala.collection has the same interface as the corresponding class in scala.collection.immutable, the latter guaranteed immutable are. The collections in the mutable sub-package have additional methods that can change the state of the collection.

Traversable
Iterable
Map
SortedMap
set
SortedSet
BitSet
Seq

Buffer
Vector
LinearSeq
Figure 6.2: The most important basic classes of the collection framework

Figure 6.2 shows the most important base classes of the collection framework shown. All collection classes have the following in common:

An instance can be created by specifying the class name and the elements in Brackets are generated, e.g. 6

Traversable (1, 2, 3)
Map ("B" -> "Berlin", "S" -> "Stuttgart")
Set ("Haskell", "Scala", "Java")
List (1, 2, 3)
HashMap (1 -> "one", 2 -> "two")

ie for each collection class the apply method is in the companion object Are defined.

A collection is represented as a string in the same way, e.g.

```
scala> Set ("Haskell", "Scala", "Java")
res0: scala.collection.immutable.Set [java.lang.String]
= Set (Haskell, Scala, Java)
scala> Map (1 -> "one", 2 -> "two")
res1: scala.collection.immutable.Map [Int, java.lang.
String] = Map ((1, one), (2, two))
```

As can be seen in the last listing, the default version is the unchangeable version chosen from a collection. Should the changeable version be used instead den, this simply has to be imported:

```
scala> import scala.collection.mutable.Map
import scala.collection.mutable.Map
scala> Map (1 -> "one", 2 -> "two")
res2: scala.collection.mutable.Map [Int, java.lang.String]
= Map ((2, two), (1, one))
```

The hierarchy of the base classes (see Figure 6.2) is designed so that Least nothing has to be defined multiple times in different places. In Scala 2.7, for example, most collections had their own map defined. The means, specifically in the list there was

```
def map [B] (f: A => B): List [B]
```

and in a set

```
def map [B] (f: A => B): Set [B]
```

only because once a list [B] and the other time a set [B] result came out. The more coherent design of the collections in Scala 2.8 means that map in Essentially defined only once in Traversable, namely as:

```
def map [B, That] (f: A => B)
(implicit bf: CanBuildFrom [Traversable [A], B, That]):
That
```

This means that there is an implicit parameter that ensures that the correct term collection comes out as a result. For this to work, every collection implement a method newBuilder, which creates a *builder* for the collection returns.

This means that a large number of collection methods are already in the trait traversable defined. Traversable's only abstract method is that method

```
def foreach [U] (f: Elem => U): Unit
```

which executes a function f with each element of the collection. By the way, you can such traversable collections can also be infinite. One example is the class scala.collection.immutable.Stream, which represent an infinite list that is *lazy* accessed. That means the next element is the

List is only calculated when it is actually needed. Differed
finite and infinite collections of the result of the measurement
method hasDefiniteSize.
Traversable's immediate subtrait, Iterable, also has a single one
abstract method, namely
def iterator: iterator [A]
The foreach method is implemented using the iterator. Nevertheless
should implement subclasses foreach for reasons of efficiency. Share further
The Collections are in Maps, Sets and Seqs, which we will describe individually below
want to introduce.
Sequences are hidden behind the Trait Seq. Sequences have an index
and can thus be understood as partial mappings from Int to the element type
the will. The index starts with 0 and ends with the number of elements with
nus one. The apply method of the sequences is used to access the elements
used via the index, e.g.
scala> val list = List ("Hello", "World")
list: List [java.lang.String] = List (Hello, World)
scala> list (1)
res3: java.lang.String = world
If a Seq can be changed, it can be changed using the update method and the index.
changed, e.g. 7
scala> val linearseq = scala.collection.mutable.LinearSeq
("One two Three")
linearseq: scala.collection.mutable.LinearSeq [java.lang.
String] = MutableList (One, Two, Three)
scala> linearseq (1) = "two"
scale> linearseq
res4: scala.collection.mutable.LinearSeq [java.lang.String
] = MutableList (one, two, three)
The two subtraits LinearSeq and Vector do not define any additional measurement
methods, but have different performance characteristics: A linear se-
quenz has efficient head and tail methods. A vector has efficient apply-
and length methods. Changeable vectors also have an efficient one
update method.
The buffers are a special feature of the collections library, another
Subclass of Seq. The buffers are only available in the changeable
sion. They offer the possibility of replacing, inserting and removing elements
distant. New elements are efficiently appended to the end of a buffer. The
are essential additional methods of Buffer
to insert:
buf insert (i, x)
// insert element x at index i
buf insertAll (i, xs) *// insert all at index i*
to remove:
buf remove i
// remove element at index i
buf remove (i, n) *// remove n elems starting at i*
buf - = x
// remove element x
buf − [illegible]
// remove all elements in xs
to attach at the end:
buf [illegible] x
// append x

buf + = (x, y, z) // *append x, y, and z*
buf ++ = xs
// *append all in xs*
to add at the beginning:
x + =: buf
// *prepend x*
xs ++ =: buf // *prepend all in xs*
Frequently used implementations of Buffer are
scala.collection.mutable.ListBuffer
scala.collection.mutable.ArrayBuffer
The trait set and its implementations represent sets. The essential
mathematical sets is that no element appears more than once in it.
can come. The apply method is defined in such a way that it checks whether the work
gument is contained in the set, and thus corresponds to the contains method.
The following listing serves as an illustration:
scala> val set = set (1,2,3)
set: scala.collection.immutable.Set [Int] = Set (1, 2, 3)
scala> set (1)
res5: Boolean = true // 1 is contained in set
scala> set (4)
res6: Boolean = false // 4 is not included in set
Depending on whether the set is changeable or not, elements can be marked with + and
++ or + = and ++ = can be added and removed with - or - =, e.g.
scale> set + 4
res7: scala.collection.immutable.Set [Int] = Set (1, 2, 3,
4)
scala> set - 1
res8: scala.collection.immutable.Set [Int] = Set (2, 3)
scala> val mSet = scala.collection.mutable.Set (1,2,3)
mSet: scala.collection.mutable.Set [Int] = Set (1, 2, 3)
scale> mSet + = 4
res9: mSet.type = Set (1, 4, 2, 3)
scale> mSet - = 1
res10: mSet.type = Set (4, 2, 3)
In addition, the usual set operations are defined in Set:
Intersection:
xs & ys
xs intersect ys
Union set:
xs | ys
xs union ys
Difference:
xs & ~ ys
xs diff ys
Subset:
xs subsetof ys
empty set (not test whether empty set!).
xs.empty
The two direct subtraits of Set are SortedSet and BitSet. A care
tedSet is a set that combines the elements with foreach or iterator in a
returns a freely selectable order. A BitSet is a set of non-
negative integers that uses little memory if the range of
possible values is small. The third immediate subtrait of Iterable is Map.
Key-value pairs are stored in a map. The apply method is like this

defines that it receives a key as an argument and the
returns the associated value. If there is no entry for the key,
an exception thrown, e.g.
scala> val map = Map ("Eins" -> "One", "Zwei" -> "Two")
map: scala.collection.immutable.Map [java.lang.String, java
.lang.String] = Map ((Eins, One), (Zwei, Two))
scala> map ("Two")
res11: java.lang.String = Two
scala> map ("Three")
java.util.NoSuchElementException: key not found: Three
The get method does essentially the same thing, but has an option as a result
nest type. This means that either the value is packed in a Some or instead of the
Exception None returned, e.g.
scala> map.get ("Two")
res12: Option [java.lang.String] = Some (Two)
scala> map.get ("Three")
res13: Option [java.lang.String] = None
A map has essentially the same features for adding and removing
methods like Set: +, + =, - and - =. Updates are possible with different syntax:
for mutable maps:
map (5) = "five"
map.update (5, "five")
map + = (5 -> "five")
for immutable maps:
map.updated (5, "five")
map + (5 -> "five")
The update method for unchangeable maps is *deprecated* , that is,
available, but should no longer be used. The only direct subtrait is
SortedMap, which is sorted according to the keys.
The equality of collections is defined in such a way that the collections are initially
divided into three
Categories are divided into: Sets, Maps and Seqs. Two collections from different
different categories are always unequal. Two collections from the same
categories are the same if and only if they contain the same elements. It applies
for example:
scala> List (1,2,3) == Vector (1,2,3)
res14: Boolean = true
scala> List (1,2,3) == Vector (1,3,2)
res15: Boolean = false
scala> import
|
scala.collection.immutable. {HashSet, TreeSet}
import scala.collection.immutable. {HashSet, TreeSet}
scala> HashSet (1,2) == TreeSet (2,1)
res16: Boolean = true

6.3 Scala and XML

The Extensible Markup Language (XML) [8] has established itself in many areas
sets, for example, computer-to-computer communication over the Internet or for the
Configuration of applications. Scala offers first class XML support:
XML elements can be written directly as literals, e.g.
scala> <b> Hello World </b>
res0: scala.xml.Elem = <b> Hello World </b>

The XML literal given above corresponds to an object of the class scala. xml.Elem with the label b and the successor Hello World 9 . The others
The main classes of the package scala.xml are:

The abstract class Node as the base class for all XML nodes.

The NodeSeq class, which represents a sequence of nodes. A single one Node can be viewed as a sequence of length 1.

The Text class for a node that contains only text, e.g. Hello World.

In an XML literal, any Scala expressions can be enclosed in curly brackets. mern (so-called *brace escapes*) may be included, e.g.

```
scala> <result> {5 + 7 + 9} </result>
res1: scala.xml.Elem = <result> 21 </result>
scala> val list = (1 to 10) .toList
list: List [Int] = List (1, 2, 3, 4, 5, 6, 7, 8, 9, 10)
scala> <result>
|
Sum of the list {list.toString} is {list.sum}
| </result>
res2: scala.xml.Elem =
<result>
The sum of List is List (1, 2, 3, 4, 5, 6, 7, 8, 9, 10)
55
</result>
```

XML literals and brace escapes can be nested as required. To lead For example, if we run the Scala script from Listing 6.3, the following is output. ben:

```
<author>
<me> </me>
</author>
<author>
<name> Jon Spencer </name>
</author>
```

Listing 6.3: Scala script to illustrate the nesting of XML and Brace Escapes

```
def author (name: String) =
<author>
{if (name == "Oliver") <me />
else <name> {name} </name>}
</author>
println (author ("Oliver"))
println (author ("Jon Spencer"))
```

By the way, by using XML literals the characters <,>, & etc. in strings automatically converted into the corresponding escape sequence. This helps against the problem that users, for example, in fields on web pages can enter XML and thus open a potential security hole. One Example for clarification is the following:

```
scala> <a> {"</a> back out & back in <a>"} </a>
res3: scala.xml.Elem <a> & lt; / a & gt; out again & amp;
back in & lt; a & gt; </a>
```

If you want a curly bracket in your XML, you have to write them twice, e.g.

```
scala> <i> def f () {{println ("Hello")}} </i>
res4: scala.xml.Elem = <i> def f () {println (& quot; Hello &
quot;)} </i>
```

Parts can be extracted using simple methods of the NodeSeq class.

As an example, consider the XML values scalabook shown in Listing 6.4 and osgibook.

Listing 6.4: XML Nodes for This Book and the OSGi Book

```
val scalabook =
<book lang = "de">
<title> Scala </title>
<author> Oliver Braun </author>
</book>
val osgibook =
<book lang = "de">
<title> OSGi for practitioners </title>
<authors>
<author> Bernd Weber </author>
<author> Patrick Baumgartner </author>
<author> Oliver Braun </author>
</authors>
</book>
```

We can extract the title node of the osgibook with the following expression - ren:

```
scala> osgibook \ "title"
res5: scala.xml.NodeSeq = NodeSeq (<title> OSGi </title>)
```

We can extract the author nodes with the following expression:

```
scala> osgibook \\ "author"
res6: scala.xml.NodeSeq = NodeSeq (<author> Bernd Weber </
author>, <author> Patrick Baumgartner </author>, <author
> Oliver Braun </author>)
```

Access to the various authors then works with those for sequences usual methods, e.g.

```
scala> (osgibook \\ "author") (2)
res7: scala.xml.Node = <author> Oliver Braun </author>
scala> for (author <- osgibook \\ "author")
|
println ("Author:" + author.text)
Author: Bernd Weber
Author: Patrick Baumgartner
Author: Oliver Braun
```

If the value of an attribute is to be calculated, the attribute must be preceded by @ be provided, e.g.

```
scala> osgibook \ "@lang"
res8: scala.xml.NodeSeq = de
```

Pattern matching is also possible directly with XML literals. In Listing 6.5, the CountAuthors function specified. If the XML node is a Book is used with the for expression from the descendants of the authors Looking for nodes. If found, the number of author-Node returned. If no authors node is found, there is probably just an author node. Therefore, 1 is returned in this case.

Listing 6.5: The countAuthors function

```
def countAuthors (xml: scala.xml.Node): Int = {
xml match {
case <book> {fields @ _ *} </book> => {
for (<authors> {authors @ _ *} </authors> <- fields)
return (authors \\ "author"). length
return 1
}
```

```
}
}
```

Let us now use the two books defined in Listing 6.4 as arguments to the Function countAuthors, we get the following results:

```
scala> countAuthors (osgibook)
res9: Int = 3
scala> countAuthors (scalabook)
res10: Int = 1
```

The scala.xml.XML object defines some very useful methods around-gang with XML, including the following:

With the load method, XML can be imported directly from a file, an input Stream, a URL or other sources.

The loadFile method can be used to convert an XML file into a node. be delt.

The save method can be used to save an XML node to a file. the.

The loadString method can be used to generate XML from a string.

6.4 Combine parsers

As soon as a Scala application receives external data in any way, these must be prepared so that they can be used in the application the. Such data can, for example, be configuration files, data that is about received on the network, or input data in a special format his. A component or program that does this decomposition and conversion is called a *parser* .

Parsers can use so-called parser genes from a description of the data rators are generated. Since the mid-1980s, however, the *Functional Programming Community has developed* a strong tendency, instead to use said *parser combiners* 10 . While parser generators are external Tools like Yacc, Bison or ANTLR are, parser combiners are used in the programming language itself used. In functional programming a function that consists of functions for a task such as parsing a new one Function combined for the same type of task, called a combiner.

The advantages of such parser combiners are obvious: They can simply are composed, are therefore more modular, and it is the entire power the programming language available for parser construction.

Scala also has a parser-combiner library, which we will use in the following want to introduce. As an example we want to parse the following input line:

Mayr, Hubertus (123456): 90 points = 1.0

The line is a data record from a database for a test. The student Hubertus Mayr with matriculation number 123456 has 90 points and thus the Grade 1.0 achieved. We want to be able to use this data in Scala. To Let there be a Student class, shown in Listing 6.6.

Listing 6.6: The Student class

```
class Student (val name: String, val matNr: Int) {
override def toString = name + "(" + matNr + ")"
}
```

For the sake of simplicity, the result of a test should then only be best as a tuple. based on the student, the points and the grade, i.e. for Hubertus Mayr:

```
val mayr = (new Student ("Mayr, Hubertus", 123456), 90,1.0)
```

First of all, we will limit ourselves to the task of correcting the character string at all.

good to parse. Once we have this, we add to our parser so that we can use the tuple obtained as a result.
In the package scala.util.parsing.combinator there are a number of parser Traits that we could use for our purposes. For example, the trait JavaTokenParsers already have some parsers, for example for strings and floating scores. The JavaTokenParsers trait extends the RegexParsers trait, that we will use. This enables parsers to be generated from regular expressions will. The base trait of RegexParsers is Parsers. In parsers they are essential parser combiners.
New in Scala 2.8 are the so-called PackratParsers, another subtrait by parsers. A Packrat parser is a special parser that handles the intermediate retains the results of all recursive calls and thus, for example, context-free Parses grammars in linear time. On Packrat parser we will at this point le do not go further.
A parser is of type Parser [T], where T is the type of the parser's result is. For example, we can have a parser that parses an integer 11 , follow- so define:

```
val int: Parser [String] = "" "\ d +" "". r
```

That is, we specify a regular expression that matches an integer, because \ d stands for a digit, and the + means one or more, i.e. a total of one or more digits. So that the backslash is not used as a control character in the String is interpreted, we have used three quotation marks. The Method r turns the string into a regular expression. We have to do more do not do. A regular expression is a parser.
In order to actually define the int parser in this way, we have to use the trait Expand RegexParsers, as shown in Listing 6.7.

Listing 6.7: The MyParsers Class

```
import scala.util.parsing.combinator._
class MyParsers extends RegexParsers {
val int: Parser [String] = "" "\ d +" "". r
}
```

To the string
Mayr, Hubertus (123456): 90 points = 1.0
To be able to parse, we first split them into the various components and define a separate parser for each. Of course we do that Solution a little easier by including the context.
The name is everything that comes before the opening round bracket 12 . The re- The usual expression for this is quite simply [^ (] * and means: read a or multiple characters that are not open parentheses. The parser sees then look like this:

```
val studentname: Parser [String] = "" "[^ (] +" "". r
```

The matriculation number is the whole number in round brackets. You can do this we reuse our int parser and two parsers for the brackets combine with it. By the way, a simple string is also a parser, ie "(" is the parser for (and ")" for). Although the characters are just side by side are written differently, we have to do this explicitly with a combiner write. There are three combiners for this type of link:
- a ~ b creates a new parser that parses first with a, then with b and returns the overall result.
- a <~ b parses just like a ~ b, but only returns the result of parser a back.
- a ~> b similarly only returns the result of b.
Since we don't need the brackets in the result, our parser sees

like this:

```
val matNr: Parser [String] = "(" ~> int <~ "):"
```

We have the colon and the space in front of it at this point the points taken. This has the advantage that we do not have too many individual ne small parser, and the disadvantage that the matNr parser cannot necessarily be reused elsewhere.

The points are again a whole number, followed by the character string points =. Between the periods, the character string periods and the = spaces can signs stand. Spaces are generated as \ W in a regular expression wrote. We only need the point value as the result of the parser, therefore let's use the combinator <~ in our parser, which looks like this:

```
val points: Parser [String] =
int <~ "" "\ W * points? \ W * = \ W *" "". r
```

We have put a question mark on the e in dots, meaning it can occur once or never. So the regular expression also fits on 1 point =.

The last partial parser we need is to parse the note. To do this must we know that after the comma only the values 0, 3 and 7, for the 4 before the comma only the 0 and the 3 and for the 5 even only the 0 are allowed. This is taken into account in the regular expression. The parser for so the grade is

```
val mark: Parser [String] =
"" "[123], [037] | 4, [03] | 5.0" "". R
```

What we are missing now is the parser for the entire line. Just as we do the individual If you have defined a parser, we only need to concatenate them for the parser with ~ hang:

```
val oneExam: Parser [Any] = studentname ~ matNr ~ points ~ mark
```

The oneExam parser gives the four results of the partial parser as a combined result result back. Therefore we simply enter Any as the result type. Later will which we convert the value accordingly.

In order to be able to use the parser to parse the line specified above, we have to put them together in one class. The class ExamParserString is shown in Listing 6.8.

Listing 6.8: The ExamParserString class

```
import scala.util.parsing.combinator._
class ExamParserString extends RegexParsers {
val int: Parser [String] = "" "\ d +" "". r
val studentname: Parser [String] = "" "[^ (] +" "". r
val matNr: Parser [String] = "(" ~> int <~ "):"
val points: Parser [String] =
int <~ "" "\ W * points? \ W * = \ W *" "". r
val mark: Parser [String] =
"" "[123], [037] | 4, [03] | 5.0" "". R
val oneExam: Parser [Any] =
student name ~ matNr ~ points ~ mark
}
```

To try it out, we also implement the ExamParserApp object

.

```
object ExamParserApp extends ExamParserString {
def main (args: Array [String]) {
val mayrString =
"Mayr, Hubertus (123456): 90 points = 1.0"
println (parseAll (oneExam, mayrString))
}
```

}

The function parseAll gets a parser, in our case oneExam, and the string to be parsed, here mayrString, as arguments and applies the Parser on the string. Let's translate the classes and run the object ExamParserApp, we see the following on the console:

[1.41] parsed: (((Mayr, Hubertus ~ 123456) ~ 90) ~ 1.0)

This output shows us that row 1 to column 41 (i.e. everything) succeeded. was parsing. The result is shown behind. Before we put the result in the convert the desired tuples, we want to extend our parser so that we can parse not just one data set but several. The necessary agile parser combiner repeats the application of the transferred parsers as long as you can. The combiner for repeated use is called rep. After we want to distribute the records over several lines, let's leave between the records whitespaces too. Therefore we use the combination tor repsep, which has a parser for the line and one for the separator as parameters meter has. So the parser for multiple records is

val exam: Parser [Any] = repsep (oneExam, "" "\ W *" "". r)

We can still change the ExamParserApp object to try it out - you- he Listing 6.10.

Listing 6.10: The ExamParserApp object for parsing multiple records

```
object ExamParserApp extends ExamParserString {
def main (args: Array [String]) {
val examString =
"" "Mayr, Hubertus (123456): 90 points = 1.0
| Painter, Brigitte (876543): 86 points = 1.3
| Reimann, Gundolf (471112): 1 point = 5.0 "" ".
stripMargin
println (parseAll (exam, examString))
}
}
```

If we run the new object ExamParserApp, the output[13] is :

[3.41] parsed: List ((((Mayr, Hubertus ~ 123456) ~ 90) ~ 1.0),
(((Maler, Brigitte ~ 876543) ~ 86) ~ 1.3),
(((Reimann, Gundolf ~ 471112) ~ 1) ~ 5.0))

That is, this time it was parsed to row 3 and column 41 and the results of all lines in a list.

Now that we are able to parse the information, we need to still bring the results into the desired form. We watch each other next look at the result of parsing a data record again and compare do it with the parser. The result was:

(((Mayr, Hubertus ~ 123456) ~ 90) ~ 1.0)

and the parser was structured as follows:

student name ~ matNr ~ points ~ mark

If we add brackets, the structure of the parser is exactly like that of the Result:

(((studentname ~ matNr) ~ points) ~ mark)

And yet there is a difference. The tilde in the parser is a method and the tilde in the result is the name of a case class that is output infix and can be written. That is, we can transform the result use pattern matching to refer to the various partial results. to grab.

First, however, the parsers for the partial results must also be modified that they return the required value. For the two parsers matNr and points is that an int. But after both to parse the number

to use the int parser, we only have to adapt it. To trans-
Form the result there is the ^^ operator. The first operand is the par
ser, the second a function that transforms the result. After we got the
Conversion of a string into an Int can be done easily with toInt,
the int parser now looks like this:

```
val int: Parser [Int] = "" "\ d +" "". r ^^ (_.toInt)
```

For the mark parser, which should return the note as a float, we first have to
replace the decimal point with a point. Then we can do the
Convert string to float with toFloat. The mark parser is
so:

```
val mark: parser [float] =
"" "[123], [037] | 4, [03] | 5.0" "". R ^^
(_.replace (',', '.'). toFloat)
```

Although the student name is a string and therefore the result of the study
dentname parsers does not have to be transformed into another type, only
let's use the ^^ operator there too. In this case, to use the method
de trim the space that was in the original string between the
Name and the round brackets stood to remove. The new student name-
The parser is thus:

```
val studentname: Parser [String] =
"" "[^ (] +" "". r ^^ (_.trim)
```

Now we can turn to the oneExam parser, which now implemen-
is animal:

```
val oneExam: Parser [(Student, Int, Float)] =
student name ~ matNr ~ points ~ mark ^^ {
case name ~ no ~ points ~ mark
=> (new Student (name, no), points, mark)
}
```

With pattern matching, we break the result down into its four components. At-
then we simply put these together to form the required triple. Dar-
in addition, we also have the type of parser to parser [(Student, Int,
Float)] changed. With the previous type of parser [Any] it would be after
correct as before, but it always makes sense to specify the more specific type.
With the exam parser, we only change the type. The implementation can be unchanged
stay cool. We group the new parsers in the ExamParser class
(see Listing 6.11).

Listing 6.11. The ExamParser class

```
import scala.util.parsing.combinator._
class ExamParser extends RegexParsers {
val int: Parser [Int] = "" "\ d +" "". r ^^ (_.toInt)
val studentname: Parser [String] = "" "[^ (] +" "". r ^^
(_.trim)
val matNr: Parser [Int] = "(" ~> int <~ "):"
val points: Parser [Int] =
int <~ "" "\ W * points? \ W * = \ W *" "". r
val mark: parser [float] =
"" "[123], [037] | 4, [03] | 5.0" "". R ^^
(_.replace (',', '.'). toFloat)
val oneExam: Parser [(Student, Int, Float)] =
student name ~ matNr ~ points ~ mark ^^ {
case name ~ no ~ points ~ mark
=> (new Student (name, no), points, mark)
}
val exam: Parser [List [(Student, Int, Float)]] =
```

```
repsep (oneExam, "" "\ W *" "". r)
}
```

We will now modify the ExamParserApp object from Listing 6.10 so that it instead of ExamParserString extends the ExamParser class (see Listing 6.12). The The rest remains unchanged.

Listing 6.12: The ExamParserApp object for parsing multiple records and a list of triples as a result

```
object ExamParserApp extends ExamParser {
def main (args: Array [String]) {
val examString =
"" "Mayr, Hubertus (123456): 90 points = 1.0
| Painter, Brigitte (876543): 86 points = 1.3
| Reimann, Gundolf (471112): 1 point = 5.0 "" ".
stripMargin
println (parseAll (exam, examString))
}
}
```

If we now execute the object, we get the following output:

```
[3.41] parsed: List ((Mayr, Hubertus (123456), 90,1.0), (
Maler, Brigitte (876543), 86,1.3), (Reimann, Gundolf
(471112), 1.5.0))
```

To extract the actual result from the ParseResult object, you can let's use the get method. That is, to continue working with the list for example we would use the two lines

```
val resultList: List [(Student, Int, Float)] =
parseAll (exam, examString) .get
```

insert into our program.

In addition to the parser combiners discussed, there are two more:

P | Q is the alternative. That is, if the parser P was successful, it returns he the result, otherwise the parser Q.

opt (P) is an options parser. If the parser P is successful and has the result nis x, opt (P) returns the value Some (x). Otherwise the result is None. This does not stop the parsing process.

6.5 A little bit of GUI

The standard Scala distribution does not come with its own GUI 14 library. othek, but with a package full of wrappers for the Java Swing classes in Package scala.swing. The aim of the developers is to provide a library that supports can be used in Scala in a very natural way and close enough to Java Swing remains so that Java programmers with Swing experience can use it well come.

To create a simple GUI, the abstract class Simple-SwingApplication can be used as the base class. The only abstract me-method that needs to be defined is the method:

```
def top: frame
```

Frames for the main window are represented by the MainFrame class. The simplest GUI can be generated by the program shown in Listing 6.13 will.

Listing 6.13: An empty window without a title

```
import scala.swing._
object MyGUI extends SimpleSwingApplication {
def top = new MainFrame
}
```

However, this GUI has neither a title nor any content. This can we change, for example by assigning a string to the title field. Listing 6.14 is the code for an empty window titled Scala Book GUI reproduced. The window created can be seen in Figure 6.3.

Listing 6.14: An empty window with a title

```
import scala.swing._
object MyGUI extends SimpleSwingApplication {
def top = new MainFrame {
title = "Scala book GUI"
}
}
```

Figure 6.3: An empty GUI window with a title

The window shown in Figure 6.3 first had to be "manually" because it defaults to a very small window in the top left corner of the screen opens. But this is also easy to change. The object defined in Listing 6.15 opens a 640x480 window, where the upper left corner has the coordinate (200,300). The numbers are clear as usual as a pixel.

Listing 6.15: An empty window with a title, a minimum size and a location

```
import scala.swing._
object MyGUI extends SimpleSwingApplication {
def top = new MainFrame {
title = "Scala book GUI"
location = new Point (200,300)
minimumSize = new Dimension (640, 480)
}
}
```

Menus and menu items are assigned to the menuBar field. To do this, Let's start with a MenuBar. We can compose the buffer content add nents. In the code in Listing 6.16, these are menus. These have again- a buffer content to which we can then add MenuItems. Finally, we attach actions to the MenuItems that are executed when the menu item was clicked.

Listing 6.16: An empty window with menu items and actions to exit and to Open a dialog window

```
import scala.swing._
object MyGUI extends SimpleSwingApplication {
def top = new MainFrame {
title = "Scala book GUI"
location = new Point (200,300)
minimumSize = new Dimension (640, 480)
val quitAction = Action ("Quit") {System.exit (0)}
val sayHelloAction = Action ("Say Hello") {
Dialog.showMessage (new FlowPanel, "Hello World!")
}
menuBar = new MenuBar {
contents + = new Menu ("File") {
contents + = new MenuItem (quitAction)
}
contents + = new Menu ("Misc") {
contents + = new MenuItem (sayHelloAction)
}
}
}
}
```

In Listing 6.16, we defined a GUI that has two menus. The File menu has the entry Quit, which terminates the program. The Misc menu has the wear Say Hello, which opens a dialog box in the Hello World! stands. The access stand after clicking the Say Hello menu item is shown in Figure 6.4.
After whole books can be filled with GUI programming, which we now only give one last, somewhat more complex example and then finish with it. A simple GUI is to be programmed for the addition of two numbers. The two numbers should be able to be entered in fields, and behind it is the result. As soon as something new has been entered in a field de, the result must also be recalculated. Figure 6.5 shows the program after entering 17 in the first field and 4 in the second.
All the code for this application is shown in Listing 6.17. For the one Given the two numbers, we take TextField objects. We write in that first at the beginning a 1 and in the second a 2. We use a for the result Label and set it to 3. In the MainFrame we take as contents a FlowPanel that contains five components: The text fields for the two numbers len, the label for the result and two more labels for the + between the Input numbers and the = in front of the result.

Listing 6.17: The Simple Adder GUI

```
import scala.swing._
import scala.swing.event._
object SimpleAdder extends SimpleSwingApplication {
val numberA = new TextField {
text = "1"
columns = 5
}
val numberB = new TextField {
text = "2"
columns = 5
}
val result = new Label ("3")
listenTo (numberA, numberB)
reactions + = {
case EditDone (_) =>
result.text = (numberA.text.toInt +
numberB.text.toInt) .toString
}
def top = new MainFrame {
title = "Simple Adder"
minimumSize = new Dimension (250, 20)
contents = new FlowPanel (numberA, new Label ("+"),
numberB, new Label ("="),
result)
}
}
```

In order to react to inputs, we use so-called events. The text field becomes after the input an event is generated to which we can react by using the Change the text in the result label.
In the SimpleSwingApplication there is a method listenTo with which we determine from whom we want to receive events. In Listing 6.17, these are the two text fields numberA and numberB. There are also the reactions, to which we can add a partial function as an additional response.
In our case this function is implemented in such a way that every EditDone-Event the text of result is recalculated.

Chapter 7

Actors - Concurrency and Multicore programming

Concurrent programming, especially using multiple cores increasingly becoming a standard task for software developers. That's because the processors no longer get faster, but that in a process sor more and more cores are located. A processor with very few cores can are usually still properly exploited by operating system processes the. Now, for example, two processes that were otherwise allowed to compute alternately can be allele work. But if there are more and more kernels, it becomes essential to divide the programs themselves into several processes or threads.

After Scala has been run on the Java Virtual Machine or on a .NET runtime is of course available from Java or .NET to concurrently (engl. *concurrent*). But Scala offers another very elegant one Possibility of abstraction based on a mathematical model of concurrent ger programming based: the *Actors* [1] .

There are implementations of the actor model in several programming languages up to actuator-based, *general purpose* programming languages such as ActorS script [2] . The syntax of the Scala implementation is heavily based on the Actor Implementation in the functional programming language Erlang [3] . Actors according to the Scala philosophy are not in the language core, but as a library available in the package scala.actors.

The basic idea of the actor model is that an actor interacts with other actors only about Messages communicated. If a message is sent to an actor, it lands in his mailbox and remains there until the actor picks it up. So that means, communication is basically asynchronous 4 .
In this chapter we give you an introduction to the world of the Scala Actors. We begin in Section 7.1 with the connection between Actors and Explain threads. Receiving and reacting to messages like an actor is shown in Section 7.2. Special actuators, namely reactors and demons, are the subject of Section 7.3. For actuators, a scheme is duling needed. Information on this can be found in Section 7.4. The chapter closes with a look at Remote Actors (see Section 7.5).

7.1 A thread is an actor

In Scala, every thread is also an actor. However, the reverse is not true because not every actor needs its own thread. To a concurrent task To do this, we usually use an actor in Scala. The simplest way Liability is the actor method of the scala.actors.Actor Companion object.
Listing 7.1 shows an example in which, in addition to the main thread, a second thread is generated by the actor method.

Listing 7.1: The TwoThreads object that creates a thread with the actor method

```
object TwoThreads {
def main (args: Array [String]) {
import scala.actors.Actor.actor
println ("Main: started")
actor {
println ("Actor: started")
for (i <- 1 to 4) {
Thread.sleep (1000)
println ("Actor:" + i)
}
println ("Actor: done")
}
for (i <- 1 to 4) {
Thread.sleep (1000)
println ("Main:" + i)
}
println ("Main: done")
}
}
```

The parameter of the actor function has the type => Unit. It's a by-name Parameter that is only executed in the actor function. Let's import the Method from the actor object and use curly braces for the gument, so actor even looks like a control structure. Everything in the argument ment, so it is executed in a separate thread. Let's run the object TwoThreads, we see something like the following on the console:

```
Main: started
Actor: started
Actor: 1
Main: 1
Actor: 2
Main: 2
Actor: 3
Main: 3
```

Main: 4
Actor: 4
Main: done
Actor: done

Although both threads sleep for 1000 milliseconds over and over again, the Management order not deterministic. As seen in the output above is, the outputs of the two threads are not strictly alternating. This means so, the behavior of the overall program is not deterministic. welcome in the world of threads!

As we have seen, the actor created with actor is also started immediately. This is also very pleasant in this case, but there is also the possibility Define an actor that must be started explicitly. We use the trait actor.

Listing 7.2: The ThreeThreads object with the MyActor inner class

```
object ThreeThreads {
import scala.actors.Actor
class MyActor (number: Int) extends Actor {
def act () {
println ("Actor" + number + ": started")
for (i <- 1 to 2) {
Thread.sleep (1000)
println ("Actor" + number + ":" + i)
}
println ("Actor" + number + ": done")
}
}
def main (args: Array [String]) {
println ("Main:
started ")
for (i <- 1 to 3)
new MyActor (i) .start ()
for (i <- 1 to 2) {
Thread.sleep (1000)
println ("Main:
"+ i)
}
println ("Main:
finished")
}
}
```

In Listing 7.2 we define the class MyActor, which adds the actor trait. In the actor trait there is a single abstract method that is implemented got to:

def act (): Unit

The body of the act method is executed as soon as the actor with the start Method is started. In Listing 7.2 we create 3 MyActor objects that we all start immediately. The output could then look like this.

Main:
started
Actor2: started
Actor3: started
Actor1: started
Main:
1

```
Actor2: 1
Actor1: 1
Actor3: 1
Main:
2
Main:
finished
Actor2: 2
Actor2: done
Actor1: 2
Actor3: 2
Actor1: done
Actor3: done
```

7.2 Receive and respond

As long as threads are independent of one another, they can also interact with other easy to generate. It becomes more difficult as soon as the threads a way to work together. In programming languages like Java this is usually done with shared data that is then Must be made thread-safe.

According to the actor model, no data is shared. Communication, and collaboration, works via messages. Here can a message can be any object. Case classes and -Objects or strings, tuples, etc. are used to use pattern matching on the measurement say to be able to react.

The! Method in the actor trait is used to send a message. That is, with the expression actor! message is assigned to the actor with the identifier actor the message message is sent. The message ends up in the actor's mailbox and stays there until the actor takes it out.

After every thread is an actor, we can move on to the main process of scaling Send a message to the shell itself, e.g. with:

```
scala> import scala.actors.Actor._
import scala.actors.Actor._
scala> self! "Hello"
```

The identifier self corresponds to a method from the Actor Companion Object that returns the actor that is currently running. The message "Hello" is now in the actor's mailbox. With the method:

```
def receive [A] (f: PartialFunction [Any, A]): A
```

We can receive the message from the actor trait and react to it. For example, in our interactive session it could look like this: hen:

```
scale> receive {
|
case msg => println ("Received message:" + msg)
| }
Received message: Hello
```

As can be seen in the type of receive method, the argument is a partial le function. That is, if we find a message in the mailbox, it doesn't matches the cases defined in receive, the message is simply ignored. For example, let's send the actor an Int, although it only works on Strings responds, the program does not crash, but continues to wait for a suitable Message is coming. This is done in the following session:

```
scala> self! 1
```

scale> receive {
|
case msg: String
|
=> println ("Received message:" + msg)
| }
If you try the last session yourself, you will find that the Shell waits indefinitely and no more prompts appear. The receive blocks until a suitable message is taken from the mailbox den can, that is, potentially infinite. After you get to the shell either, otherwise you have to explicitly cancel it at some point 5 .
To receive a message, receiveWithin can also be used to set a timeout Interval can be specified. After the specified period of time, the Actor sent the scala.actors.TIMEOUT object as a message. The actor can then react to it. Otherwise an exception is thrown.
Listing 7.3: The Timeout object with a MyActor class that uses the receive method Within uses

```
object timeout {
import scala.actors._
import scala.actors.Actor._
class MyActor (timeout: Long) extends Actor {
def act () {
println ("Actor started, waiting" +
timeout + "ms for strings")
receiveWithin (timeout) {
case msg: String =>
println ("Actor: received" + msg)
case TIMEOUT =>
println ("Actor: TIMEOUT")
}
}
}
def main (args: Array [String]) {
var myActor = new MyActor (100)
myActor.start ()
myActor! "Hello"
myActor = new MyActor (0)
myActor! "Hello Again"
myActor.start ()
myActor = new MyActor (100)
myActor.start ()
}
}
```

The MyActor class in Listing 7.3 uses receiveWithin and responds with a own case on the TIMEOUT object. If the object is executed, we see one such or similar output:

```
Actor started, waiting 100ms for strings
Actor started, waiting 0ms for strings
Actor started, waiting 100ms for strings
Actor: received Hello Again
Actor: received Hello
Actor: TIMEOUT
```

The TIMEOUT object is a completely normal object. So we don't have to respond with a special case. For example, if we replace the receive

Within block from Listing 7.3 as follows:

```
receiveWithin (timeout) {
case msg => println ("Actor: received" + msg)
}
```

and react to every message and no longer just to msg: String,
we get the last issue:

```
Actor: received TIMEOUT
```

We can also react to several messages with one actor. In Listing 7.4 an actor is shown that first sends a string, then an int as a message want to process. It is not important which message arrives first. The actor blocks until it has received a string message. The subsequently required int message is already in its before the string message Mailbox arrived and can then be removed second.

Listing 7.4: The TwoMessages object with an actor that contains two receive blocks

```
object TwoMessages {
import scala.actors._
import scala.actors.Actor._
class MyActor extends Actor {
def act () {
receive {
case msg: String =>
println ("Actor: got String:" + msg)
}
receive {
case i: Int =>
println ("Actor: got Int:" + i)
}
}
}
def main (args: Array [String]) {
val myActor = new MyActor
myActor.start ()
myActor! 1
myActor! "Hello"
}
}
```

If we execute the object TwoMessages, we see the following output on the Console:

```
Actor: got String: Hello
Actor: got Int: 1
```

We can also use a receive block in a loop for multiple messages respond to each other. In Listing 4.7 on page 57 we had a shared Counter object that represents a counter that is used by all objects of the SharedCounter class is shared. In Listing 7.5 we show same approach with an actor.

Listing 7.5: An application with a SharedCounter-Actor

```
object counter {
import scala.actors._
import scala.actors.Actor._
case object increment
case object value
case object stop
object SharedCounter extends Actor {
private [this] var count = 0
```

```
def act () {
var continue = true
while (continue) {
receive {
case increment => count + = 1
case value => sender! count
case Stop => continue = false
}
}
}
}
def printValueOfSharedCounter () = {
SharedCounter! Value
receiveWithin (100) {
case i: Int =>
println ("value of shared counter:" + i)
case TIMEOUT =>
println ("shared counter not available")
}
}
def main (args: Array [String]) {
SharedCounter! Increment
SharedCounter! Increment
SharedCounter.start ()
printValueOfSharedCounter ()
SharedCounter! Increment
printValueOfSharedCounter ()
SharedCounter! Stop
SharedCounter! Increment
printValueOfSharedCounter ()
SharedCounter.restart ()
printValueOfSharedCounter ()
SharedCounter! Stop
}
}
```

First we define three case objects for the various messages. The SharedCounter object has a variable count that is used to count and de- defines the act method. This time, however, should not only receive a message but all messages up to the message stop. We do this with a a while loop and a flag.

When the message increment is received, count is incremented. At Value becomes the sender of the message, which can be determined with the method sender can return the current value of count. If you stop, continue set to false and thus the act method and the entire actor terminated.

The method printValueOfSharedCounter is used to query and give the current SharedCounter value. After we finished at one SharedCounter don't want to wait indefinitely, we use receiveWithin and define a response to TIMEOUT.

Finally, in the main method, we increment, start and stop the SharedCounter. An actor that has already started and stopped can be start again. We also ask the current one four times Stand off. If we run the Count object, we see the following on the console- de issues:

value of shared counter: 2

value of shared counter: 3
shared counter not available
value of shared counter: 4

Although the SharedCounter only works after two incremental Messages was started, the messages were not lost. Even after We can stop sending messages, but we don't get any Answer more. After restarting, the actor processes the intermediate messages arrived in time.

A disadvantage of the SharedCounter approach with an actor, as we see it in Listing 7.5 is the fact that we care for every message the Actor processed, must switch to the thread of the actor. this means Overhead and, for example, if we use several such actors, resources Waste of resources because everyone uses their own thread. We can do this first of all by sprinkling Thread.currentThread outputs clear.

Listing 7.6: An application with many SharedCounter-Actor and outputs, which Thread is currently running

```
object Counter2 {
import scala.actors._
import scala.actors.Actor._
case object increment
case object stop
class SharedCounter (i: Int) extends Actor {
private [this] var count = 0
def act () {
var continue = true
while (continue) {
receive {
case increment => {
println ("Actor" + i + ":" + Thread.currentThread)
count + = 1
}
case Stop => continue = false
}
}
}
}
def main (args: Array [String]) {
val counters = for (i <- 0 to 9)
yield new SharedCounter (i)
for (i <- 0 to 9) counters (i) .start ()
for (i <- 0 to 9) counters (i)! Increment
for (i <- 0 to 9) counters (i)! Increment
Thread.sleep (1000)
for (i <- 0 to 9) counters (i)! Stop
}
}
```

Listing 7.6 shows a modified version of Listing 7.5. Instead of an object SharedCounter we define a class SharedCounter. The act method in response to the increment message, we have an output of the current ellen threads added. The return of the value of count and the output We have omitted gabe for the sake of clarity. In order to generate To be able to differentiate between the ten SharedCounter, we use a class Parameter, which we then also output.

We create ten SharedCounter objects, start them and send each one twice the message increment. Before we stop them, let's put the main Thread sleep a while. If we didn't, threads from the Thread pool can be reused because an actor may already have ended, before another is even started 6 .
If we run the Counter2 object, we see the following or a similar input on the console:

```
Actor 0: Thread [ForkJoinPool-1-worker-3,5, main]
Actor 1: Thread [ForkJoinPool-1-worker-1,5, main]
Actor 2: Thread [ForkJoinPool-1-worker-2,5, main]
Actor 3: Thread [ForkJoinPool-1-worker-0,5, main]
Actor 0: Thread [ForkJoinPool-1-worker-3,5, main]
Actor 3: Thread [ForkJoinPool-1-worker-0,5, main]
Actor 2: Thread [ForkJoinPool-1-worker-2,5, main]
Actor 1: Thread [ForkJoinPool-1-worker-1,5, main]
Actor 4: Thread [ForkJoinPool-1-worker-4,5, main]
Actor 4: Thread [ForkJoinPool-1-worker-4,5, main]
Actor 5: Thread [ForkJoinPool-1-worker-5,5, main]
Actor 5: Thread [ForkJoinPool-1-worker-5,5, main]
Actor 6: Thread [ForkJoinPool-1-worker-6,5, main]
Actor 6: Thread [ForkJoinPool-1-worker-6,5, main]
Actor 7: Thread [ForkJoinPool-1-worker-7,5, main]
Actor 7: Thread [ForkJoinPool-1-worker-7,5, main]
Actor 8: Thread [ForkJoinPool-1-worker-8,5, main]
Actor 8: Thread [ForkJoinPool-1-worker-8,5, main]
Actor 9: Thread [ForkJoinPool-1-worker-9,5, main]
Actor 9: Thread [ForkJoinPool-1-worker-9,5, main]
```

The essence of the output is that each actor has its own thread. So ten different threads appear in the output.
Scala offers a very easy 7 way to program actors that they don't need their own thread. We just have to react or Use reactWithin instead of receive or receiveWithin. The basic idea is that the reaction to a message is decoupled from the context. That means it must only a few instructions are executed, but no context is established. This means that any thread can be used to create the instructions. perform sings.
A special feature resulting from this approach is that calling react never returns. That means, unlike receive, react does not give Result back, and code that comes after the react is never executed. In particular, this also means that a react is not embedded in a loop can be. The end of the loop is never reached, and neither can anyone give second pass of loop.

Listing 7.7: An application with many SharedCounter-Actors that use react

```
object Counter3 {
import scala.actors._
import scala.actors.Actor._
case object increment
case object stop
class SharedCounter (i: Int) extends Actor {
def act () = act (0)
def act (count: Int) {
react {
case increment => {
println ("Actor" + i + ":" + Thread.currentThread)
```

```
act (count + 1)
}
case stop =>
}
// this will never be executed
println ("Actor" + i + "stopped")
}
}
def main (args: Array [String]) {
val counters = for (i <- 0 to 9)
yield new SharedCounter (i)
for (i <- 0 to 9) counters (i) .start ()
for (i <- 0 to 9) counters (i)! Increment
for (i <- 0 to 9) counters (i)! Increment
Thread.sleep (1000)
for (i <- 0 to 9) counters (i)! Stop
}
}
```

In Listing 7.7 we changed the code of the SharedCounter class so that that the react method is used instead of receive. After we're not at the while loop, we recursively call act again, since we are for the counter can no longer use any changeable variables. Therefore define we have a method act that receives the current counter reading as an argument. We start with the count 0. If the message Stop is received, must we do nothing. But it is important that we react to Stop, otherwise it would Actor keep waiting. If we run the Counter3 object, we see that the println expression after the react block is never evaluated:

```
Actor 0: Thread [ForkJoinPool-1-worker-1,5, main]
Actor 3: Thread [ForkJoinPool-1-worker-3,5, main]
Actor 0: Thread [ForkJoinPool-1-worker-1,5, main]
Actor 3: Thread [ForkJoinPool-1-worker-3,5, main]
Actor 4: Thread [ForkJoinPool-1-worker-1,5, main]
Actor 5: Thread [ForkJoinPool-1-worker-3,5, main]
Actor 4: Thread [ForkJoinPool-1-worker-1,5, main]
Actor 5: Thread [ForkJoinPool-1-worker-3,5, main]
Actor 6: Thread [ForkJoinPool-1-worker-1,5, main]
Actor 7: Thread [ForkJoinPool-1-worker-3,5, main]
Actor 6: Thread [ForkJoinPool-1-worker-1,5, main]
Actor 7: Thread [ForkJoinPool-1-worker-3,5, main]
Actor 8: Thread [ForkJoinPool-1-worker-1,5, main]
Actor 9: Thread [ForkJoinPool-1-worker-3,5, main]
Actor 8: Thread [ForkJoinPool-1-worker-1,5, main]
Actor 9: Thread [ForkJoinPool-1-worker-3,5, main]
Actor 2: Thread [ForkJoinPool-1-worker-2,5, main]
Actor 1: Thread [ForkJoinPool-1-worker-0,5, main]
Actor 1: Thread [ForkJoinPool-1-worker-0,5, main]
Actor 2: Thread [ForkJoinPool-1-worker-0,5, main]
```

Also, in the output above, we can see that for all ten Actors only four threads were used. This means that the approach with react requires uses significantly fewer resources. We can even take it to the extreme and let all actors run in the main thread (see Section 7.4). We also see that for example Actor 2 for the two independent Reactions uses two different threads.

The presented approach with react is even a bit nicer because there are no changeable variables can be used. But there are several cases in the react Blocks that end with a recursive call have the potential risk of to forget one of them. As a way out, the actor class provides the two methods the loop and loopWhile are available. With that we can do the code again make it look a bit more imperative [8].

Listing 7.8: The SharedCounter class with react and loopWhile

```
class SharedCounter (i: Int) extends Actor {
private [this] var count = 0
def act () {
var continue = true
loopWhile (continue) {
react {
case increment => {
println ("Actor" + i + ":" + Thread.currentThread)
count + = 1
}
case Stop => continue = false
}
}
println ("Actor" + i + "stopped") // never reached
}
}
```

8 ... if we really want that ;-).

Listing 7.8 shows the SharedCounter class using react and loopWhile. The code looks much like it did in Listing 7.6, with while through loopWhile and receive have been replaced by react. But here too the Output after the loopWhile block never executed.

So far we have only communicated with an actor via asynchronous messages. A reply also came as a message, which we explicitly use receive or react had to receive. There is still another possibility to send the answer directly to a Assign a draftsman even though it does not yet exist. We use for Send instead of the method! the method !!, we get a future object back. This encapsulates the value that will come back as an answer in the future becomes. We don't have to change anything on the actor itself.

Listing 7.9: An application with a SharedCounter object and access to the response word about a future

```
object FutureCounter {
import scala.actors._
import scala.actors.Actor._
case object increment
case object value
case object stop
object SharedCounter extends Actor {
private [this] var count = 0
def act () {
var continue = true
while (continue) {
receive {
case increment => count + = 1
case value => {
println ("SharedCounter is sleeping")
Thread.sleep (1000)
println ("SharedCounter is awake")
Channel ! count
}
```

```
case Stop => continue = false
}
}
}
}
def main (args: Array [String]) {
SharedCounter.start ()
SharedCounter! Increment
SharedCounter! Increment
val value = SharedCounter !! Value
println ("Value-request sent")
println ("Value =" + value)
println ("Value =" + value ())
SharedCounter! Stop
}
}
```

Listing 7.9 shows how the response can be accessed using a future object. We use the same SharedCounter object as in Listing 7.5 with an addition three lines in the response to the Value object. This addition is for illustrative purposes only. The actor is called with Thread.sleep put to sleep, with status messages on the console before and after are given.

In the main method we send the Message Value to the SharedCounter the !! method and assign the result to the identifier value. Subsequent At the end we output value with and without an empty pair of brackets. Let's leave that Application, we see the following output:

```
Value request sent
Value = <function0>
SharedCounter is sleeping
SharedCounter is awake
Value = 2
```

The output of value without curly braces is immediate, and as < function0 > . This means that value is a 0-digit Function. If we use value (), value.apply () is actually evaluated. tet. After it is a future, this call blocks until the value is available, i.e. until the SharedCounter has woken up, the answer and it can be called up in the mailbox. With value.isSet you can rigens to check whether the value is already available.

7.3 Demons and Reactors

Scala also offers some special actors. The DaemonActor offers the same Interface like the actor. The difference is that an application is also then is terminated if there are still running DaemonActors. On current actors is being serviced. That is, if we don't all have the SharedCounter objects the message stop had ended, the application could never have ended overall will.

After a SharedCounter is an auxiliary object that is not an end in itself exists, it makes perfect sense to implement it as a DaemonActor. In Listing 7.10 is an implementation of the SharedCounter as a DaemonActor.

Listing 7.10: An application with many SharedCounter DaemonActors

```
object Counter5 {
import scala.actors._
import scala.actors.Actor._
```

```
case object increment
case object value
object SharedCounter extends DaemonActor {
def act () = act (0)
def act (count: Int) {
react {
case increment => act (count + 1)
case value => {
Channel ! count
act (count)
}
}
}
}
def main (args: Array [String]) {
SharedCounter.start ()
SharedCounter! Increment
SharedCounter! Increment
SharedCounter! Value
receive {
case i => println ("Value =" + i)
}
}
}
```

This time the SharedCounter is implemented directly as an object again. Since it's a DaemonActor, we don't have to shut it down. We start the SharedCounter and use it. Although it is still running, the program will successfully completed after output of Value 2. So we don't have to explicitly End zit, for example with a stop message.

A reactor is a very lightweight actor. The different characteristics of the reactor versus the actor are:

The sender is not transmitted implicitly with the message.

There is only react, no receive, ie no exclusive thread.

The reactor manages less state than the actor.

If a sender should be transmitted, the Subtrait ReplyReactor can be used. The Trait Reactor still needs a type parameter for which as Lower Bound Zero is specified. Otherwise we can use the reactor analog to use as an actor.

Listing 7.11: An application with a StringBuildReactor

```
object StringBuildReactor {
import scala.actors.Reactor
import scala.actors.Actor._
object MyStringBuildReactor extends Reactor [String] {
def act () = act (new StringBuilder)
def act (str: StringBuilder) {
react {
case      => println (str)
case s => act (str ++ = s)
}
}
}
def main (args: Array [String]) {
MyStringBuildReactor.start ()
"Hello world and hello reader!" split
```

```
"" map
{str => str.head.toUpper + str.tail} foreach
{MyStringBuildReactor! _}
MyStringBuildReactor! ""
}
}
```
Listing 7.11 shows an example of a reactor. The MyString BuildReactor only receives strings and appends them with a string Builders at each other. If the empty string is sent, it returns the entire chain and ends.

After the reactor has started, the words from the specified A string sent individually. Before that, the first letter in each case is converted into a Converted to uppercase. Then the empty string is sent det. The output is then:

HelloWorldAndHelloReader!

7.4 Scheduler

Some schedulers are defined in the package scala.actors.scheduler. As we seen in some editions in section 7.2, the default is the ForkJoinScheduler used. This scheduler manages a lot of Threads (*thread pool*) in which the individual actors can run. In Listing 7.7 on page 204 we used react to get the actors to only few threads to use. In the sample output there were four threads. Speech-let's define the scheduler method from the trait actor with a single ThreadedScheduler object, all actors will run in just one thread.

Listing 7.12: An application with many SharedCounter-Actors, which in a thread to run

```
object Counter6 {
import scala.actors._
import scala.actors.Actor._
case object increment
case object stop
class SharedCounter (i: Int) extends Actor {
import scala.actors.scheduler.SingleThreadedScheduler
override def scheduler = new SingleThreadedScheduler
def act () = act (0)
def act (count: Int) {
react {
case increment => {
println ("Actor" + i + ":" + Thread.currentThread)
act (count + 1)
}
case stop =>
}
}
}
def main (args: Array [String]) {
val counters = for (i <- 0 to 9)
yield new SharedCounter (i)
for (i <- 0 to 9) counters (i) .start ()
for (i <- 0 to 9) counters (i)! Increment
for (i <- 0 to 9) counters (i)! Increment
Thread.sleep (1000)
```

for (i <- 0 to 9) counters (i)! Stop
}
}
In Listing 7.12, we redefined the scheduler method. Let's leave them Counter6 application, we see output like the following:

Actor 0: Thread [main, 5, main]
Actor 1: Thread [main, 5, main]
Actor 2: Thread [main, 5, main]
Actor 3: Thread [main, 5, main]
Actor 4: Thread [main, 5, main]
Actor 5: Thread [main, 5, main]
Actor 6: Thread [main, 5, main]
Actor 7: Thread [main, 5, main]
Actor 8: Thread [main, 5, main]
Actor 9: Thread [main, 5, main]
Actor 0: Thread [main, 5, main]
Actor 1: Thread [main, 5, main]
Actor 2: Thread [main, 5, main]
Actor 3: Thread [main, 5, main]
Actor 4: Thread [main, 5, main]
Actor 5: Thread [main, 5, main]
Actor 6: Thread [main, 5, main]
Actor 7: Thread [main, 5, main]
Actor 8: Thread [main, 5, main]
Actor 9: Thread [main, 5, main]

That means, all actors run in the main thread. Besides the two featured there are also the following schedulers:
the ResizableThreadPoolScheduler which, as the name suggests, has one Use thread pool. The thread pool is increased if necessary, for example if many actors should run in their own thread.
The DaemonScheduler as the standard scheduler for the DaemonActors.
Instead of redefining the scheduler method in each actor, the JVM can Property actors.enableForkJoin can be set to false. This becomes the ResizableThreadPoolScheduler as the standard scheduler for actors. Au-
There is also the property actors.corePoolSize for changing the Size of the thread pool used.

7.5 Remote Actors

With the package scala.actors.remote, actors can easily made available over the network. To do this, the object defines RemoteActor some methods that we want to introduce below.
To bind an actor to a port, there is the alive method. The me-
method register registers an actor under one name. In this way several actors can be addressed under one port with different names will be.

Listing 7.13: The RemoteActor object, which has two actors under different names Exposes port 9010

case object stop
object RemoteActor {
import scala.actors.Actor. {
actor, loop While, react, self}
import scala.actors.remote.RemoteActor. {

```
alive, register}
def remoteActor (name: String, remoteName: Symbol) =
actor {
alive (9010)
register (remoteName, self)
println (name + ": Waiting for messages ...")
var continue = true
loopWhile (continue) {
react {
case stop => {
println (name + ": Exiting")
continue = false
}
case i: Int => println (name + ":" + i + ": Int")
case msg => println (name + ":" + msg)
}
}
}
def main (args: Array [String]) {
remoteActor ("Echo1", 'echo1)
remoteActor ("Echo2", 'echo2)
}
}
```

An example of two RemoteActors is shown in Listing 7.13. To the To be able to stop the actor, we define a Case object stop. The same defi- we will also refer to the client code below.

In order to use two actors of the same kind, we implement a remoteActor-Method that we use the name (for local output) and the network name (for registration) handed over. The network name must be an icon. The Actor is started immediately by using the actor method. He will registered under port 9010 and the transferred network name.

It then issues a status message and waits for messages. There He differentiates between the object Stop, Ints and all other messages.

If we start the program, we see the two lines

```
Echo2: Waiting for messages ...
Echo1: Waiting for messages ...
```

in that order or vice versa on the console. After clicking on Messages waited, the shell does not return to the prompt.

On the client side, we use the select method to access a remote Actor to access. As arguments we need a node with network werkname or IP address and the port as well as the name under which the RemoteActor is registered, again as an icon.

Listing 7.14: The SendToRemoteActor object that sends messages to two different RemoteActors sends under different names on the same node

```
case object stop
object SendToRemoteActor extends Application {
import scala.actors.Actor.actor
import scala.actors.remote.Node
import scala.actors.remote.RemoteActor.select
val node = Node ("127.0.0.1", 9010)
actor {
val c = select (node, 'echo1)
val d = select (node, 'echo2)
c! "Hello RemoteActor"
```

```
d! "Hello RemoteActor"
for (i <- 1 to 10) {
c! i
d! i
}
c! Stop
d! Stop
}
}
```

In Listing 7.14, we showed the client side. To stop the RemoteActors To be able to pen, the case object Stop is defined first. In the application an actor with actor is generated, which sends the RemoteActors messages. To use a RemoteActor, the select method is used with the Node and the name used as arguments. Then the two alternately sent some messages. After both have received stop, the application that provides the RemoteActors is terminated. Before that was still output the following:

```
Echo2: Hello RemoteActor
Echo1: Hello RemoteActor
Echo1: 1: Int
Echo1: 2: Int
Echo1: 3: Int
Echo1: 4: Int
Echo1: 5: Int
Echo1: 6: Int
Echo1: 7: Int
Echo1: 8: Int
Echo1: 9: Int
Echo1: 10: Int
Echo2: 1: Int
Echo2: 2: Int
Echo2: 3: Int
Echo2: 4: Int
Echo1: Exiting
Echo2: 5: Int
Echo2: 6: Int
Echo2: 7: Int
Echo2: 8: Int
Echo2: 9: Int
Echo2: 10: Int
Echo2: Exiting
```

The actors model is also used in the Akka framework, which we will show you in chapter 11.

Chapter 8
Software quality - Document and test

Good code alone is not enough. Even when programming languages like Scala well suited to programming understandably, the source code should be carefully be documented. And not only when it comes to software, to be passed on. Carefully documented means not too much and not to less. In particular, the Application Programming Interface (API), i.e. anything that can be used from outside should be described as can be understood easily and without great effort.
High quality software has as few errors as possible. To prove this is Not possible in many areas, but at least too expensive. Although it is very good approaches in the field of formal methods 1 are rarely found their way into the normal programming routine.
In any case, the software must be tested. In small terms, that means for many programmers "try it out a little". That is certainly helpful, yes however, it is better to specify test cases and execute them automatically to let. This should basically go hand in hand with the programming. A test Driven development in which the tests are written first and then the software is one of the "high schools" in this area.
In this chapter we deal with the API documentation and testing. The focus is on how Scala is documented and how the available test frameworks are used. In from-Section 8.1 starts with the use of Scaladoc. The following three sections introduce the essential Scala test frameworks, which by the way

all can also be used for testing Java code. ScalaCheck (see Section 8.2) is a framework with which test data is automatically generated can be. The framework that most of the different types of Tests that can be performed is ScalaTest (see Section 8.3). The capital tel ends with the description of the Specs framework, a BDD 2 library (it- see section 8.4). To compare the test frameworks, we develop all possible tests for a very simple software for managing video stores. These are available as an Sbt project at http://github.com/obcode/moviestore_ test frameworks available.

8.1 Scaladoc

We already presented the Scaladoc tool in Section 2.1.3. Well want we will bring you closer to how you can document in the source code- nen. Comments that are automatically included in the API documentation with Scaladoc are to be taken, two conditions must be met:

Scaladoc comments must start with / ** and end with * /. You can- extend over several lines. Usually we start the new en lines with *.

Scaladoc comments can only be correctly assigned if they are attached to meaningful places:

- **in** front of a class, a trait or an object definition (class, trait, object)
- **in** front of a package object, not in front of a package (package object)
- before a member definition (def, val, var)
- before type member definition (type)

Annotations and modifiers must be placed between the Scaladoc comment and the respective keyword can be placed.

Scaladoc supports the following wiki syntax:

Inline elements

- Italic font: " text " becomes *text* .
- bold font: " 'text' " becomes **text** .
- Underline: __text__ becomes text.
- Monospace: 'text' becomes text.
- Superscript text: ^ text ^ becomes
text
.
- Subscript: ,, text ,, becomes *text* .
- Entity Links: [[scala.collection.Set]] becomes a link to the entity.
- external links: [[http://obraun.net/ Oliver Braun's website]] becomes a link that is displayed as "Oliver Braun's website".

Block elements

- Paragraphs: begin or end with a blank line
- Source code: starts with {{{and ends with}}}
- Headings: Through = before and after the text. A = corresponds to the first Level, two = the second etc.

Enumerations: sequence of similar enumeration elements without break

- Disordered bullet items: begins with at least one space chen and -. As long as the same number of leading spaces are used, we are on the same level. More spaces mean a sublevel.
- Ordered enumeration elements: As unordered with 1., I., I., A. or a. in front of *all* elements, for example

/ **

* 1st first
* 1st second
* /
to
1. first
2nd second
The individual stars on the left are ignored. That is, one line which only contains an asterisk and a space is treated as a blank line, and the stars are not included in the source code.
HTML elements are only supported for backward compatibility and should no longer be used. Earlier versions of Scaladoc under-
do not yet support wiki syntax.
Scaladoc supports various so-called *tags* . A Scaladoc comment is structured in such a way that a descriptive part can come first and then a series of tags. A day begins with an @ sign followed by a Identifier. Depending on the day, the first following word has a special meaning. The content of the day ends with the comment or the beginning of the next Tags. The following tags are supported by the current Scaladoc version:
Parameter tags
- @param <name> <body>: Describes the parameter with the identifier <name>.
- @tparam <name> <body>: Describes the type parameter with the description draftsman <name>.
- @return <body>: Describes what is returned (only for methods allowed).
- @throws <name> <body>: Describes an exception of the type <name>, thrown by the method or constructor.
Usage tags
- @see <body>: Refers to another place for more information.
- @note <body>: Describes preconditions and postconditions or restrictions requirements or requirements.
- @example <body>: Example usage and associated description.
Inventory tags
- @author <author>: The author. If there are several authors for each one same day.
- @version <version>: Version of the commented artifact.
- @since <version>: Since which version included.
- @deprecated <body>: Marks the artifact as obsolete. In the current Scaladoc version it is crossed out.
Other tags
- @todo <body>: Documented something that has not yet been implemented.
If a member is inherited from a class or a trait, the Scaladoc comment adopted. Individual areas, the free description or tags can be overwritten.
It is also possible to define macros. With
@define <name> <body>
a macro with the name <name> is defined. So then everyone will Deposits of $ <name> in comments related unit 3 by <body> replaced. Macros are also inherited and can be overwritten.

Listing 8.1: A class with Scaladoc comments

```
/ **
*
* This class is ``documented''
*
```

```
* 1. first about this class
*
- sublevel
*
- so
* 1. second about this class
* 1. third
*
* $ ob
* @ version 1.0
*
* @ define ob @ author Oliver Braun [[mailto : ob @ obraun.net
"<ob @ obraun.net>]]
* @ define DC [[org.obraun.scala.DocumentedClass]]
* /
class DocumentedClass (val id: Int) extends
DocumentedTrait {
DocumentedClass.ids + = id
/ **
* The ID type.
* /
type ID = Int
/ **
* Another constructor without any params.
* /
def this () = this (0)
/ **
* Create new $ DC object with the sum of
* 'this.id' and 'that.id' as id.
*
* @ todo something to do
* @ param that another
* $ DC object
*
* @ return new DocumentedClass-object
* /
def + (that: DocumentedClass) = {
val newID = this.id + that.id
if (DocumentedClass ids newID)
throw DocumentedClassObjectExistsException
new DocumentedClass (this.id + that.id)
}
def abstractMethod [T <: AnyVal] (x: T) = id
/ **
* @ deprecated will be removed in 5 years
* /
val x = 7
/ **
* The 'toString' method
*
* {{{
* println (DocumentedClass (19))
*}}}
*
```

*/
override def toString = "DocumentedClass-Object #" + id
}
Listing 8.1 shows sample documentation for a DocumentedClass class that uses various features of Scaladoc. The generated documentation mentation can be seen in Figure 8.1.
A good source to learn more about the look and feel of Scaladoc too learn are the sources and API documentation pages of the Scala distribution.
Below we'll be starting on the various testing frameworks with ScalaCheck.

8.2 ScalaCheck

The first tool for automating unit tests that we introduce to you want is ScalaCheck [4]. ScalaCheck emerged as a port of QuickCheck [5], has but meanwhile also features that are not available in QuickCheck.

8.2.1 Basics

The main idea is to check *properties* using automatic table generated test data. The property is the test unit in ScalaCheck. To the We start creating a property with the org.scalacheck method.
Prop.forAll, which has a function as a parameter and represents a property that should apply to all input values. For example, we can use the communication Specify the tative law for the addition of two whole numbers as follows:
forAll {(a: Int, b: Int) => a + b == b + a}
Mathematically, we would only write this in a different syntax. To make such a perty now simply to check in the Scala shell, we first have to check the ScalaCheck jar file from http://code.google.com/p/scalacheck/ underload. Then we start the Scala shell with
$ scala -cp scalacheck-version.jar
where version is intended as a placeholder for the current version. Now we can define and check the property:

```
scala> import org.scalacheck.Prop.forAll
import org.scalacheck.Prop.forAll
scala> val propCommutativePlus = forAll {
|
(a: Int, b: Int) => a + b == b + a
| }
propCommutative: org.scalacheck.Prop = Prop
scala> propCommutativePlus.check
+ OK, passed 100 tests.
```

After we have defined the property, we can use the method check check. As we can see in the issue, ScalaCheck has made 100 tests carried out successfully. This means that random data were generated for 100 cases and checked the property for this. Of course, this is not proof! It could It may well be that there are not considered cases for which the property is not applies. Conversely, we can prove that the property does not apply as soon as a Test fails. To demonstrate this, we claim that one list is the same remains when we reverse them with reverse;

```
scala> val propReverse = forAll {
|
(l: List [AnyVal]) => l reverse == l
| }
propReverse: org.scalacheck.Prop = Prop
```

```
scala> propReverse.check
! Falsified after 2 passed tests.
> ARG_0: List ("- 100", "true")
```

We see that the property is not holding up. Interestingly, ScalaCheck has this can only be determined during the second test. The first generated list has the claim not yet refuted. ScalaCheck also shows with which list the Property was falsified: List (-100, true).

Sometimes it is necessary or desirable to narrow the test area ken. Let's consider the following property:

```
forAll {(a: BigInt, b: BigInt) => a * b / b == a}
```

So of course this only makes sense for b! = 0. Using the implication operator ==> this can be formulated:

```
forAll {(a: BigInt, b: BigInt) =>
b! = 0 ==> (a * b / b == a)
}
```

If the condition cannot be met or is very difficult to meet, the property not to be tested. ScalaCheck then stops, as in the following session can be seen:

```
scala> import org.scalacheck.Prop._
import org.scalacheck.Prop._
scale> val propTrivial = forAll {
|
(a: Int, b: Int) => a == b ==> (b == a)
| }
propTrivial: org.scalacheck.Prop = Prop
scala> propTrivial.check
! Gave up after only 5 passed tests. 500 tests were
discarded.
```

Properties can be combined with &&, ||, ==, all and atLeastOne. For two properties p and q hold:

p && q holds if p and q hold.
p || q holds when p or q hold.
p == q holds if p holds exactly where q holds.
all (p, q) corresponds to p && q.
atLeastOne (p, q) corresponds to p || q.

Especially when combining several properties into one, the information is mation interesting what exactly caused the test to fail. To properties can be created using one of the two methods |: and: | With be provided with a label. This is then displayed in the output. The Label is on the side of the | and the property on the side of the:.

Listing 8.2: A property with labels

```
import org.scalacheck.Prop._
val labeledProp = forAll {(a: String, b: String) =>
val res = a + b
("String =" + res |: all (
"length" |: res.length == a.length + b.length,
"reverse" |: res.reverse == b.reverse + a.reverse,
"head" |: a.length> 0 ==> (res.head == a.head),
"headWrong" |: b.length> 0 ==> (res.head == b.head)
)
)
}
```

Listing 8.2 shows a property with labels. Let's test the property, se- we hen a 6 in the Scala shell:

```
scala> labeledProp.check
! Falsified after 0 passed tests.
> Labels of failing property:
headWrong
String = HelloWorld
> ARG_0: Hello
> ARG_1: World
```

The Properties class is ideal for testing several properties at once at. The class itself is also a property that applies when everyone is in it contained properties apply. Listing 8.3 shows an example.

6 We added the strings Hello and World used in the output ourselves. Due to of Unicode, in numerous attempts in the Scala shell, only Asian characters were always closed see :-).

Listing 8.3: A ScalaCheck specification

```
import org.scalacheck._
object MyScalaCheckSpec extends Properties ("Int-Tests") {
import Prop.forAll
property ("Commutativity Plus") = forAll {
(i: Int, j: Int) => i + j == j + i
}
property ("Commutativity Mult") = forAll {
(i: Int, j: Int) => i * j == j * i
}
property ("Associativity Plus") = forAll {
(i: Int, j: Int, k: Int) => (i + j) + k == i + (j + k)
}
property ("Associativity Mult") = forAll {
(i: Int, j: Int, k: Int) => (i * j) * k == i * (j * k)
}
property ("Distributivity") = forAll {
(i: Int, j: Int, k: Int) => i * (j + k) == (i * j) + (i * k)
}
}
```

We can then simply translate and extract the MyScalaCheckSpec object. to lead:

```
$ fsc -cp scalacheck-version.jar MyScalaCheckSpec
$ scala -cp scalacheck-version.jar :. MyScalaCheckSpec
+ Int-Tests.Commutativity Plus: OK, passed 100 tests.
+ Int-Tests.Commutativity Mult: OK, passed 100 tests.
+ Int-Tests.Associativity Plus: OK, passed 100 tests.
+ Int-Tests.Associativity Mult: OK, passed 100 tests.
+ Int-Tests.Distributivity: OK, passed 100 tests.
```

The include method can be used to insert one Properties object into another will. This allows test cases to be assigned systematically at first and later test by using include as a single Properties object.

8.2.2 Generators

An essential part of the ScalaCheck framework are the generators for the Generation of the random values that are used in the tests. For the Data types previously used in the properties, the generators are already part of ScalaCheck. To implement new generators, there is a some basic functions and combiners. With the function choose des org.-scalacheck.Gen objects can take random values from an Int, Long, or Double interval can be generated. You can use for-Komprehension several can then be combined to form a new value. For example, can the following tupleGen generator generates tuples, the first of which Components between 10 and 20. The second component is then between between twice and three times the first component. With the me- method sample we can generate a tuple:

```
scala> import org.scalacheck.Gen._
import org.scalacheck.Gen._
scala> val tupleGen = for {
|
a <- choose (10.20)
|
b <- choose (2 * a, 3 * a)
| } yield (a, b)
tupleGen: org.scalacheck.Gen [(Int, Int)] = Gen ()
scala> tupleGen.sample
res0: Option [(Int, Int)] = Some ((17,37))
```

As can be seen, the tuple is returned as an option. This applies to all generators. In addition to choose, there is also oneOf and frequency. With both will from given values a random one is returned. This is what happens with oneOf for all with the same probability, with frequency the relative frequency can be specified as an int for each value. With

```
val stringGen1 = oneOf ("Hello", "World", "and", "Reader")
```

each time the generator is accessed, one of the four strings is returned, and on average everyone equally often. With

```
val stringGen2 = frequency (
(4, "Hello"),
(2, "World"),
(1, "and"),
(3, "Reader")
)
```

Hello is generated four times as often as and on average. Also for case classes we can easily define our own generator. Listing 5.24 shows On page 122 we have the three case classes for the abstract class Lecture:

```
case class Course (title: String) extends Lecture
case class Exercise (belongsTo: Course) extends Lecture
case class tutorial (belongsTo: Course) extends Lecture
```

Are defined. A generator for this is implemented in Listing 8.4.

Listing 8.4: A generator for lectures

```
val genCourse = for {
title <- oneOf ("Prog 1", "Prog 2", "FP", "OOP")
} yield course (title)
val genExercise = for {
course <- genCourse
} yield exercise (course)
val genTutorial = for {
course <- genCourse
} yield tutorial (course)
val genLecture = oneOf (genCourse, genExercise, genTutorial)
```

We can try out our genLecture generator in the Scala shell:

```
scala> genLecture.sample
res1: Option [Product with Lecture] = Some (Course (Prog 2))
scala> genLecture.sample
res2: Option [Product with Lecture] = Some (Exercise (Course
(Prog 2)))
scala> genLecture.sample
```

```
res3: Option [Product with Lecture] = Some (Exercise (Course
(FP)))
```

It is also possible to set conditions for the generated values with the suchThat-Specify method. For example generates:

```
val smallEvenIntGen = choose (0.200) suchThat (_% 2 == 0)
```

only even Ints between 0 and 200. With containerOf, by default for different container values are generated, e.g.

```
scala> val intListGen = containerOf [List, Int] (genInt)
intListGen: org.scalacheck.Gen [List [Int]] = Gen ()
scala> intListGen.sample
res4: Option [List [Int]] = Some (List (235412, 18767, 0, ...
```

ScalaCheck already offers support for some containers. By definition of an implicit conversion into a buildable, additional be added. With containerOf1 non-empty containers and with containerOfN Containers with a specified size can be created.

A special generator is arbitrary from the object org.scalacheck.-Arbitrary. This generates any values for all supported types. One A look at the API documentation shows which types these are. For example we can with:

```
import org.scalacheck.Arbitrary._
val evenIntGen = arbitrary [Int] suchThat (_% 2 == 0)
```

generate any even ints. A list of tuples consisting of one For example, we get BigInt and its square with:

```
val intList = for {
list <- arbitrary [List [BigInt]]
} yield list map (x => (x, x * x))
```

For a separate type T, arbitrary can be used if an implicit There is a conversion that has Arbitrary [T] as its result type, i.e. a View.

Listing 8.5: Implicit conversion from Lecture to Arbitrary [Lecture]

```
implicit def arbLecture: Arbitrary [Lecture] =
Arbitrary {
val genCourse = for {
title <- oneOf ("Prog 1", "Prog 2", "FP", "OOP")
} yield course (title)
val genExercise = for {
course <- genCourse
} yield exercise (course)
val genTutorial = for {
course <- genCourse
} yield tutorial (course)
oneOf (genCourse, genExercise, genTutorial)
}
```

In Listing 8.5, such a function is available for the lectures by using the Arbitrary factory method defined. Then we can use arbitrary ry generate a list of lectures, as the following session shows:

```
scala> val listOfLecturesGen = arbitrary [List [Lecture]]
listOfLecturesGen: org.scalacheck.Gen [List [Lecture]] =
Gene()
scala> listOfLecturesGen.sample
res5: Option [List [Lecture]] = Some (List (Exercise (Course (
Prog 1)), Tutorial (Course (OOP)), Tutorial (...
```

Finally, with the classify method from org.scalacheck.Prop, in information about the generated values can be collected and specified.

Listing 8.6: Property using classify

```
def ordered (l: List [Int]) = l == l.sort (_> _)
val listRevRev = forAll {l: List [Int] =>
classify (ordered (l), "ordered") {
classify (l.length> 5, "large", "small") {
l.reverse.reverse == l
}
}
}
```

In Listing 8.6 there is a function ordered that checks whether a list is sorted, and a property listRevRev is specified. For each generated list, checks whether it is sorted and whether it is large or small. An example session results then the following output:

```
scala> listRevRev.check
+ OK, passed 100 tests.
> Collected test data:
81% large
11% small, ordered
8% small
```

Should only be collected and evaluated what percentage of each value have been generated, the collect method can be used. The following sit- The illustration is used to illustrate:

```
scala> val lectureProp = forAll {l: Lecture =>
|
collect (l) {
|
l == l
|
}
| }
lectureProp: org.scalacheck.Prop = Prop
scala> lectureProp.check
+ OK, passed 100 tests.
> Collected test data:
12% Course (FP)
12% Exercise (Course (Prog 2))
11% Tutorial (Course (Prog 1))
11% Course (Prog 1)
11% Course (Prog 2)
10% Course (OOP)
9% Exercise (Course (OOP))
8% Tutorial (Course (FP))
6% Tutorial (Course (OOP))
5% Exercise (Course (FP))
4% Tutorial (Course (Prog 2))
1% Exercise (Course (Prog 1))
```

8.2.3 Automated testing with Sbt

To conclude the section on ScalaCheck, we want to use an example explain how ScalaCheck can be used with Sbt. For a direct comparison in the following chapters we will use the same example with Sbt and the respective gen test framework.

A simple video library management system, shown in Listing 8.7 is shown. First we create a Sbt project, as in section 2.2.2

was discussed. Under src / main / scala / we create the file Movie-Store.scala with the content shown in Listing 8.7. At this point we refrain from explaining the code and give you the chance to try out the code Practice reading and understanding Scala code.

Listing 8.7: The Movie and MovieStore classes

```
case class Movie (title: String, filmrating: Int)
class MovieStore {
private [this] var available = Map [Int, Movie] ()
private [this] var rent = Map [Int, Movie] ()
def addToStore (movie: Movie) {
MovieStore.serial + = 1
available + = (MovieStore.serial -> movie)
}
def addToStore (movies: Traversable [Movie]) {
movies foreach (addToStore (_))
}
def rentMovie (serial: Int): Option [Movie] = {
val movieOption = available get serial
movieOption match {
case None => None
case Some (movie) =>
available - = serial
rent + = (serial -> movie)
movieOption
}
}
def returnMovie (serial: Int) = {
val movie = rent (serial)
rent - = serial
available + = (serial -> movie)
}
def availableMoviesForAge (age: Int) =
available.filter {
case (_, Movie (_, r)) => r <= age
}
def availableMovies = available
def rentMovies = rent
}
object MovieStore {
private var serial = 0
}
```

The file src / test / scala / MovieStoreScalaCheck.scala with the tests is shown in Listing 8.8. We have two arbitrary instances and six there Properties defined.

Listing 8.8: The MovieStoreScalaCheck object for testing with ScalaCheck

```
import org.scalacheck._
object MovieStoreScalaCheck
extends Properties ("MovieStore") {
import Gen._
import Arbitrary _
implicit def arbMovie: Arbitrary [Movie] =
Arbitrary (for {
title <- arbitrary [String]
film rating <- oneOf (6,12,16,18)
```

```
} yield Movie (title, filmrating)
)
implicit def arbSetMovie: Arbitrary [Set [Movie]] =
Arbitrary (for {
pairs <- arbitrary [Set [(String, Int)]]
} yield pairs map {case (t, f) => Movie (t, f)}
)
import Prop._
property ("Add") = forAll {m: Movie =>
val movieStore = new MovieStore
movieStore addToStore m
movieStore.availableMovies.size == 1
movieStore.rentMovies.size == 0
}
property ("AddAndRent") = forAll {m: Movie =>
val movieStore = new MovieStore
movieStore addToStore m
val keys = movieStore.availableMovies.keys
movieStore rentMovie keys.head
movieStore.availableMovies.size == 0
movieStore.rentMovies.size == 1
}
property ("AddAndTryRent") = forAll {m: Movie =>
val movieStore = new MovieStore
movieStore addToStore m
val keys = movieStore.availableMovies.keys
movieStore rentMovie (keys.head + 1)
movieStore.availableMovies.size == 1
movieStore.rentMovies.size == 0
}
property ("AddAddRentReturn") = forAll {
(m: Movie, n: Movie) =>
val movieStore = new MovieStore
movieStore addToStore m
movieStore addToStore n
val keys = movieStore.availableMovies.keys
val serial = keys.head
val movieOption = movieStore rentMovie serial
movieOption match {
case None => throw new NoSuchElementException
case Some (movie) => movieStore returnMovie serial
}
movieStore.availableMovies.size == 2
movieStore.rentMovies.size == 0
}
property ("AddSet") = forAll {
(ms: Set [Movie]) =>
val movieStore = new MovieStore
movieStore addToStore ms
val setOfMovies: Set [Movie] =
(movieStore.availableMovies: \ Set [Movie] ()) {
case ((_, v), s) => s + v
}
setOfMovies == ms
```

```
}
property ("AddSetAge") = forAll {
(ms: Set [Movie], age: Int) =>
val movieStore = new MovieStore
movieStore addToStore ms
val setOfMoviesForAge: Set [Movie] =
(movieStore.availableMoviesForAge (age): \
Set [Movie] ()) {
case ((_, v), s) => s + v
}
setOfMoviesForAge ==
ms.filter {case Movie (_, f) => f <= age}
}
}
```

If we now add the downloaded ScalaCheck JAR to the lib copy, we can enter the command test in the Sbt console and hen the following:

```
> test
...
[info] == MovieStoreScalaCheck ==
[info] + MovieStore.Add: OK, passed 100 tests.
[info] + MovieStore.AddAndRent: OK, passed 100 tests.
[info] + MovieStore.AddAndTryRent: OK, passed 100 tests.
[info] + MovieStore.AddAddRentReturn: OK, passed 100
Testing.
[info] + MovieStore.AddSet: OK, passed 100 tests.
[info] + MovieStore.AddSetAge: OK, passed 100 tests.
[info] == MovieStoreScalaCheck ==
...
[success] Successful.
```

Sbt will automatically run the tests in the test directory. And one more little more can be automated with sbt: it is not necessary that Download the ScalaCheck-Jar yourself and copy it to lib. Instead we can configure the sbt project to update the jar with a sbt downloaded automatically and copied to lib_managed. To do this, Let's create a configuration in the project / build / MovieStore.scala file for the project, as shown in Listing 8.9.

Listing 8.9: A project definition that manages the ScalaCheck jar

```
import sbt._
class MovieStoreProject (info: ProjectInfo) extends
DefaultProject (info) {
val scalacheck = "org.scalacheck"% "scalacheck"%
"1.7"% "test" from
"http://scalacheck.googlecode.com/files/scalacheck_
2.8.0-1.7.jar "
}
```

8.3 ScalaTest

The second test framework that we would like to introduce to you is ScalaTest. Around To use ScalaTest, we first have to download the current Jar from http: // www. download scalatest.org/. ScalaTest supports different types of Tests that we would like to briefly introduce in the following sections. An introductory tion in the used additional frameworks like JUnit 7 or TestNG 8 würde go far beyond the scope of this book. Since ScalaTest itself is very is catchy, we will only be able to show examples here. Explain for it For all types, however, we immediately test the MovieStore class (see Listing 8.7) using Sbt.

8.3.1 ScalaTest and JUnit

JUnit is a Java unit test framework. Even if JUnit versions 3 and 4 is supported by ScalaTest, we limit ourselves here to the cooperation work with JUnit 4. For an introduction to JUnit, please visit the JUnit website at http://www.junit.org/. You can also find the current JUnit Jar download.

ScalaTest provides the necessary support in the package org.scalatest.junit for JUnit with. If we include the contained trait JUnitSuite mix, we have the ScalaTest assertions as well as the JUnit assertions Available. Listing 8.10 shows an example of a test suite.

Listing 8.10: ScalaTest and JUnit

```
import org.scalatest.junit.JUnitSuite
class MovieStoreScalaTestJUnit extends JUnitSuite {
import org.junit.Assert._
import org.junit.Test
val m: Movie = Movie ("At the limit", 6)
@Test def add () {
val movieStore = new MovieStore
movieStore addToStore m
assertEquals (movieStore.availableMovies.size, 1)
assertEquals (movieStore.rentMovies.size, 0)
}
@Test def addAndRent () {
val movieStore = new MovieStore
movieStore addToStore m
val keys = movieStore.availableMovies.keys
movieStore rentMovie keys.head
assert (movieStore.availableMovies.size == 0)
assert (movieStore.rentMovies.size == 1)
}
@Test def exceptionTest () {
val movieStore = new MovieStore
intercept [NoSuchElementException] {
movieStore.availableMovies (12)
}
}
}
```

The methods with the @Test annotation correspond to the tests. To-
In addition, the @Before and @After annotations for initiali-
Before or after the tests, "cleanups" can be used.

The test method add uses JUnit assertions (assertEquals), the method addAndRent Scala test assertions (assert). In contrast to ScalaCheck, we can define the test data ourselves. Each test is then carried out exactly once guided.

The exceptionTest method uses the ScalaTest intercept method. This test is only successful if a NoSuchElementException is thrown.

To run the test suite with Sbt, the class from Listing 8.10 must be included in the test directory of the Sbt project, and the ScalaTest and JUnit Jar must copied to lib /. Of course we can do the project configuration Extend Listing 8.9 so that both are managed. To complement this we simply use the following two definitions:

```
val junit = "org.junit"% "junit"% "4.8.2"% "test" from
"http://github.com/KentBeck/junit/downloads/junit
-4.8.2.jar "
val scalatest = "org.scalatest"% "scalatest"% "1.2"% "
test"
```

After the Jar for ScalaTest is in a repository that Sbt knows, you have to we do not give a source for this. Then we run sbt update again and after sbt test see the following output:

```
...
[info] == MovieStoreScalaTestJUnit ==
[info] Test Starting: add
[info] Test Passed: add
[info] Test Starting: addAndRent
[info] Test Passed: addAndRent
[info] Test Starting: exceptionTest
[info] Test Passed: exceptionTest
[info] == MovieStoreScalaTestJUnit ==
...
[success] Successful.
```

8.3.2 ScalaTest and TestNG

TestNG is another test framework for Java, which together with ScalaTest can be used. After the required TestNG jar with its dependencies If the Maven repository is in the Maven repository, which Sbt knows, we first expand ours Project configuration at the following val:

```
val testng = "org.testng"% "testng"% "5.13"% "test"
```

and download the jars with sbt update. The JUnit test suite is in a few Steps converted into a TestNG test suite. Compared to Listing 8.10, we have to just change the imports and the mixed-in trait. In Listing 8.11 the re-result shown.

Listing 8.11: ScalaTest and TestNG

```
import org.scalatest.testng.TestNGSuite
class MovieStoreScalaTestTestNG extends TestNGSuite {
import org.testng.Assert._
import org.testng.annotations.Test
val m: Movie = Movie ("At the limit", 6)
@Test def add () {
val movieStore = new MovieStore
movieStore addToStore m
assertEquals (movieStore.availableMovies.size, 1)
assertEquals (movieStore.rentMovies.size, 0)
}
@Test def addAndRent () {
val movieStore = new MovieStore
movieStore addToStore m
val keys = movieStore.availableMovies.keys
movieStore rentMovie keys.head
assert (movieStore.availableMovies.size == 0)
assert (movieStore.rentMovies.size == 1)
}
```

```
@Test def exceptionTest () {
val movieStore = new MovieStore
intercept [NoSuchElementException] {
movieStore.availableMovies (12)
}
}
}
```

If we run the tests, the following output for the TestNG suite is added:

```
...
[info] == MovieStoreScalaTestTestNG ==
[TestNG] Running:
Command line suite
[info] initialize
[info] Suite Starting: MovieStoreScalaTestTestNG
[info] Test Starting: add
[info] Test Passed: add
[info] Test Starting: addAndRent
[info] Test Passed: addAndRent
[info] Test Starting: exceptionTest
[info] Test Passed: exceptionTest
[info] Suite Completed: MovieStoreScalaTestTestNG
===============================================

Command line suite
Total tests run: 3, Failures: 0, Skips: 0
===============================================

[info] == MovieStoreScalaTestTestNG ==
...
```

8.3.3 ScalaTest and BDD

BDD stands for *behavior-driven development* and as such represents the textual writing the program behavior in the foreground. Of course this must be Behavior can then be verified by a suitable test.

ScalaTest offers three traits that differ only in the way they are the specification text is to be formulated: Spec, WordSpec and FlatSpec. Listing 8.12 shows our specification using the WordSpec trait.

Listing 8.12: ScalaTest with the WordSpec trait

```
import org.scalatest.WordSpec
import org.scalatest.matchers.ShouldMatchers
class MovieStoreScalaTestWordSpec extends WordSpec with
ShouldMatchers {
val m = Movie ("At the limit", 6)
"A MovieStore" when {
"added one movie" should {
val movieStore = new MovieStore
movieStore addToStore m
"have one movie in availableMovies" in {
assert (movieStore.availableMovies.size == 1)
}
"have no movie in rentMovies" in {
assert (movieStore.rentMovies.size == 0)
}
}
"added and rent one movie" should {
val movieStore = new MovieStore
```

```
movieStore addToStore m
val keys = movieStore.availableMovies.keys
movieStore rentMovie keys.head
"have no movie in availableMovies" in {
assert (movieStore.availableMovies.size == 0)
}
"have one movie in rentMovies" in {
assert (movieStore.rentMovies.size == 1)
}
}
"empty" should {
val movieStore = new MovieStore
("throw NoSuchElementException" +
"when lookup a serial") in {
evaluating {
movieStore.availableMovies (12)
} should produce [NoSuchElementException]
}
}
}
}
```

The lines with the texts and when, should or in describe the behavior The tests are in the corresponding blocks. The goal is the test document as legible as possible. Hence the part that refers to the NoSuchElementException tests, programmed to be more fluid and readable. Since we only need the ScalaTest-Jar, we can do the tests without any further Run configuration of Sbt immediately. See in addition to the previous edition we the following lines:

```
...
[info] == MovieStoreScalaTestWordSpec ==
[info] A MovieStore (when added one movie)
[info] Test Starting: A MovieStore (when added one movie)
should have one movie in availableMovies
[info] Test Passed: A MovieStore (when added one movie)
should have one movie in availableMovies
[info] Test Starting: A MovieStore (when added one movie)
should have no movie in rentMovies
[info] Test Passed: A MovieStore (when added one movie)
should have no movie in rentMovies
[info] A MovieStore (when added and rent one movie)
[info] Test Starting: A MovieStore (when added and rent
one movie) should have no movie in availableMovies
[info] Test Passed: A MovieStore (when added and rent one
movie) should have no movie in availableMovies
[info] Test Starting: A MovieStore (when added and rent
one movie) should have one movie in rentMovies
[info] Test Passed: A MovieStore (when added and rent one
movie) should have one movie in rentMovies
[info] A MovieStore (when empty)
[info] Test Starting: A MovieStore (when empty) should
should throw NoSuchElementException when lookup a
serial
[info] Test Passed: A MovieStore (when empty) should
should throw NoSuchElementException when lookup a
```

serial
[info] == MovieStoreScalaTestWordSpec ==
...
When using Spec instead of WordSpec, we have to use < description > when and < description > should by describe (< description >) so- as < description > in through it (< description > replace). The use The use of FlatSpec does not allow the texts to be nested.

8.3.4 Functional, integration and acceptance tests

FeatureSpec can be used to describe and test scenarios of features the. The textual approach is even more important than with the BDD approaches presented Description in the foreground. Listing 8.13 shows an example of its usage of the FeatureSpec trait.

Listing 8.13: ScalaTest with the FeatureSpec trait

```
import org.scalatest.FeatureSpec
import org.scalatest.GivenWhenThen
import org.scalatest.matchers.MustMatchers
class MovieStoreScalaTestFeatureSpec extends FeatureSpec
with GivenWhenThen with MustMatchers {
feature ("The user can add a movie to the moviestore") {
scenario ("added one movie to an empty moviestore") {
given ("an empty moviestore")
val movieStore = new MovieStore
and ("a movie")
val m = Movie ("At the limit", 6)
when ("added the movie to the moviestore")
movieStore addToStore m
then ("availableMovies contains one movie")
movieStore.availableMovies.size must be === 1
and ("rentMovies contains no movie")
movieStore.rentMovies.size must be === 0
}
scenario ("added one movie to an empty moviestore" +
"and rent it") {
given ("an empty moviestore")
val movieStore = new MovieStore
and ("a movie")
val m = Movie ("At the limit", 6)
when ("added the movie to the moviestore")
movieStore addToStore m
and ("rent it")
val keys = movieStore.availableMovies.keys
movieStore rentMovie keys.head
then ("availableMovies contains no movie")
movieStore.availableMovies.size must be === 0
and ("rentMovies contains one movie")
movieStore.rentMovies.size must be === 1
}
scenario ("added no movie, but try to get one from" +
"availableMovies") {
given ("an empty moviestore")
val movieStore = new MovieStore
when ("trying to get a movie from availableMovies")
```

```
then ("NoSuchElementException should be thrown")
evaluating {
movieStore.availableMovies (12)
} must produce [NoSuchElementException]
}
}
}
```

In addition to the FeatureSpec trait, the GivenWhenThen and the MustMatchers-Trait mixed in. This means that scenarios of Fea-Describe tures in great detail. All texts are also included in the Run, which looks like this:

```
...
[info] == MovieStoreScalaTestFeatureSpec ==
[info] Feature: The user can add a movie to the
moviestore
[info] Test Starting: Feature: The user can add a movie
to the moviestore added one movie to an empty moviesto
[info] Test Passed: Feature: The user can add a movie to
the moviestore added one movie to an empty moviestore
[info] Given an empty moviestore
[info] And a movie
[info] When the movie is added to the moviestore
[info] Then availableMovies contains one movie
[info] And rentMovies contains no movie
[info] Test Starting: Feature: The user can add a movie
to the moviestore added one movie to an empty moviesto
and rent it
[info] Test Passed: Feature: The user can add a movie to
the moviestore added one movie to an empty moviestore
nd rent it
[info] Given an empty moviestore
[info] And a movie
[info] When the movie is added to the moviestore
[info] And rent it
[info] Then availableMovies contains no movie
[info] And rentMovies contains one movie
[info] Test Starting: Feature: The user can add a movie
to the moviestore added no movie, but try to get one f
m availableMovies
[info] Test Passed: Feature: The user can add a movie to
the moviestore added no movie, but try to get one fro
availableMovies
[info] Given an empty moviestore
[info] When trying to get a movie from availableMovies
[info] Then NoSuchElementException should be thrown
[info] == MovieStoreScalaTestFeatureSpec ==
...
```

8.3.5 The FunSuite

The last possibility to specify tests in ScalaTest is the FunSuite, whereby Fun stands for function. A test is a function named test that is saved as a The first parameter list is the name and the second is the code to be executed becomes. If we formulate our tests with FunSuite, they look like in Listing 8.14 out.

Listing 8.14: ScalaTest with the FunSuite trait

```
import org.scalatest.FunSuite
import org.scalatest.matchers.ShouldMatchers
class MovieStoreScalaTestFunSuite extends FunSuite
with ShouldMatchers {
val m: Movie = Movie ("At the limit", 6)
test ("add") {
val movieStore = new MovieStore
movieStore addToStore m
movieStore.availableMovies.size should be === 1
movieStore.rentMovies.size should be === 0
}
test ("addAndRent") {
val movieStore = new MovieStore
movieStore addToStore m
val keys = movieStore.availableMovies.keys
movieStore rentMovie keys.head
movieStore.availableMovies.size should be === 0
movieStore.rentMovies.size should be === 1
}
test ("exceptionTest") {
val movieStore = new MovieStore
evaluating {
movieStore.availableMovies (12)
} should produce [NoSuchElementException]
}
}
```

These tests now look more for code and less for specifics.
tion. As can be seen, we can use the MustMatchers or here the
Use ShouldMatchers in ScalaTest regardless of the test type. The output
Our FunSuite then looks like this:

```
...
[info] == MovieStoreScalaTestFunSuite ==
[info] Test Starting: add
[info] Test Passed: add
[info] Test Starting: addAndRent
[info] Test Passed: addAndRent
[info] Test Starting: exceptionTest
[info] Test Passed: exceptionTest
[info] == MovieStoreScalaTestFunSuite ==
...
```

8.4 Specs

The third Scala testing framework is called *Specs* [9] and is a BDD library. JUnit can also be integrated into specs. Specs also offers an integration on from ScalaCheck and various mocking frameworks. Give below we give you a small overview of specs and its features and use them the step-by-step structure of a specification for the MovieStore from Listing 8.7.

8.4.1 A specs specification

The basic idea of testing with Specs is to create and review a spec cification. To do this, we define an object that extends the Specification class. tert, as shown in Listing 8.15.

Listing 8.15. An object that extends the Specification class

```
import org.specs._
object MovieStoreSpecs extends Specification
```

In order to be able to start right away with Sbt, we are expanding the project definition the following line:

```
val specs = "org.scala-tools.testing"% "specs_2.8.0"% "
1.6.5 "%" test "
```

After a sbt update we can already run the specs test. From-
The input from Sbt regarding specs is then:

```
...
[info] == MovieStoreSpecs ==
[info] total specification
[info] == MovieStoreSpecs ==
...
```

In order to translate the specification again and again during further development and to run, we start the interactive sbt shell with sbt and enter ~ test a. This means that the Sbt command test get immediately every time you save rigged, which executes the tests and translates them beforehand.

But now back to the specification. We're still giving the specification a name that we pass to Specification as a class parameter.
We also describe the system to be tested, the movie
Store. The current status of our specification can be seen in Listing 8.16.

Listing 8.16. The MovieStore specification with a name and the system

```
object MovieStoreSpecs extends
Specification ("MovieStore Specification") {
"A MovieStore" should {}
}
```

We now see the following additional lines in the sbt output:

```
[info] A MovieStore should
[info] o PENDING: not yet implemented
```

Can can also be used instead of should if there is a better description exercise results. We can also define our own words. For example we can with the definition

```
def provide = addToSusVerb ("provide")
```

also specify:

```
"A MovieStore" should provide {}
```

Within the system we describe example 10 , our tests, with a String and the method in or alternatively >>. We can do these examples too nest in each other. Listing 8.17 shows the framework for the first example. given, where we want to check two different properties.

Listing 8.17: Nested Examples in the Specification

```
"A MovieStore" should {
"when added one movie" >> {
"contain one movie in availableMovies" >> {
}
"contain no movie in rentMovies" >> {
}
}
}
```

If we save the file, we see the additional descriptions in the Sbt
Output:

```
[info] A MovieStore should
[info]
o when added one movie
[info]
```

o contain one movie in availableMovies
[info]
o contain no movie in rentMovies

Specs supports the test-first approach by using the hulls of the two games are allowed to leave blank, as shown in Listing 8.17. But there are also those Ability to already write the implementation of the test, but the test not yet to arm. On the one hand there is the possibility of a ski Write statement at the beginning of the example. On the other hand, we can Trait PendingUntilFixed from the package org.specs.specification mix in and use its pendingUntilFixed method. The edition does not change it. The examples are fully programmed in Listing 8.18, but set to *pending* .

Listing 8.18: Two examples on with skip or pendingUntilFixed *pending* set are

```
import org.specs._
import org.specs.specification.PendingUntilFixed
object MovieStoreSpecs extends
```

[10] In English, the tests are called *Examples* . We translate this with *examples* .

```
Specification ("MovieStore Specification") with
PendingUntilFixed {
val movie = Movie ("Step Across the Border", 0)
"A MovieStore" should {
"when added one movie" >> {
val movieStore = new MovieStore
movieStore addToStore movie
"contain one movie in availableMovies" >> {
pendingUntilFixed {
movieStore.availableMovies.size must _ == 1
}
}
"contain no movie in rentMovies" >> {
skip ("not yet implemented")
movieStore.rentMovies.size must _ == 0
}
}
}
}
```

The advantage of pendingUntilFixed compared to skip is that the test application of pendingUntilFixed is still executed and displayed, as soon as it was successful:

```
...
[info] A MovieStore should
[info]
x when added one movie
[info]
Fixed now. You should remove the 'pending
until fixed 'declaration (PendingUntilFixed.scala: 68)
[info]
x contain one movie in availableMovies
[info]
Fixed now. You should remove the 'pending
until fixed 'declaration (PendingUntilFixed.scala: 68)
[info]
o contain no movie in rentMovies
...
```

In order not to overlook this, the entire test even fails.

8.4.2 Matchers

We saw the first matcher in Listing 8.18: must _ ==. For the Properties that are to be checked with a test are specified in Specs a Many such matchers are used. The basic use of a mat chers is:
<object> must <matcher> (<parameter>)
An example of such an expression is:
"hello" must beMatching ("h. *")
Some of the matchers that Specs bring with them begin with be or have. At the-The matchers can be written in two words. For example, can instead of the above expression, the following can be written:
"hello" must be matching ("h. *")
This makes the specification look more readable. Other very readable examples are:
"hello" must not be matching ("z. *")
List ("hello") must not have size (2)
Map ("hello" -> "world") must have the key ("hello")
"hello" must be matching ("h. *") and
not be matching ("z. *")
Matchers are case classes derived from org.specs.matcher.Matcher and have an apply method. The apply method must have a by-Have name parameters of the type of the object to be checked. Result must be a triple, consisting of a truth value as a statement whether the test was successful, and two strings that are returned in the event of success or failure. be practiced.
This also makes it possible to write your own matchers. In Listing 8.19, the Implementation of the matcher haveOnlyMoviesForTheAgeOf shown.
Listing 8.19: The haveOnlyMoviesForTheAgeOf matcher

```
import org.specs.matcher.Matcher
case class haveOnlyMoviesForTheAgeOf (age: Int)
extends Matcher [Map [Int, Movie]] {
def apply (movies: => Map [Int, Movie]) = {
((movies filter {
case (_, (Movie (_, f))) => f> age
}). isEmpty,
"only allowed movies",
"not only allowed movies"
)
}
}
```

With this we can use the following expression in an example check:
movieStore.availableMoviesForAge (age) must
haveOnlyMoviesForTheAgeOf (age)
It is also possible to define matchers yourself who start with be or have as ex-trawort can be written. To do this we need an implicit conversion from Result [T] from the package org.specs.specification to a class se that has a method named without be or have. In Lis-ting 8.20 is the implicit conversion and the class OnlyMoviesForTheAge-OfResult shown.
Listing 8.20: The OnlyMoviesForTheAgeOfResult class and an implicit conversion Result [Map [Int, Movie]]

```
import org.specs.specification.Result
implicit def toOnlyMoviesForTheAgeOfResult (
result: Result [Map [Int, Movie]])
= new OnlyMoviesForTheAgeOfResult (result)
class OnlyMoviesForTheAgeOfResult (
result: Result [Map [Int, Movie]]) {
def onlyMoviesForTheAgeOf (age: Int) =
result.matchWithMatcher (
haveOnlyMoviesForTheAgeOf (age))
}
```

With this we can now specify the condition as follows:

```
movieStore.availableMoviesForAge (age) must
have OnlyMoviesForTheAgeOf age
```

Matchers can be used with and, or, xor, verifyAll and verifyAny to create new can be combined. When and unless the application of mat-can be adapted to specific conditions. Plus there is still *Eventually matchers* who use a matcher multiple times and even one Waiting time between attempts can be passed.

The Specs library defines a large number of matchers that are used for the different which data types can be used. So we can finally get the Lines

```
movieStore.availableMovies.size must _ == 1
movieStore.rentMovies.size must _ == 0
```

replace by:

```
movieStore.availableMovies must have size 1
movieStore.rentMovies must have size 0
```

The entire specification developed up to this point for testing the MovieStore with the Specs framework is shown in Listing 8.21.

Listing 8.21: The specs specification for the MovieStore

```
import org.specs._
object MovieStoreSpecs extends
Specification ("MovieStore Specification") {
val movie = Movie ("Step Across the Border", 0)
"A MovieStore" should {
"when added one movie" >> {
val movieStore = new MovieStore
movieStore addToStore movie
"contain one movie in availableMovies" >> {
movieStore.availableMovies must have size 1
}
"contain no movie in rentMovies" >> {
movieStore.rentMovies must have size 0
}
}
"when added a set of movies" >> {
val movieStore = new MovieStore
movieStore addToStore Set (
movie,
Movie ("At the Limit", 6),
Movie ("The Matrix", 16),
Movie ("Bad Taste", 18),
Movie ("Bad Lieutenant", 16)
)
"return only movies which are allowed" +
```

```
"for the given age" >> {
import org.specs.matcher.Matcher
case class haveOnlyMoviesForTheAgeOf (age: Int)
extends Matcher [Map [Int, Movie]] {
def apply (movies: => Map [Int, Movie]) = {
((movies filter {
case (_, (Movie (_, f))) => f> age
}). isEmpty,
"only allowed movies",
"not only allowed movies"
)
}
}
import org.specs.specification.Result
implicit def toOnlyMoviesForTheAgeOfResult (
result: Result [Map [Int, Movie]])
= new OnlyMoviesForTheAgeOfResult (result)
class OnlyMoviesForTheAgeOfResult (
result: Result [Map [Int, Movie]]) {
def onlyMoviesForTheAgeOf (age: Int) =
result.matchWithMatcher (
haveOnlyMoviesForTheAgeOf (age))
}
val age = 15
movieStore.availableMoviesForAge (age) must
have onlyMoviesForTheAgeOf age
}
}
}
}
```

8.4.3 Mocks with Mockito

Imagine if we were to use more complex video library software in develop a team. We are still responsible for the MovieStore class responsibly. However, there is also a module for customer management on which another team member is working. For a new version of the movie class Store we want to save the customer number for the rented films.
Strictly speaking, instead of the map [Int, Movie] we want a map [Customer-Use ID, Map [Int, Movie]]. For example, we want to use this to When a film is being played, check whether the customer has already rented five films. He is not supposed to get a sixth film. In addition, in the customer denverwaltung the option to be implemented for an existing customer to deactivate. Then he is not allowed to rent films at all.
In order to test our customized class, we now also need to test the classes of the Implement customer management. Of course, this means a certain wall, in which errors can creep in, which then make testing difficult do. Usually a different approach is taken today. Instead of a united To implement the interface, it is *mocked* (to mock = something ting). There are also a number of so-called mocking libraries with we can very easily create an object that behaves as if it were implementing the interface.
Mockito [11] is one such library. Specs offers a connection to Mockito and two more mocking libraries: EasyMock [12] and JMock [13] . also Specs also contains its own lightweight mocking framework.

In the following we want to take a look at the Mockito connection. As an accessory game, the traits shown in Listing 8.22 are used.

Listing 8.22: The Customer and CustomerID traits

```
trait CustomerID
trait customer {
val id: CustomerID
def isDisabled: Boolean
}
```

In the MovieStore specification, we use Mockito by using the Trait Mix in Mockito from org.specs.mock. Can use the mock method we then create mock objects. The following lines define a customer and a CostumerID mock object:

```
val customer = mock [customer]
val customerID = mock [CustomerID]
```

In order to link the customerID with the customer, write let's just practice:

```
customer.id returns customerID
```

We can do this in an example with:

```
customer.id mustEqual customerID
```

testing. We also give a result for isDisabled:

```
customer.isDisabled returns false
```

In this case this simple definition is sufficient. For methods with parameters there there is also the possibility of defining a function with answers that the pa-uses parameters. Mocks even have one major advantage over that actual implementation: we can easily check whether a method was called and even how often. We can get through this, for example the expression

```
there was atLeastOne (customer) .isDisabled
```

check whether the method isDisabled in the rentMovie method is at least was called at least once. In that case we can assume that it has been checked whether the customer is blocked.

In order to be able to use Mockito with Sbt, we are expanding the project definition to:

```
val mockito = "org.mockito"% "mockito-all"% "1.8.5"%
"test"
```

8.4.4 Literate Specifications

Even if Literate Specifications are at the time this book is being written, are still in the alpha stage, we do not want to leave them unmentioned. The The idea is to specialize systems as informal text, perhaps even with images. fify. Parts of the text are specs examples that can be executed. The Specs website includes an example of such a specification that we are listing in 8.23.

Listing 8.23: A Literate Specification (Source: Specs website)

```
class HelloWorldSpecification extends HtmlSpecification
with Textile {
"The greeting application" is <t>
h3. Presentation
This new application should say "hello" in different
languages.
For example, <ex> by default, saying hello by default
should use English </ex>
{greet must _ == "hello"}
Then, other languages, like <ex> French and German should
```

```
be supported too </ex>
{eg {
greet ("French") must _ == "bonjour"
greet ("German") must _ == "hello"
}
}
<ex> Japanese should be supported also </ex>
{notImplemented}
</t>
}
```

Here are some explanations:
The name of the system is The greeting application.
The system is specified by the XML element <t> </t>.
By using the Textile-Trait, the heading with h3. Presentation can be generated.
The names of the specs examples are in <ex> </ex> elements.
The Scala code for the examples is directly behind it in curly brackets.
mern.
The eg function encapsulates several expectations.
Another feature of Literate Specifications are data tables. In Listing 8.24 an example is shown.

Listing 8.24: An example of the use of data tables (source: Specs website)

```
All those small examples should be ok: {
"examples are ok" inTable
"a" | "b" | "sum" |
1 ! 1 ! 2
|
1 ! 2! 3
|
1 ! 3! 4th
| {(a: Int, b: Int, sum: Int) =>
a + b must be equalTo (sum)
}
}
```

With this outlook on new features of Specs, we want to start the chapter about Complete documentation and testing. In summary, it can be said:
Testing is important, and in the Scala environment there are some testing frameworks that
be really fun! In the following chapters we will now come to an agreement employ other Scala frameworks.

Chapter 9

Web programming with lift

Lift [1] is a framework with which web applications are developed in Scala can. Lift is a so-called *full stack web application framework* . This means, Lift brings everything essential that we need for a web application could: a template engine, AJAX and Comet support, a Persis solution, link and access management and a complete user management ment. There are also a number of other useful modules such as Textile support for using Wiki syntax in input fields or

a PayPal integration.
We will show you some of the lift features in this chapter using the present the setting of a web application and provide you with an got into the framework give.
The web application that we want to create is called *Talk Allocator* . Sense and purpose of the application should be to give users the opportunity to choose from a Pick a suitable one from a multitude of lecture topics to work on and want to present. The system can then be used, for example, at a university le for assigning seminar, project or presentation topics to the students be used.
We begin in section 9.1 with the introduction to the lift development and show you how to use the prototype provided by the lift team get up and running. In Section 9.2 we deal with the boat strapping, i.e. with the things that were done when the lift application was started should be. A first look at the rendering with templates and snippets We throw pets in Section 9.3. Lift has built-in support for loading user administration and the SiteMap (see Section 9.4). Also brings elevator an OR mapper, the use of which we want to introduce in Section 9.5. len. The chapter closes with a discussion of the implementation of the snipping pets in Section 9.6. The code created in this chapter is available at http://github.com/obcode/talkallocator_lift.

9.1 Quick start with lift

We don't have to start developing our lift application with an empty start drawing. The lift team offers the possibility of an initial, executable Create a lift project for Maven or Sbt. We use Sbt, da this is now the preferred variant in the Scala community.
If you still want to work with Maven, you should for the sake of simplicity use a version 2.2 or higher. This already contains an archetype for lift. In of the currently available Maven version 2.2.1 these are the numbers:
250: remote -> liftweb-archetype-blank (Archetype - blank project for liwftweb)
251: remote -> liftweb-archetype-hellolift (Archetype - hellolift sample liwftweb application)
So we start here with Sbt. To do this, we have to start the initial project times download. To do this, we use a prototype that is available via the Lift GitHub Account [2] is provided. The prototype we used below is called lift_21_sbt and uses Scala 2.8.0 and Lift 2.1. We also use Git [3] as a version control system and can easily clone the prototype with it:
$ git clone git: //github.com/lift/lift_21_sbt.git
talk allocator
With the above command we clone the Git repository under the directory name talkallocator. If you don't have git installed, you can also download the project from http://github.com/lift/lift_21_sbt/ Download downloads as tgz or zip files. A look inside the cloned or the unpacked directory shows the structure shown in Listing 9.1.
Listing 9.1: Files and directories of the lift prototype

```
+ - project
|
+ - build
|
|
+ - LiftProject.scala
```

```
|
+ - build.properties
+ - src
+ - main
|
+ - resources
|
|
+ - props
|
|
+ - default.props
|
+ - scale
|
|
+ - bootstrap
|
|
|
'- liftweb
|
|
|
'- Boot.scala
|
|
+ - code
|
|
+ - comet
|
|
+ - lib
|
|
|
+ - DepencyFactory.scala
|
|
+ - model
|
|
|
+ - User.scala
|
|
+ - snippet
|
|
|
+ - HelloWorld.scala
|
|
```

```
+ - view
|
+ - webapp
|
+ - images
|
|
+ - ajax-loader.gif
|
+ - index.html
|
+ - static
|
|
+ - index.html
|
+ - templates-hidden
|
|
+ - default.html
|
|
+ - wizard-all.html
|
+ - WEB-INF
|
+ - web.xml
+ - test
+ - resources
+ - scale
+ - code
|
+ - AppTest.scala
|
+ - snippet
|
+ - HelloWorldTest.scala
+ - LiftConsole.scala
+ - RunWebApp.scala
```

We start Sbt in the talkallocator directory. After Sbt has the necessary gen libraries does not download without request, we give the com- command update on. To try out the running web application we enter jetty-run under Sbt. This command starts the embedded Jetty web server 4 . If you now open a browser and http: // localhost: 8080 /, you should see the information shown in Figure 9.1 see the website.

The sample application includes user management. You can register trier, log in and log out again. If it is on port 25 on your computer SMTP server listens, you can already send a "forgotten password" email send. All of this happens with relatively little code. Let's go back one more time to the files from Listing 9.1. The project directory contains the configuration ration for the Sbt project, and tests are located under src / test. The actual A lift application therefore only consists of the files in the src / main directory, which we want to look at individually below.

The resources / props / default.props file is empty in the prototype. she can Properties contain such as
db.driver = com.mysql.jdbc.Driver
It is also possible to define your own properties. In the scala directory the Scala files, under webapp all others such as images, static HTML pages and templates. There are two subdirectories in the scala directory nits.
The bootstrap directory contains the liftweb / Boot.scala file, which is included in the Starting the web application is used. We will look at this file in the Take a closer look at section 9.2 or adapt it to our needs. Important is, that this file has the class Boot in the package bootstrap.liftweb with a Method boot defined. Exactly this method is used by the lift servlet when starting th executed.
The three files in the code directory contain the necessary Scala classes and objects for the running application. We will look at this area in Section 9.3 together with the templates in the src / main / webapp directory. to take. The directory name code is chosen arbitrarily. We will later replace it with the org directory, as we are using the package org.obraun.talkallocator.

9.2 Bootstrapping

First of all we want to adapt the class bootstrap.liftweb.Boot. In the The main issue is the boot method, which is activated when the web application is started.
to be led. As in the prototype, we also want a database for storage the user, but also the information. The prototype developed for this The code held is shown in Listing 9.2.

Listing 9.2: Code of the lift prototype for the database connection

```
if (! DB.jndiJdbcConnAvailable_?) {
val vendor =
new StandardDBVendor (
Props.get ("db.driver") openOr "org.h2.Driver",
Props.get ("db.url") openOr
"jdbc: h2: lift_proto.db; AUTO_SERVER = TRUE",
Props.get ("db.user"), Props.get ("db.password"))
LiftRules.unloadHooks.append (
vendor.closeAllConnections_! _)
DB.defineConnectionManager (
DefaultConnectionIdentifier, vendor)
}
Schemifier.schemify (true, Schemifier.infoF _, User)
```

We can use this code to explain the first lift concepts. First the method jndiJdbcConnAvailable_? of the DB object checked, whether we can get a JDBC connection from JNDI 5 . Lift defines a ne variety of methods using the suffix _? or _! have to indicate whether asked for something or not. After we take care of our database want to take care of the binding itself, we omit the if statement. That what is within the block, but we will still need some of it.
We need a StandardDBVendor object for the database connection. We want to use this to manage an H2 database 6 . In the prototype code, Props.get tries to access properties that are, for example, in the data part resources / props / default.props could be. Props.get delivers a ne property as a value of the type Box [String]. A box is similar to

an option with a few additional features. If the box is empty, the method
de openOr returns its argument, otherwise the content of the box. After we don't
ne properties 7 , we can use the first two arguments of the

5 Java Naming and Directory Interface

6 http://www.h2database.com/

7 Of course it makes sense to leave the Props.get statements in the code. With this we can later You can easily switch to another database management system. For didactic reasons but let's remove them here.

StandardDBVendor constructor directly specify the respective strings. The third and fourth arguments, the DB user and the password, are also not required. does. But since the constructor needs a value of the type Box [String], we simply pass an empty box by specifying the Empty object.

The next concept that we would like to introduce to you is the LiftRules-Object. This object serves as a container for almost everything that is confi can be gured. In the corresponding line of code in Listing 9.2, the unloadHooks-Collection a function for closing all connections. hangs. This is then carried out when the lift application is shut down. It makes sense to keep it that way. Also the line to define the We leave the database connection as the ConnectionManager unchanged.

A part of the O / R mapper from Lift is used with the Schemifier. The me- method schemify ensures that the database has the correct schema to save the user objects. The "right" scheme is in the class com.model.User, which we will cover in the next section.

After we also want to save the lectures in a separate table, add we simply add the Talk class as an additional argument for schemify. In order to If this can be compiled, we of course first have to pass the Talk class to implement. We ask you to be patient until section 9.5.

The code that replaces the lines in Listing 9.2 in the Talk Allocator is shown in Listing 9.3 to see.

Listing 9.3: Code of the talk allocator for the database connection

```
val vendor =
new StandardDBVendor (
"org.h2.Driver",
"jdbc: h2: talkallocator.db; AUTO_SERVER = TRUE",
Empty, Empty)
LiftRules.unloadHooks.append (
vendor.closeAllConnections_! _)
DB.defineConnectionManager (
DefaultConnectionIdentifier, vendor)
Schemifier.schemify (true, Schemifier.infoF _, User, Talk)
```

The next line in the prototype is:

```
LiftRules.addToPackages ("code")
```

This informs the lift framework, in the package code according to classes and Search for objects for the so-called *snippets* (see Section 9.3). We change the line from in

```
LiftRules.addToPackages ("org.obraun.talkallocator")
```

because we want to use this package for our code. The meeting and Adaptation of the following lines, which are necessary for the SiteMap, we practice on section 9.4. We'll also leave the last five statements for now as they are, so that the current contents of the Boot.scala file are as in Listing 9.4 shows.

Listing 9.4: The partially revised Boot.scala file

```
package bootstrap.liftweb
import net.liftweb._
```

```
import util._
import common._
import http._
import sitemap._
import Loc._
import mapper._
// still needed until rebuilt
import code.model._
class boot {
def boot {
val vendor =
new StandardDBVendor (
"org.h2.Driver",
"jdbc: h2: talkallocator.db; AUTO_SERVER = TRUE",
Empty, Empty)
LiftRules.unloadHooks.append (
vendor.closeAllConnections_! _)
DB.defineConnectionManager (
DefaultConnectionIdentifier, vendor)
Schemifier.schemify (true, Schemifier.infoF _,
User, talk)
LiftRules.addToPackages ("org.obraun.talkallocator")
// not yet adjusted
val entries = List (
Menu.i ("Home") / "index",
Menu (Loc ("Static", Link (List ("static"), true,
"/ static / index"),
"Static Content"))) :::
User.sitemap
LiftRules.setSiteMap (SiteMap (entries: _ *))
LiftRules.ajaxStart =
Full (() =>
LiftRules.jsArtifacts.show ("ajax-loader"). Cmd)
LiftRules.ajaxEnd =
Full (() =>
LiftRules.jsArtifacts.hide ("ajax-loader"). Cmd)
LiftRules.early.append (
_.setCharacterEncoding ("UTF-8"))
LiftRules.loggedInTest = Full (() => User.loggedIn_?)
S.addAround (DB.buildLoanWrapper)
}
}
```

The LiftRules for ajaxStart and ajaxStop define the on and off dazzle an image. With the following statement, the used th character set set to UTF-8. The loggedInTest is used to differentiate whether a user is successfully logged in or not, e.g. to display different menu items.

Finally, the object S from the package net.liftweb.http comes into Game. This object represents the current status of the HTTP request and - Response. For example, it can be used for cookie management or for local zation / internationalization. With the addAround method a wrapper around the entire request. In the specific case it is Wrapper defined by the buildLoanWrapper method from the DB object, which turns the entire request into a database transaction.

Let's start the web application with the Sbt command jetty-run with the changed boot class, the start page looks like http: // localhost: 8080 / as seen in Figure 9.2.

We see an error message saying that a snippet could not be found-de. The rest of the application still works. The snippet is in Package code, but we have the package org.obraun.talkallocator for the snippets given. We deal with snippets and the presentation in the following section.

For those who like to have their code together in one package and not a want to use the extra package bootstrap.liftweb, there is this possibility-of course. To use the class org.obraun.talkallocator.Boot to we only have to change a few things:

1. We move the Boot.scala file from the bootstrap / directory - liftweb to org / obraun / talkallocator relative to src and change the package name accordingly.
2. We are expanding the Bootable class.
3. We add an element init- in the webapp / WEB-INF / web.xml file -param by setting the bootloader to the new class (see list ting 9.5).

own boot class

```
<? xml version = "1.0" encoding = "ISO-8859-1"?>
<! DOCTYPE web app
PUBLIC "- // Sun Microsystems, Inc.//DTD Web Application
2.3 // EN "
"http://java.sun.com/dtd/web-app_2_3.dtd">
<web-app>
<filter>
<filter-name> LiftFilter </filter-name>
<display-name> Lift Filter </display-name>
<description>
The filter that intercepts lift calls
</description>
<filter-class>
net.liftweb.http.LiftFilter
</filter-class>
<init-param>
<param-name> bootloader </param-name>
<param-value>
org.obraun.talkallocator.Boot
</param-value>
</init-param>
</filter>
<filter-mapping>
<filter-name> LiftFilter </filter-name>
<url-pattern> / * </url-pattern>
</filter-mapping>
</web app>
```

9.3 Rendering templates and snippets

Lift's rendering concept, which is also used in the prototype, is the use of templates. Scala-Functions, so-called *snippets* , are integrated. There is also the possibility possibility, without templates, only with the help of Scala functions, so-called *views* ,

to render. In the following we restrict ourselves to the use of templates tes and snippets.
If http: // localhost: 8080 / is called, the template with the name men default.html from the templates-hidden directory under wepapp rendered and shipped [8] . A look at the file shows HTML with some peculiarities. What we can easily customize is the title of the page as it is this is the usual HTML title tag in the head. We replace that existing day by:
<title> Talk Allocator </title>
After the title we already see two lift-specific tags:
<lift: CSS.blueprint />
<lift: CSS.fancyType />
This is the integration of two snippets. The tags have the Form <lift: snippet_name />, where the snippet_name is a method of a class or an object. In the snippets above, these are the Methods blueprint and fancyType of the CSS object of the lift framework.
The meaning of the snippet tag is to run the appropriate method and replace the day with the result. That of course means that the methods must return a value of type scala.xml.NodeSeq.
In the body of the template we can still add the heading from app to talk Change allocator. A little further down in the file we see two more cher snippet tags:
<lift: Menu.builder />
<lift: Msgs showAll = "true" />
The builder method of the object Menu executed. This renders the menu with the SiteMap content. In the two-The tenth snippet tag is not a method. If no method is specified, the render method, which means in this case the render method of the object Msgs. This gives messages from the lift framework such as error messages genes, warnings or notifications. The showAll attribute, the is read in the render method, it can be specified whether all message applications are to be issued.
The last lift tag in the default.html file is:

[8] The template is not really the entry point. More details below.

<lift: bind name = "content" />
This is not a snippet tag, but belongs to a separate class of tags: the *bind tags* . The bind tag defines a place with a name in which what can be inserted. And that brings us to the real entry point into the application. Of course, you must have guessed correctly, when call from http: // localhost: 8080 / not the file default.html, but index.html delivered. The index.html file included in the lift prototype in the webapp directory is shown in Listing 9.6.

Listing 9.6: The index.html file from the lift prototype

```
<lift: surround with = "default" at = "content">
<h2> Welcome to your project! </h2>
<p>
<lift: helloWorld.howdy>
<span> Welcome to your Lift app at <b:time/> </span>
</lift:helloWorld.howdy>
</p>
</ lift: surround>
```

What we see as the topmost XML element in the index.html file is the Matching the bind tag from the default.html file. That surround tag takes the template specified with the with attribute and replaces the bind Tag with the name content with its own content, i.e. from <h2> to

</p>. This content contains a snippet tag that the howdy method of the class HelloWorld calls. This time the start and end tags are separated from each other, and there is the following in between:
<span> Welcome to your Lift app at <b:time/> </span>
In this way we can pass a NodeSeq as an argument to a snippet.
give. That means, there are snippets without and snippets with a NodeSeq as argument. The argument used is valid XML, but it also contains
a specialty: the tag <b: time />. This tag is in the howdy method
replaced. Let's take a look at the method:

```
import net.liftweb.util.Helpers.bind
def howdy (in: NodeSeq): NodeSeq =
bind ("b", in, "time" -> date.map (d => Text (d.toString)))
```

Using bind of the Helpers object causes <b: time /> to pass through
replaces a text node with the current date. The bind method expects
tet the following parameters:
A namespace, i.e. the prefix before the colon - in this case b.
The NodeSeq in which to replace - in this case in.
One or more mappings of element names (time) to the replacement
Element (date.map (d => Text (d.toString)))).
The date field is of the type Box [Date]. The important thing about the field is that it is lazy
val was defined. This ensures that the current time is only available upon access
is determined. Since HelloWorld is not an object but a class,
a new object is created each time index.html is loaded.
For the talk allocator, we'll modify the index.html file, as shown in Listing 9.7
is pictured.

Listing 9.7. The Talk Allocator's index.html file

```
<lift: surround with = "default" at = "content">
<h2> Welcome to the talk allocator </h2>
<h4> Talks that have not yet been awarded are </h4>
<lift: Talks.available />
<h4> Are already taken </h4>
<lift: Talks.allocated />
</ lift: surround>
```

We use the template default and give those not yet and those already assigned
given talks. We have specified two snippet tags for this purpose. So this
works, we need to create a class or an object talks with the two
Implement available and allocated methods. That must be
Then in the sub-package one snippets the lift framework as part of the
Bootstrapping announced packages. After we got that in the boot class
Have added package org.obraun.talkallocator to the LiftRules,
we save our snippets in org.obraun.talkallocator.snippet. Loading
before we do this, however, let's deal with the next two sections.
ten first with the supplied user administration, the SiteMap and the
Lift's own OR mapper [9] .

9.4 User administration and SiteMap

The lift framework contains user management that we already have in the prototype
have seen. Lift offers the MegaProto-
User. In the following we adapt the file User from the prototype to our requirements
needs. Strictly speaking, we only take what we don't need
from the User class and the Companion object. The ones we use
The User.scala file is shown in Listing 9.8.

[9] Object-relational mapping, for storing objects in a relational database.

Listing 9.8. The User Class with Companion Object for User Management

```
package org.obraun.talkallocator
package model
import net.liftweb.mapper._
import net.liftweb.common._
class User extends MegaProtoUser [User] {
def getSingleton = User
}
object User extends User with MetaMegaProtoUser [User] {
override def dbTableName = "users"
override def screenWrap = Full (
<lift: surround with = "default" at = "content">
<lift: bind />
</ lift: surround>
)
override def skipEmailValidation = true
}
```

The User class adds the MegaProtoUser trait. This trait defines a user who can be saved using the OR mapper. The the only abstract method that needs to be implemented is getSingleton. This method must return an object, the *meta-server* for this class. This meta server provides the necessary information for the database etc. available and in our case is the companion object.

By mixing in the trait MetaMegaProtoUser to the object User we have all the functionality you need. We also take over some speeches definitions from the lift prototype. We give a separate table name for the Storage of the user. The screenWrap method is used to development of the web pages of the user administration, and finally leave we allow new users to register without email validation.

Next, let's go back to the boot class and define the SiteMap. The lines required for this are shown in Listing 9.9.

Listing 9.9: Creating a SiteMap in the Boot Class

```
val ifLoggedIn = If (() => User.loggedIn_ ?,
() => RedirectResponse ("/ index"))
val ifAdmin = If (() => User.superUser_ ?,
() => RedirectResponse ("/ index"))
val entries = List (
Menu.i ("Home") / "index",
Menu (Loc ("Add", List ("add"),
"Add / delete talk", ifAdmin)),
Menu (Loc ("Choose", List ("choose"),
"Select Talk", ifLoggedIn))
) ::: User.sitemap
LiftRules.setSiteMap (SiteMap (entries: _ *))
```

We want a SiteMap with a start page. Only when the user is logged in, a page for selecting a talk should also be added. If the user is an admin, he also receives a page to create new talks and delete talks. In addition, the Default SiteMap for user management can be added.

To do this, we define entries, a list of menu items. The first menu entry is the easiest way to create an entry With the method i of the Menu object we create an entry that is named as and Linktext gets the argument passed. We add to the result

add a path to the / method.
We use the Loc object to create the two entries Add and Choose.
We pass a name, a link, a link text to its apply method
and a LocParam. A link is represented as a list of directories, also we would have to specify admin / add List ("admin", "add") for the link. One
Finally, LocParam modifies an entry. In our example we have
the two LocParams, ifLoggedIn and ifAdmin, for clarity
ber defined as vals. The LocParam used in both cases is an ob-
object of the class If. The first parameter is a predicate, which is a function that
returns a boolean. The second parameter specifies the behavior that
should be executed if the predicate does not apply. The so implemented
We concatenate the list with the User.sitemap. After all, we use that
Elements of the entries list individually, therefore as entries: _ *, for creation
of a SiteMap object and pass this to the method setSiteMap of the
LiftRules object.

9.5 Persistence

Next we implement a Talk class for the talks that are
database should be persisted via the OR mapper. A talk should be included
Have a field for a title and a field for the presenter. Without OR mapping
we would define the class as follows:

```
class Talk (val title: String, var speaker: User)
```

Because of the use of the OR mapper, we need to create this basic framework
puff it up just a little, as shown in Listing 9.10.

Listing 9.10: The Talk class

```
class Talk extends LongKeyedMapper [Talk] with IdPK {
def getSingleton = Talk
object title extends MappedString (this, 100)
object speaker extends MappedLongForeignKey (this, user)
}
```

To use the OR mapper, we need to add a mapper trait to the class
Mix in talk. We choose the LongKeyedMapper trait, which is a long-
Value used as primary key in the database. After we have the primary
If you don't want to define the key yourself, we add a suitable implementation
through the IdPK trait. This gives every talk object a unique
term key with the identifier id.
As in the User class (see Listing 9.8), we have to use the get-
Define singleton. Analogous to the user, we also use the compa-
nion object. We have to define the fields a little differently for the OR mapper,
namely as objects. The type of column in the database results from each
because trait used. We want the title as a string with a maximum
Save 100 characters in length. We use the MappedString trait for this.
The first parameter is the Talk object to which this field belongs, the second
Parameter indicates the maximum length. To manage the presenter, use
we zen a MappedLongForeignKey, i.e. a long value that is
key is used. We pass the object to the
this field belongs and the user object as the target for the foreign key.
The Talk companion object that is still required is shown in Listing 9.11.

Listing 9.11: The Talk Object

```
object Talk extends Talk with LongKeyedMetaMapper [Talk] {
override def dbTableName = "talks"
}
```

The Talk object extends the Talk class and adds the LongKeyedMeta-

Mapper added. Analogous to the user administration, we have the OR Mapper needs functionality and can change it as needed. We give the table in which the talks are stored the name talks.
This allows us to use Talk objects in our web application that are database. Access to the fields of the Talk objects is included quite normally possible. For example, if we have a Talk object named ner myTalk, we can access the title with myTalk.title. The Creating, changing and saving objects works a little differently than usual.
We create a talk object with the create method of the Talk Companion Object. We set a value for a field using the apply method of the field representative object. With the following expression we generate for example wise a talk object with the title "News from Scala":
Talk.create.title ("News from Scala")
With the save method we save the object in the database.
There are various methods of searching for objects in the database of the companion object. The find method, for example, is given as a parameter ter a QueryParam and returns a box that is either empty or that contains found object. In Listing 9.12, the createExampleTalks that we add to the Talk object. The one used in the method QueryParam is generated by the By object and looks for the value talk im Title field.

Listing 9.12. The createExampleTalks method from the Talk object

```
def createExampleTalks () = {
Cunning (
"Scala 2.8.0 - What's new?",
"Scala - OSGi Bundles from Outer (Java) Space"
) .foreach {
talk =>
if (find (By (title, talk)). isEmpty)
create.title (talk) .save
}
}
```

By adding to the line
Talk.createExampleTalks ()
In the boot class, when the web application is started, a check is made to see whether the two
Talks already exist in the database. If not, they will be newly placed. The respective unset field speaker has the value in the database ZERO. The value NULL can also be explicitly used with the method call myTalk.-speaker (Empty).
To create two sample users when the application starts, add Let's add the user object to the create method given in Listing 9.13. ExampleUsers and call them in the boot class.

Listing 9.13: The createExampleUsers method from the user object

```
def createExampleUsers () {
if (find (By (email, "admin@obraun.org")). isEmpty) {
create.email ("admin@obraun.org")
.firstName ("Hugo")
.lastName ("Admin")
.password ("talkadmin")
.superUser (true)
.validated (true)
.Save
```

```
}
if (find (By (email, "user@obraun.org")). isEmpty) {
create.email ("user@obraun.org")
.firstName ("Egon")
.lastName ("User")
.password ("talkuser")
.validated (true)
.Save
}
}
```

9.6 Implementation of the snippets

What is still missing from the finished Talk Allocator are the snippets and the templates for selecting and administering the talks. The template for the We already showed the start page in Listing 9.7. The start page should then be like in Figure 9.3 will look like shown.

Figure 9.3: Talk Allocator start page

We want to implement the two required snippets first. There- to create a file Talks.scala in the sub-package snippet of the package ges org.obraun.talkallocator. We need two methods available and allocated, each of which has a NodeSeq as a result. With the already assigned talks should be followed by the speaker with first and last name in brackets can be specified. Since that's only a small difference, we'll implement a method talksAsTable that has a flag as a parameter indicating which Talks, free or assigned, should be displayed. The object Talks with the three methods are given in Listing 9.14.

Listing 9.14: The Talks object with the first snippets

```
package org.obraun.talkallocator
package snippet
import scala.xml._
import net.liftweb._
import mapper._
import util.Helpers._
import common._
import http.S._
import http.SHtml._
import model._
object talks {
def available = talksAsTable (true)
def allocated = talksAsTable (false)
def talksAsTable (available: Boolean) = {
def speaker (speakerID: MappedLong [Talk]) = {
val speaker = User.find (
By (User.id, speakerID)
) .get
Text (speaker.firstName + "" + speaker.lastName)
}
val talks = Talk.findAll (
if (available) NullRef (Talk.speaker)
else NotNullRef (Talk.speaker)
)
<table>
{talks.map {
talk =>
<tr>
```

```
<th> {talk.title} </th>
{if (! available)
<th width = "20%">
({speaker (talk.speaker)})
</th>
}
</tr>
}
}
</table>
}
}
```

The talksAsTable method consists of three parts: a function for give the speaker, the calculation of the talks to be displayed and the formulas calculation of the result value. After the speaker is a foreign key in the talk is included, we pass the value to the speaker function. In the radio tion speaker, we determine the associated user object with the method User.find. After find returns a box, we pack the object with get out. Then we create an object of the type from the first and last name scala.xml.Text.

We use the findAll method to determine the talks. Free talks have in of the database in the column speaker the value NULL. Via the query In this way, we can determine all free talks using the NullRef parameter. Conversely, we find with NotNullRef all talks that have already been given.

The NodeSeq that talksAsTable eventually returns is a table. Out Each talk is made up of its own line, either just the title or the title and contains speakers.

Figure 9.4: Start page of the talk allocator with a talk assigned

After Egon User has decided on a talk, the start page looks at Example as in Figure 9.4. So that Egon User can even have a talk we have to implement the template and the snippet for it- Ren. Listing 9.15 shows the template for the selection page. The page should look like then as in Figure 9.5.

Listing 9.15: The choose.html template for selecting a talk

```
<lift: surround with = "default" at = "content">
<h2> Select Talk </h2>
<lift: Talks.choose form = "post" />
</ lift: surround>
```

As can be seen in Listing 9.15, we choose the same structure with the default Template. This time, the snippet tag has an attribute form. pet to the form. It should be implemented as a method choose in the talk Object. This method aims to do the following:

Figure 9.5: Selection page of the talk allocator

1. If the user clicks on the button "Do not accept a talk", "is sure to put that no talk is assigned to him. If he already had a talk, he will join this the speaker is set back to ZERO.
2. All available talks are displayed as a radio button list. Does the User already selected a talk, it is at the top and is already marked. If none have been selected yet, none will be pre-selected Clicking the "Select" button immediately does not lead to any changes. change.
3. If the user selects a talk and confirms this with the button "Off select ", the corresponding talk is assigned to him. A previously chosen one is released again.

Listing 9.16: The Talks.choose method

```
def choose = {
val user = User.currentUser.open_!
val chosen = Talk.findAll (By (Talk.speaker, user.id))
val available = Talk.findAll (NullRef (Talk.speaker))
var newTitle: Option [String] = None
def chooseTalk (maybeTitle: Option [String]) = {
val hasOld =! chosen.isEmpty
maybeTitle match {
case None if hasOld =>
chosen.head.speaker (Empty) .save
case Some (title) =>
Talk.find (By (Talk.title, title)) match {
case Full (talk) =>
if (hasOld) {
val old = chosen.head
if (old.title! = talk.title) {
old.speaker (Empty) .save
talk.speaker (user.id) .save
}
} else talk.speaker (user.id) .save
case _ => error ("Talk" + title + "not found")
}
case _ =>
}
redirectTo ("/")
}
val talks = radio (
(chosen ::: available) .map {_.title.toString},
if (chosen.isEmpty)
Empty
else
Full (chosen.head.title),
title => newTitle = Some (title)
) .toForm
val choose = submit (
"Choose",
() => chooseTalk (newTitle)
)
val chooseNone = submit (
"Don't take on any talk",
() => chooseTalk (None)
)
talks: + choose: + chooseNone
}
```

The method choose is shown in Listing 9.16. In the first part a nige vals and one var defined. With User.currentUser we get that logged in user in a box that we open with open_! unpacking. Access with open_! throws an exception if no user is logged in. Due to on our SiteMap, the corresponding page can only be seen if a user zer is logged in. Then we calculate the list of those already selected Talks and assign them chosen. Although only a maximum of one talk can be assigned can, in such cases in functional programming with Lis- th worked. This is also done, for example, by generating the radio button

a little bit tighter below. Determining the available talks
we already know from the talksAsTable method. For the possibly excellent
For the selected title, we use a local variable that we preset with None.
We store the logic of the method described above in the function choose-
Talk, which gets the value from newTitle. Is it
at None, the talk that may have already been selected is reset,
to which pass an empty box to the speaker object and the Talk object with
save is written to the database. If a title was given, the
Talk determined. The various cases are then processed.
At the end of the chooseTalk function, you will be redirected to the start page. The to it
The redirectTo method used belongs to the S object that contains the current status
of the HTTP request and response.
After the chooseTalk function, we still have to get the result, i.e. the node
Define Seq. We can create a group of radio buttons with the method
radio of the SHtml object. The three parameters are:

1. The different options, with us the different talks. After the
If the value of chosen is a list, we can add it, regardless of whether it is empty or not,
fold in front of the list of available talks.
2. The pre-selected option as a box. Empty does not correspond to any prediction
choice.
3. The function performed with the selected option. We assign them
The selected option is packed in a Some of the variable newTitle.

The radio buttons generated in this way still have to be converted into a NodeSeq using
toForm.
to be converted.
We define the two buttons with the submit method, which has a label
for the button and a function to execute after clicking. In
In both cases we use our help function chooseTalk. Finally hand
Let's add the two buttons to the NodeSeq of the radio buttons and give them
this as a result of the snippet. This gives us full functionality
Implemented into the Talk Allocator for selecting a talk.
What now follows is the administration page with the options for Talks
create and delete. The template for this, shown in Listing 9.17,
contains two snippet tags. The first consists of a start day, an end day
and a bit of XML in between. This XML in between becomes the snippet
Pass Talks.add as an argument. It contains two self-defined tags with
the prefix talk. At these points we will add something with the add method
put. The second snippet tag (for deletion) has no argument for the snippet
Talks.delete. The administration page should look like Figure 9.6.

Listing 9.17: The add.html template for adding and deleting talks

```
<lift: surround with = "default" at = "content">
<h2> New Talk </h2>
<lift: Talks.add form = "post">
<table>
<tr>
<td>
<talk: title />
</td>
</tr>
<tr>
<td>
<talk: add />
</td>
</tr>
```

```
</table>
</lift:Talks.add>
<h2> Delete talk </h2>
<lift: Talks.delete form = "post" />
</ lift: surround>
```

Figure 9.6: Administration page of the Talk Allocator

The add method of the Talks object is shown in Listing 9.18. After a Variable for the new title to be entered in the text field, we define the auxiliary function addTalk. This creates and saves a new talk with the given title, unless it is the empty string or a talk with the title already exists. We use for the generation of the NodeSeq the bind method of the Helpers object from the net.liftweb.util package. With this method we can change parts of an existing NodeSeq.

Listing 9.18: The Talks.add method

```
def add (html: NodeSeq) = {
var title = ""
def addTalk (title: String) = {
if (title! = "" &&
Talk.find (By (Talk.title, title)). IsEmpty) {
Talk.create.title (title) .save
}
}
bind ("talk", html,
"title" -> text ("",
t => title = t.trim),
"add" -> submit ("add",
() => addTalk (title))
)
}
```

The first argument to bind is the namespace. In the template in Listing 9.17 we have the namespace talk for the two tags that we want to replace elected. The second argument is the NodeSeq to replace in - in in our case the argument of the add method with the name html. The white The other arguments are of type BindParam. The first of these replaces the day title in the namespace talk through a text field using the method de SHtml.text. The first argument to text is the predefined content. The second argument, functionality, assigns the entered text without leading and adding trailing spaces to the variable title. The day talk: add will by a button with the label "Add", which deactivates the addTalk function leads, replaced.

Listing 9.19: The Talks.delete method

```
def delete = {
import scala.collection.mutable.Set
val toDelete = Set [Talk] ()
val talks = Talk.findAll
def deleteTalks (toDelete: Set [Talk]) {
toDelete.foreach {
talk =>
if (! talk.delete_!)
error ("Could not delete:" + talk.toString)
}
}
val checkboxes = talks.flatMap (talk =>
checkbox (
false,
```

```
if (_) toDelete += = talk
): +
Text (talk.title): +
<br />
)
val delete = submit (
"Clear",
() => deleteTalks (toDelete)
)
checkboxes ++ delete
}
```

The Talks.delete method for the second snippet tag of the template of the The administration page is shown in Listing 9.19. By the use of Checkboxes can be deleted several talks at the same time. For the talks that are to be deleted, we use a changeable set. To delete All talks should be available without exception, including those that have already been given.

The auxiliary function deleteTalks deletes all transferred talks. For every talk let's create a checkbox that is not checked. If it has been marked, will the talk added to toDelete. Next to the checkbox, the title of the talk can still be specified explicitly. [10] We create the button for deleting in the same way to the previous buttons.

We are done with our little lift web application. We could you in the context of this chapter, of course, only show a small section of Lift. Lift can of course do much, much more.

[10] There is also an overloaded version of checkbox, with which we create a sequence of checkboxes could generate. However, this shows the entire talk and not just the title. Ok we could Of course, redefine toString in the Talk class. As you can see, there are always several possibilities opportunities!

Chapter 10 Lightweight Web programming with scalatra

In addition to extensive web frameworks such as the one provided in Chapter 9 There are also lighter weight alternatives in Scala. One of them is Scalatra [2] , inspired by the Ruby web framework Sinatra [1] , which we bring to you in want to introduce this chapter using an example.

The *final grade calculator* serves as a simple example . This is intended to note for one of the two computer science courses Bachelor of Science and Diplom calculate from three partial grades. In a web application it should be possible to transfer the course and the three partial grades necessary for the calculation and to display the overall grade with the grade achieved.

In Section 10.1 we will first of all, independently of our example, Start with a prototype provided by the Scalatra team. Then create we len the final grade calculator and explain the steps in section 10.2.

The code created for this is available at http://github.com/obcode/ finalgradecalculator_scalatra.

10.1 Quickstart with Scalatra

The start with Scalatra is analogous to that with the lift (see 9.1). There is a proto- types that we can download and customize. To do this, we clone the

1 http://www.sinatrarb.com/
2 http://www.scalatra.org/

Repository, change to the directory, load the required resources via Sbt and start the web application by starting the embedded jet:

```
$ git clone \
git: //github.com/scalatra/scalatra-sbt-prototype.git \
finalgradecalculator
Cloning into finalgradecalculator ...
...
$ cd finalgradecalculator
$ sbt update
Getting Scala 2.7.7 ...
...
$ sbt jetty
[info] Building project scalatra-sbt-prototype 0.1.0-
SNAPSHOT against Scala 2.8.0
...
```

If we then open the URL http: // localhost: 8080 / in the browser, which we with "Hello, world!" welcomed. The Scalatra web application consists of a a single Scala file, the contents of which are shown in Listing 10.1.

Listing 10.1: The Scalatra prototype

```
package com.example
import org.scalatra._
class MyScalatraFilter extends ScalatraFilter {
get ("/") {
<h1> Hello, world! </h1>
}
}
```

With Scalatra, both filters and servlets, based on the Java Package javax.servlet. The Trait ScalatraFilter expands tert the Java interface Filter. The ScalatraServlet class extends the Java Class HttpServlet from the sub-package http.

A Scalatra filter or servlet provides the following methods:

before - This method is executed before a request is returned becomes.

get (< path >) - response to a GET request with the path < path > . Loading if part of the path starts with a colon, this part is used as a parameter to hand over. We will use this in section 10.2.

post (< path >) - response to a POST request with the path < path > .

put (< path >) - response to a PUT request with the path < path > .

delete (< path >) - response to a DELETE request with the path < path > .

error - Executed when there is an error.

after - Is placed after the appropriate get, post, put or delete block executed.

10.2 The Final Grade Calculator

After we've got the Scalatra prototype up and running, let's build gradually convert it to a Final Grade Calculator (FGC). We postpone this First, place the MyScalatraFilter class in the desired location and fit

Name and package. The result is shown in Listing 10.2.

Listing 10.2: The FGCFilter class

```
package org.obraun.finalgradecalculator
import org.scalatra._
class FGCFilter extends ScalatraFilter {
get ("/") {
<h1> Final Grade Calculator </h1>
}
}
```

In order for the filter to be found, we have to open the web.xml file in the directory Adjust nis src / main / webapp / WEB-INF. The entire file is in Listing 10.3 to see.

Listing 10.3. The web.xml file

```
<? xml version = "1.0" encoding = "UTF-8"?>
<web-app xmlns: xsi = "http://www.w3.org/2001/XMLSchema-
instance "
xmlns = "http://java.sun.com/xml/ns/javaee"
xmlns: web = "http://java.sun.com/xml/ns/j2ee/web-app_2_4.
xsd "
xsi: schemaLocation = "http://java.sun.com/xml/ns/j2ee
http://java.sun.com/xml/ns/j2ee/web-app_2_4.xsd "
version = "2.4">
<filter>
<filter-name> scalatra </filter-name>
<filter-class>
org.obraun.finalgradecalculator.FGCFilter
</filter-class>
</filter>
<filter-mapping>
<filter-name> scalatra </filter-name>
<url-pattern> / * </url-pattern>
</filter-mapping>
</web-app>
```

If we now restart the jetty with Sbt, we see at the URL http: // localhost: 8080 / in the browser now the response of the FGC filter.

We begin with the actual implementation of the final grade calculator with a get method to which we pass the parameters in the URL. The path should be structured as follows:

/ calculate / grade / mark1 / mark2 / mark3

instead of the course and the three grades, the actual values are given should. That means, a valid URL would be for example:

http: // localhost: 8080 / calculate / dipl / 1,3 / 2,0 / 1,7

This is supported in Scalatra through the following path:

/ calculate /: grade /: mark1 /: mark2 /: mark3

In the get method we can then access the values with the param method. to grab. The reaction to a GET request with such a URL is shown in Listing 10.4 reproduced.

Listing 10.4: The method for calculating the grade for a GET request

```
get ("/ calculate /: grade /: mark1 /: mark2 /: mark3") {
val grade = params ("grade")
val mark1 = params ("mark1") replace (',', '.') toDouble
val mark2 = params ("mark2") replace (',', '.') toDouble
val mark3 = params ("mark3") replace (',', '.') toDouble
def isValid (mark: Double) =
(1.0 <= mark) && (mark <= 5.0)
```

```
if (! isValid (mark1) ||
! isValid (mark2) ||
! isValid (mark3)) redirect ("/ error")
def rating (m: Double): String = {
val adjusted = (m * 10) .toInt / 10.0
if (adjusted <= 1.2)
return "passed with distinction"
if (adjusted <= 1.5) return "very good passed"
if (adjusted <= 2.5) return "passed well"
if (adjusted <= 3.5) return "satisfactory passed"
if (adjusted <= 4.0) return "sufficiently passed"
return "failed"
}
def calcMark (p1: Double, p2: Double, p3: Double) = {
require (p1 + p2 + p3 == 100)
val mark = (
(mark1.toDouble) * p1 +
(mark2.toDouble) * p2 +
(mark3.toDouble) * p3
) / 100
mark.toString.replace ('.', ',') + "," + rating (mark)
}
grade.map {_. toLower} match {
case "ba" =>
<h1> Bachelor of Science:
{calcMark (6,22,72)}
</h1>
case "dipl" =>
<h1> Dipl.-Inform .:
{calcMark (32,8,60)}
</h1>
case _ => redirect ("/ error")
}
}
```

First, the parameters are read out and a double is generated from the notes. power. If the values are not valid grades, we will guide to access the path / error. The rating function calculates the rating or the Wording of the note, whereby only the whole note and the first position after the Comma is significant. The calcMark function calculates the overall grade the three individual grades, the first with p1%, the second with p2% and the third is weighted with p3%. The strings ba and dipl.

In addition to the path with all parameters, we also want the two paths / calcu- Allow late / ba and / calculate / dipl. In response, a formula should lar for entering the grades. The code for this is in the listing 10.5.

Listing 10.5. Reaction to a GET request with the paths / calculate / ba or / cal- culate / dipl

```
def calculateForm (
grade: String, grade: String,
mark1: String, mark2: String, mark3: String
) = {
<body>
<h1> {gradename} </h1>
```

```
<form action = '/ post' method = 'POST'>
<input name = 'grade' value = {grade} type = 'hidden' />
<table>
<tr>
<tr>
<td> {mark1}: </td>
<td> <input name = 'mark1' type = 'text' /> </td>
</tr>
<tr>
<td> {mark2}: </td>
<td> <input name = 'mark2' type = 'text' /> </td>
</tr>
<tr>
<td> {mark3}: </td>
<td> <input name = 'mark3' type = 'text' /> </td>
</tr>
<td> </td>
<td> <input type = 'submit' /> </td>
</tr>
</table>
</form>
</body>
}
get ("/ calculate / ba") {
calculateForm (
"Bachelor of Science",
"ba",
"Grade of the bachelor thesis",
"Overall subject examination grade",
"Average grade for all modules"
)
}
get ("/ calculate / dipl") {
calculateForm (
"Graduate computer scientist",
"dipl",
"Grade of the diploma thesis",
"Grade of the colloquium",
"Overall subject examination grade"
)
}
```

The two reactions differ only in five places. Hence we have Factors out the form into the calculateForm function. The two Forms are shown side by side in Figure 10.1.

As can be seen in Listing 10.5, when the form is submitted, the path / post headed. We can keep the code developed so far and do not have to write anything twice, but can use a redirect respond. The additional code is shown in Listing 10.6.

Listing 10.6: Response to a POST request with the path / post

```
post ("/ post") {
redirect ("/ calculate /" +
params ("grade") + "/" +
params ("mark1") + "/" +
params ("mark2") + "/" +
```

```
params ("mark3")
)
}
```

We determine the parameters and use them to create a path on which the block from Listing 10.4 must respond.

In order to be able to enter something at the root of the path, we change the Response to the path / ab, as shown in Listing 10.7.

Listing 10.7: Response to a GET request with the path /

```
get ("/") {
<body>
<h1> Final Grade Calculator </h1>
<form action = '/ postgrade' method = 'POST'>
<input type = 'radio' name = 'grade' value = 'ba' />
Bachelor of Science
<input type = 'radio' name = 'grade' value = 'dipl' />
Computer scientist
<input type = 'submit' />
</form>
</body>
}
```

So we start by entering http: // localhost: 8080 / with the form from Figure 10.2.

Finally, we need the reaction to the POST request with the Path / postgrade that the submission of the form from Listing 10.7 triggers. The-

Figure 10.2: Choice of degree program

this reaction and a reaction to all other requests using the notFound-Methods are shown in Listing 10.8.

Listing 10.8: Response to a POST request with the path / postgrade and response to all requests that have not yet been defined

```
post ("/ postgrade") {
redirect ("/ calculate /" + params ("grade"))
}
notFound {
"Wrong entry"
}
```

Even if Scalatra is nowhere near as extensive as Lift, we could here only offer an initial introduction and do not cover everything. About what has been discussed

In addition, the current Scalatra version offers support for uploading Files, the administration of sessions and the integration of the template engine Scalate [3] .

Chapter 11

Akka - Actors and Software Transactional memory

After we learned about Scala's built-in actors in Chapter 7, throw In this chapter we take a look at the Akka [1] framework , which is based on the Actors-Model is based and the Scala standard approach goes a lot further leads. Akka's self-declared goal is simpler scalability, fault tolerance,

Concurrency and access over the network through the use of actors.
By connecting actors and software Transactional Memory (STM) [2] the level of abstraction is increased and thus a basis is created on which it's easier to write correct concurrent and scalable applications. For Akka relies on fault tolerance in the field of telecommunications te concept *Let it crash* [3] . And ultimately, Akka actors can be completely transparent be distributed.
On the following pages we want to give you an introduction to Akka. Analogous for the previous chapters, we will gradually introduce an example application tion and address the essential concepts. To build it we refer to the simple one used in Chapter 8 (see Listing 8.7 on page 229) Video library management (MovieStore) and expand it.
In Section 11.1 we will set up an Akka project with Sbt to then create the To transform MovieStore into an Akka-Actor in section 11.2. With the We deal with user and session management in Section 11.3. In

1 http://akkasource.org/
2 STM is an approach in which access to shared memory in transactions is analogous to database transactions. See also [ST95].
3 The idea of *Let it crash* or *Embrace failure* comes from the programming language Erlang (see also [Arm07]). There supervisors are used, for example when a process is aborted can terminate other processes in order to then start all again in an orderly manner.

In Section 11.4 we use Akka's Transactional Memory software to ten structures for available and rented films from several MovieStores to be able to use them together without running the risk of an inconsistent th state to generate. Finally, in Section 11.5 we will show you the im- implementation of the service and the client and how the entire application then lets try it out in the Scala Shell. The code created in this chapter is available at http://github.com/obcode/moviestore_akka.

11.1 Quickstart with Akka

We use Sbt again to develop our Akka application. We generate First create a new project in an empty directory:

```
$ mkdir moviestore
$ cd moviestore
$ sbt
Project does not exist, create new project? (y / N / s) y
Name: moviestore
Organization: org.obraun
Version [1.0]: 0.9
Scala version [2.7.7]: 2.8.0
sbt version [0.7.4]:
Getting Scala 2.7.7 ...
```

Next we configure our project to use the Akka plugin can be. The necessary Plugins.scala file is shown in Listing 11.1 see.

Listing 11.1: The project / plugins / Plugins.scala file

```
import sbt._
class plugins (info: ProjectInfo)
extends PluginDefinition (info) {
val akkaPlugin = "se.scalablesolutions.akka"%
"akka-sbt-plugin"% "0.10"
}
```

This can be done with the Akka plug-in, which must match the Akka version used Sbt project by mixing in the AkkaProject trait into an Akka project be made. The MyProject.scala file required for this is in the listing 11.2.

Listing 11.2. The project / build / MyProject.scala file

```
import sbt._
class MyProject (info: ProjectInfo)
extends DefaultProject (info) with AkkaProject
```

With this definition we have a dependency on the core module of acka defined. Dependencies on other modules can be made using the Trait AkkaProject provided method akkaModule can be added den, e.g.

```
val akkaKernel = akkaModule ("kernel")
```

to use the Akka microkernel, which allows Akka to be used as a stand to use alone service. We do not need any further for our sample application teren Akka modules. After a sbt update everything is available locally, and we can start developing the MovieStore.

11.2 The MovieStore

We start with the MovieStore as we developed it in Chapter 8. Around To save you having to page back, we have included the contents of Listing 8.7 Page 229 reproduced again in Listing 11.3.

Listing 11.3: The Movie and MovieStore classes from Chapter 8

```
case class Movie (title: String, filmrating: Int)
class MovieStore {
private [this] var available = Map [Int, Movie] ()
private [this] var rent = Map [Int, Movie] ()
def addToStore (movie: Movie) {
MovieStore.serial + = 1
available + = (MovieStore.serial -> movie)
}
def addToStore (movies: Traversable [Movie]) {
movies foreach (addToStore (_))
}
def rentMovie (serial: Int): Option [Movie] = {
val movieOption = available get serial
movieOption match {
case None => None
case Some (movie) =>
available - = serial
rent + = (serial -> movie)
movieOption
}
}
def returnMovie (serial: Int) = {
val movie = rent (serial)
rent - = serial
available + = (serial -> movie)
}
def availableMoviesForAge (age: Int) =
available.filter {
case (_, Movie (_, r)) => r <= age
}
def availableMovies = available
def rentMovies = rent
```

```
}
object MovieStore {
private var serial = 0
}
```

We are now converting the MovieStore for our Akka application. The Movie Store service should later not only manage the films but also create a user account have administration. Each user who uses the service should have a separate session be generated. We don't want to implement all of this in one class. animals. So first we make a trait out of the MovieStore class. The We keep the MovieStore object and the Movie class unchanged.

In the Trait MovieStore, we want to respond to messages that the management implementation of the films. Therefore we expand it with the Trait Actor from the Akka Core Package. The Trait MovieStore sees in its first mutation as shown in Listing 11.4.

Listing 11.4: First changes to the MovieStore

```
package org.obraun.moviestore
import se.scalablesolutions.akka.actor.Actor
trait MovieStore extends Actor {
protected [this] var available = Map [Int, Movie] ()
protected [this] var rent = Map [Int, Movie] ()
def rentMovieAge (age: Int, serial: Int) = {
val movieOption = available get serial
movieOption match {
case None => None
case Some (movie @ Movie (_, r)) =>
if (r <= age) {
available - = serial
rent + = (serial -> movie)
movieOption
} else None
}
}
...
}
```

After defining the package, we import the Akka actor trait. The Both maps should no longer be private, but inherited can. The rentMovieAge method is new and solves the rent-Movie that ignored the age when renting it. The methods add-ToStore, returnMovie and availableMoviesForAge we take over changed. So we left them out in Listing 11.4. The two methods We do not accept availableMovies and rentMovies.

What is still missing for the definition of the actor is the implementation of the method

def receive: PartialFunction [Any, Unit]

which is the only abstract method included in the Akka-Actor-Trait. The im-Implementation of this method corresponds to what is done in Scala-Actors with a receive or react block is made. Before we get into the implementation first of all, let's define the various messages to which the MovieStore trait react or which it should be able to send. The Messages are shown in Listing 11.5. We will have more messages later complete.

Listing 11.5: The messages for the MovieStore trait

```
package org.obraun.moviestore
sealed trait message
case class AvailableList (age: Int) extends Message
```

```
case class RentMovie (age: Int, serial: Int)
extends message
case class Return (serial: Int) extends Message
case class ResultList (movies: List [(Int, String, Int)])
extends message
case class SuccessfullyRent (serial: Int) extends Message
case class Error (msg: String) extends Message
```

The three messages AvailableList, RentMovie and Return should be vieStore. The messages ResultList, Successfully-
Rent and Error are used for answers. The reaction to the messages

we define in the method rentalManagement, which in the Trait MovieStore then also serves as an implementation of receive. The two methods are shown in Listing 11.6.

Listing 11.6: The receive and rentalManagement methods of the MovieStore trace

```
def receive = rentalManagement
protected def rentalManagement: Receive = {
case AvailableList (age) =>
val result = availableMoviesForAge (age)
println ("Calculated" + result)
self.reply (
ResultList (
result.toList.map {
case (s, movie) =>
(s, movie.title, movie.filmrating)
}
)
)
case RentMovie (age, serial) =>
val maybeMovie = rentMovieAge (age, serial)
maybeMovie match {
case None =>
self.reply (Error ("Movie not available"))
case Some (movie) =>
self.reply (SuccessfullyRent (serial))
}
case Return (serial) => returnMovie (serial)
}
```

The type Receive is a type synonym for PartialFunction [Any, Unit]. As with the Scala Actors, we react with the help of Pattern Matching on the various messages. Something new is the expression self.
reply (...). In Akka, actors are controlled via ActorRefs. These are re-
references to actors. The self field of an actor contains the reference to itself itself. In the ActorRef-Trait there are methods like! for sending measurement sages or, as used in Listing 11.6, reply to send a message to the sender of the received message.

On the Message AvailableList is the map of the available, for the age allowed films are determined. This is converted into a list of triples that Consists of serial number, title and the age limit. We do this to be able to change the internal representation of films later, oh-
ne having to adapt the client. The list is then converted into a ResultList Message packed and sent back with self.reply.

In the case of a RentMovie message - depending on whether the film is rented which can or may - answered with a SuccessfullyRent or error message-words. When returning a film via the Message Return no response is word provided.

11.3 User and Session Management

Next we want to implement session management. To do this, Let's create a class User, the implementation of which is shown in Listing 11.7.

Listing 11.7. The Class and the User Object

```
package org.obraun.moviestore
import java.util.Calendar
class User private (
val name: String,
val dateOfBirth: Calendar,
val id: Int
) {
override def toString = id + ":" + name + "(" + age + ")"
def age = {
val today = Calendar.getInstance
val age = today.get (Calendar.YEAR) -
dateOfBirth.get (Calendar.YEAR)
today.set (Calendar.YEAR,
dateOfBirth.get (Calendar.YEAR))
if (today before dateOfBirth)
age-1
else
age
}
}
object user {
private [this] var id = 0
def apply (name: String, dateOfBirth: Calendar) = {
id + = 1
new User (name, dateOfBirth, id)
}
def unapply (x: Any) = {
x match {
case c: User => Some (c.name, c.dateOfBirth, c.id)
case _ => None
}
}
}
```

A user has an ID, a name and a birthday. With the age the age of the user can be calculated. After the ID should be unique, we prevent with the private modifier in front of the class parameters that a

ne instance of the class can be created with new. Instead we define in the Companion object, an apply method that applies an object with a unique ID generated and returned. We define the unapply method so that we can work with User objects can make pattern matching.

We still need a few messages for session management. These are in Listing 11.8 shown. With the messages Login and Logout a user can Log in or out user. With ShowAvailable the user asks the list of films permitted for him. Rent a film with Rent.

Listing 11.8: Additional messages for the trait session management

```
case class Login (userID: Int) extends Message
case class Logout (userID: Int) extends Message
```

case class ShowAvailable (userID: Int) extends Message
case class Rent (userID: Int, serial: Int) extends Message
The implementation of the SessionManagement trait is shown in Listing 11.9. ben.

Listing 11.9: The Session Management trait

```
package org.obraun.moviestore
import se.scalablesolutions.akka.actor. {Actor, ActorRef}
import se.scalablesolutions.akka.actor.Actor.actorOf
trait Session Management extends Actor {
protected var users: Map [Int, User]
protected var sessions = Map [Int, ActorRef] ()
abstract override def receive =
sessionManagement orElse super.receive
def sessionManagement: Receive = {
case login (id) =>
val user = users.get (id)
user match {
case None =>
self.reply (Error ("User id" + id + "not known!"))
case Some (user) =>
sessions.get (id) match {
case None =>
log.info ("User [% s] has logged in",
user.toString)
val session = actorOf (
new session (user, self)
)
session.start
sessions + = (id -> session)
case _ =>
}
}
case Logout (id) =>
log.info ("User [% d] has logged out", id)
val session = sessions (id)
session.stop
sessions - = id
case msg @ ShowAvailable (userID) =>
sessions (userID) forward msg
case msg @ Rent (userID, _) =>
sessions (userID) forward msg
}
override def shutdown = {
log.info ("Session management is shutting down ...")
sessions foreach {case (_, session) => session.stop}
}
}
```

The trait session management extends the trait actor. The abstract field users corresponds to a map with UserIDs as keys and user objects as values The session management essentially receives login and logout Messages and creates and ends the associated sessions. The implementation the session management will be done after the session management speak. The currently existing sessions are stored in the sessions field in a Map is saved, which assigns the associated session to the UserIDs as ActorRef.

net.
In order to be able to react to additional messages, the receive abstractly redefined. This means that the Trait SessionManagement can be stacked (see also section 4.3.2 on page 88). After receive a partial function we can use the orElse method. This means that the The sessionManagement method is used if it is used at the point, i.e. for the se message, is defined. Otherwise, the one in the class that has the trait SessionManagement adds, defined method receive through the pressure super.receive used.
The actual management of the sessions takes place in the session-Management. In response to the message login, an attempt is made to use the id belonging user to determine. If this is not possible, an error message sent back. If this is the case, a check is carried out to determine whether a Session exists. Only if no session is found does the Method log issued a message from the trait actor. Where this Logmel Once landing, it can be configured on the Akka platform. At-then a new session is created, started and in the sessions map saved.

A session is also an actor. To get an instance of an actor in Akka create, becomes a function that can create the actor, in our case new Session, to the actorOf method of the Actor Companion object. give. This generates the actor and returns the associated ActorRef. The actor can then be started via the ActorRef. The classes-Session parameters, as we will see below, are the user and the reference to the MovieStore.
In response to the logout message, the session is stopped and removed.
The two messages ShowAvailable and Rent are sent to the respective session forwarded. By using the ActorRef method, forward remains the sender of the message remains unchanged. Because of this, a reply comes as Reaction in the session not with session management, but with the original original sender.
If the Session Management Actor is ended with stop, the other The unreachable sessions are also ended. We implement this by redefining the shutdown method from the actor trait.

Listing 11.10: The Session Class

```
package org.obraun.moviestore
import se.scalablesolutions.akka.actor. {Actor, ActorRef}
class session (user: User, moviestore: ActorRef)
extends Actor {
private [this] val age = user.age
def receive = {
case msg @ ShowAvailable (_) =>
self.reply (
moviestore !! AvailableList (age) getOrElse
Error ("Cannot show movies!")
)
case Rent (_, serial) =>
self.reply (
moviestore !! RentMovie (age, serial) getOrElse
Error ("Cannot rent movie #" + serial)
)
}
}
```

The Session class is shown in Listing 11.10. The age of the user is only calculated once, when creating the session. The receive method reacts to the two messages sent by session management to the session can be sent on. The sense and purpose in both cases is the the request for the age of the user. This allows the user to do a Don't "cheat" request and really only get the films that are for him allowed are. The session sends the requests to the ActorRef, which the MovieStore represents. The method used for this !! waiting for one Answer. This is sent back with reply. After the answer word is an option, it is either sent out for forwarding packs or replaced by an error message.

11.4 Transactional Memory Software

With software transactional memory (STM) the idea of database transaction transferred to main memory to work with multiple threads on the same To be able to access data. The difficult task of setting locks and doing so Avoiding deadlocks becomes unnecessary. Of the ACID [4] properties, one In a database transaction, STM transactions offer the first three (ACI). The Of course, durability makes little sense in main memory. But it is important that the changes are visible to all threads.

With the support of STM we can manage our video library very much. fold in such a way that each client has a separate one beyond the session MovieStore-Actor is started, which processes the client's requests regardless of treated everyone else. The maps with the available and rented films but should be used jointly by everyone.

So the challenge is to manage the two data structures in such a way that everyone can access it, but the state is always consistent. This means For example, when renting a film must be available in and out rent to be taken into it. This can be done in one transaction with STM, ie either both were successful or the previous state is for the others Actors visible.

What we need for this are transactional references (instances of the class Ref) in which the data is stored. Access to such refs is only possible within transactions. The value a ref picks up should itself be unchangeable. The first changes we made to the Trait MovieStore converting the two fields available and rent into transactional references (see Listing 11.11).

Listing 11.11: The available and rent fields of the MovieStore trait are transactional credentials

```
import se.scalablesolutions.akka.stm.local.Ref
protected val available: Ref [Map [Int, Movie]]
protected val rent: Ref [Map [Int, Movie]]
```

We have changed three things compared to the original version:

[4] **A** Tomic - **C** onsistent - **I** solated - **D** urable

1. We made a val out of the var. The ref must always be the same stay. The content changes.
2. We changed the type from a map to a ref.
3. We made the two fields into abstract fields. This is natural not necessary to use STM. We could also use the Ref but we want the same ref in the other MovieStores too use.

To get through the references to the content, we have to use the get use. We change the content of a reference using the age method.

Finally, we use atomic to add a block to a transaction close. The changed compared to the previously developed MovieStore Methods are shown in Listing 11.12.

Listing 11.12: The methods of the MovieStore trait used for integrating STM had to be changed

```
import se.scalablesolutions.akka.stm.local.atomic
def addToStore (movie: Movie) {
MovieStore.serial + = 1
atomic {
available age (_ + (MovieStore.serial -> movie))
}
}
def rentMovieAge (age: Int, serial: Int): Option [Movie] =
atomic {
val movieOption = available.get.get (serial)
movieOption match {
case None => None
case Some (movie @ Movie (_, r)) =>
if (r <= age) {
available age (_ - serial)
rent age (_ + (serial -> movie))
movieOption
} else None
}
}
def returnMovie (serial: Int) = {
atomic {
val movie = rent.get.apply (serial)
rent age (_ - serial)
available age (_ + (serial -> movie))
}
}
def availableMoviesForAge (age: Int) =
atomic {
available.get.filter {
case (_, Movie (_, r)) => r <= age
}
}
```

All code blocks in which we access available and rent include we eat with atomic and turn it into a transaction. The serial number in the MovieStore Companion object we did not have a transactional re-reference made. Instead we provide in our service (see section 11.5) sure that addToStore can only be used in the "main MovieStore", to generate a serial number and insert a new movie.

To add a film to the available films, we will use older a function as an argument. This function gets the old one as a parameter Content and calculates the new one as a result.

To rent a film, we make the entire body of the method de rentMovieAge a transaction, since we first check whether the film is available and then borrow it. When determining the movie, the first is get necessary to get the map from the ref. The second get then takes action the key to the map and returns a [Movie] option. also we have to make the changes to available and rent again with the old to lead.

The changes to returnMovie and availableMoviesForAge are analogous on the changes to the other two methods: get for access and age for change. We need more in our video library management do not adjust to use STM for the maps.

In order to have a new one in the session management instead of the existing MovieStore to create for each session, we change exactly in the trait session management two places:

1. We do not use self as ActorRef to create the new session, but transfer a newly created MovieStore:

```
val session = actorOf (
new Session (user, newMovieStore)
)
```

2. To create the new MovieStore, we add those under point 1 abstract method used

```
def newMovieStore: ActorRef
```

one.

We are making another change to the Session class: If a session sion actor is stopped, it must stop its MovieStore. In addition re- let's define the shutdown method as follows:

```
override def shutdown = moviestore.stop
```

Everything else that is still necessary, we will do in service and in Implement client, which we will discuss in the following section.

11.5 Client and Service

Now that we've implemented all of the functionality, we need to we just put them together for the MovieStoreService:

```
package org.obraun.moviestore
class MovieStoreService
extends MovieStore
with Session Management
```

In the MovieStoreService class we have to set the fields available and rent a value from the MovieStore trait:

```
import se.scalablesolutions.akka.stm.local.Ref
protected val available = Ref (Map [Int, Movie] ())
protected val rent = Ref (Map [Int, Movie] ())
```

To replace the abstract users field from SessionManagement with a concrete Providing value and being able to add some movies to try out let's define the ExampleData trait, which is shown in Listing 11.13.

Listing 11.13. The ExampleData trait with some example users and films

```
package org.obraun.moviestore
trait ExampleData {
import java.util. {Calendar, GregorianCalendar}
var users = List (
User (
"Jon Spencer",
new GregorianCalendar (1970, Calendar.APRIL, 12)
),
User (
"Ilse Kling",
new GregorianCalendar (1997, Calendar.MAY, 17)
)
) map {case user @ User (_, _, id) => (id -> user)} toMap
val movies = set (
Movie ("Step Across the Border", 0),
```

```
Movie ("At the Limit", 6),
Movie ("The Matrix", 16),
Movie ("Bad Taste", 18),
Movie ("Bad Lieutenant", 16)
)
}
```

We add the ExampleData trait to the MovieStoreService class.
The expression addToStore (movies) in the body of the class represents the example films are then available in the MovieStore. Finally we have to do one more Implementation for the abstract method newMovieStore from Session-Specify management (see Listing 11.14).

Listing 11.14: The newMovieStore method for creating a new MovieStore Actors with the transactional references

```
import se.scalablesolutions.akka.actor.Actor.actorOf
def newMovieStore =
actorOf (
new MovieStore {
protected val available: Ref [Map [Int, Movie]] =
service.available
protected val rent: Ref [Map [Int, Movie]] =
service.rent
override def addToStore (movie: Movie) = ()
override def addToStore (
movies: Traversable [Movie]
) = ()
}
).begin
```

The method newMovieStore creates an actor from an anonymous class, which adds the Trait MovieStore. The two maps available and rent are set to the reference of the MovieStoreServices. We can do this of course not with this.available or this.rent. Therefore must let's look at a self-type annotation (see Section 5.7.8) with another Define identifier. The commonly used identifier self can be found in an Akka-Actor cannot be used because it is the ActorRef acts. We have therefore chosen the identifier service, ie the definition the class starts with

```
class MovieStore ... {service =>
```

So that no films can be added to the MovieStores created in this way. nen, we redefine addToStore with the constant value () of type Unit. The created actor is finally started with start.

To make the MovieStoreService available as a service over the network we only have to use the init method, as shown in Listing 11.15, redefine. We start a RemoteNode on the local computer on port 9999 and register the self-ActorRef under the name moviestore: service.

Listing 11.15: Redefinition of the init method in the MovieStoreService

```
override def init = {
import se.scalablesolutions.akka.remote.RemoteNode
RemoteNode.start ("localhost", 9999)
RemoteNode register ("moviestore: service", self)
}
```

Since we are working with Sbt, we can start a Scala shell via sbt console, where all the libraries and classes in our project are available to our Test MovieStoreService. The following session shows the start of the services in the Akka framework:

```
scala> import org.obraun.moviestore._
import org.obraun.moviestore._
scala> import se.scalablesolutions.akka.actor.Actor._
import se.scalablesolutions.akka.actor.Actor._
scala> val movieStoreService =
|
actorOf [MovieStoreService] .start
...
00: 22: 31.065 [run-main] INFO ssakka.remote.RemoteNode $
- Registering server side remote actor [org. Brown.
moviestore.MovieStoreService] with id [moviestore:
service]
00: 22: 31.066 [run-main] DEBUG ssakka.actor.Actor $ - [
Actor [org.obraun.moviestore.MovieStoreService
: 1283512328095]] has started
...
```

To be able to test the service, we implement a simple client, the we can use in another Scala shell. The client code is in the listing 11.16.

Listing 11.16: The MovieStoreClient

```
package org.obraun.moviestore
import se.scalablesolutions.akka.remote.RemoteClient
class MovieStoreClient (userID: Int) {
val movieStore =
RemoteClient.actorFor (
"moviestore: service",
"localhost",
9999
)
def login = movieStore! Login (userID)
def logout = movieStore! Logout (userID)
def rent (serial: Int) = {
val result = movieStore !! Rent (userID, serial)
result match {
case Some (SuccessfullyRent (_)) =>
println ("Successfully rent movie #" + serial)
case Some (Error (msg)) =>
println ("error:" + msg)
case msg =>
println ("error: something unexpected happened"
+ msg)
}
}
def show = {
val result = movieStore !! ShowAvailable (userID)
result match {
case Some (ResultList (movies)) =>
for ((serial, title, filmrating) <- movies)
println (serial + "" + title + "(" + filmrating + ")")
case msg =>
println ("error while receiving movielist:" + msg)
}
}
def returnM (serial: Int) = movieStore! Return (serial)
```

}
In the MovieStoreClient class, the connection to the MovieStore-
Service established via the RemoteClient object. Even if the client is in
This example is running on the same host, it could be on another
Calculator running. It would then just have to add localhost to the name of the host
on which the MovieStoreService is running.
The three methods login, logout and returnM send the required
good message with! to the MovieStoreService and therefore do not wait
an answer. The two methods rent and show also send their message
!! and assign the result, the response message, to a val. With the help of
Pattern matching, the answer is evaluated and printed accordingly with println
issued. To try it out, we start with sbt in a second terminal
console another Scala shell and, as shown in the following session,
to work with the service:


```
scala> import org.obraun.moviestore._
import org.obraun.moviestore._
scala> val client = new MovieStoreClient (1)
...
INFO: Successfully initialized GlobalStmInstance using
factoryMethod 'org.multiverse.stms.alpha.AlphaStm.
createFast '.
client: org.obraun.moviestore.MovieStoreClient = org.
obraun.moviestore.MovieStoreClient@51493995
scala> import client._
import client._
scala> login
11: 33: 58.819 [run-main] DEBUG ssakka.remote.
RemoteClientHandler - [id: 0x273d6d53] OPEN
11: 33: 58.860 [run-main] INFO ssakka.remote.
RemoteClient - Starting remote client connection to [
localhost: 9999]
...
scala> show
...
1 At the limit (6)
2 Bad Taste (18)
3 The Matrix (16)
4 Bad Lieutenant (16)
5 Step Across the Border (0)
scala> rent (1)
...
Successfully rent movie # 1
scala> show
...
2 Bad Taste (18)
3 The Matrix (16)
4 Bad Lieutenant (16)
5 Step Across the Border (0)
```

You can also open other Scala shells and from there you can
their UserID or register with the same.
At this point we want to take a brief look at the very powerful Akka-
Framework quit, even if we like many other interesting features
for example the Akka microkernel, persistence, lift integration and error handling

could not discuss tolerance in the context of this book. The under http: //doc.akkasource.org/ documentation provided is very good and catchy, so that there is nothing to deepen your knowledge of Akka more stands in the way.

Closing word

So this is it: my introduction to Scala. I hope you had read it Just as much fun as I do thinking up, writing and programming. The, what I've shown you in this book relates to the one in October 2010 current versions of Scala, the tools and the frameworks. Although in the development moves a lot, the content will certainly remain useful and long current, and only new features are added. For example, Scala is sion 2.9 get parallel collections. The one on the website for this book http://scala.obraun.net/ I will send the linked code to new customize sions.

The Scala world and the universe of functional programming have, however much more to offer than what I presented on the previous pages. could ren. The Scalaz framework 5 implements further concepts of the functional programming, and many Scala enthusiasts dare at least one Looking in the direction of a purely functional language such as Haskell. If you have any questions or comments, please do not hesitate to contact me to write to scala@obraun.net. If you still need further information or want to convince your boss or client to switch to Scala I will try to help you with that. I would be happy to hear from To hear you.

Made in the USA
Monee, IL
13 March 2021

62679620R00125